MENSA

MENSA

The Society for the Highly Intelligent

Victor Serebriakoff

Foreword by Isaac Asimov

STEIN AND DAY/*Publishers*/**New York**

First published in the United States of America in 1986
Copyright © 1985 by Victor Serebriakoff
All rights reserved, Stein and Day, Incorporated
Printed in the United States of America

STEIN AND DAY/Publishers
Scarborough House
Briarcliff Manor, N.Y. 10510

Library of Congress Cataloging-in-Publication Data
Serebriakoff, Victor.
Mensa: the society for the highly intelligent.
Includes index.
1. Mensa – History. 2. Intellect. I. Title.
BF431.S442 1986   367   85-40964
ISBN 0-8128-3091-1

Contents

Acknowledgements

I have to acknowledge the many kind friends who have helped me with this book. My wife Win, John McNulty, Madsen Pirie, and Harold Gale have taken on the task of a careful and critical reading of the MSS and they have eliminated errors where I have not been too wrongheaded to accept correction. The many faults, errors and inaccuracies that are left are poor things but they are mine own.

The number of those who have contributed to the book in one way or another is too large for it to make sense to name them all but Harper Fowley, Harold Gale, Ruth Whittle, Philip Poole, Adrian Berrill, Christopher Cruice Goodall, Kenneth Passmore Brown, Eric Hills, Judge Brian Galpin, Sir Clive Sinclair, Jaques Schupbach, Ralph Spicer, Paul Griffin, Rudolph Schroeder, Sydney Jackson, Nigel Searle, Sushil Bilaney, Margot Seitelman, Sander Rubin, Udo Schulz, Jonathan Causer, and many, many more whose names do not come to mind just now have been very helpful.

So have many others who have been kind enough to answer my call and offer the contributions which have been crowded out by the growing bulk of these pages.

I can only express gratitude to all of them and to Mensa in general. The encouragement, the immediate, imaginative, willing and practical help I have had is none the less welcome because it can be always relied on in Mensa and from Mensans.

This is also probably the best place to acknowledge many I mentioned in earlier drafts whose names have been edited out in the drastic pruning of the manuscript which was needed to bring the book down to the size required. These are the names of just a few of the people who have kept Mensa going and growing through the years; just some of those who have made an impression on this observer.

Here is my thanks from myself and from Mensa to: Joan and Peter Needs, the late Joe Wilson, Erika Omasta, James Hayes, Ralph Spicer, Al Rubinstein, Brian Heald, Dr Emerson Coyle, Herb Ahrend, Sam Naber, Evelyn Glor, Len Ahearn, Margaret Brandt, Angus Henry, Michael MacGuinness, Harper Fowley, George Hopkins, Arthur Gardner, David Warren, Antony Hill, Dr George Atherton, Nils Kleinjan, Jean Marc L'Officier, Dr John Good, Eileen Donovan, Dr Jack Cohen, Ferdinand Heger, Jaqueline Bellanger, Christopher Frost, Professor Philip Vernon, Rosemary Ashford, Ron Meadows, Len Rickard, Helen Kupper, Ian Palmer, Maurice Salzedo, Lorraine Boyce, Velma Jeremiah, Anne Hinds, Fred Schumacher, Sue Sparrow, George Thomas, Mennotti Cossu, James Sprague, Karl Schnoelzer, Jorma Maekinen, Julian Parr, the late Raymond Allen, Dr Beverley Burgess, Paul Victor, Jaqueline Berlet, Pennti Wuorenjuuri, Cary Horch, Tom Napier.

These are those that came to mind. There are many more that ought to have come to mind and did not. There are even more where I remember the person, the contribution and the face but have forgotten the name. I ask forgiveness of those I have neglected.

The extract from the Simplex Intelligence Test GNV 5 used by kind permission of George G. Harrap & Co. Ltd, London, Toronto, Wellington and Sydney. Copyright. All rights reserved.

Rien dans l'Univers ne peut resister a l'ardeur convergente d'un nombre suffisament grand d'intelligences groupées et organisées.

Teilhard de Chardin

There is a kinship, a kind of freemasonry between all persons of intelligence, however antagonistic their moral outlook.

Norman Douglas

Foreword

MENSA AND I

by Isaac Asimov

I first heard of Mensa in 1961, when a charming young woman, Gloria Salzberg, who was herself a member, urged me to join. I was quite willing until I heard I would have to take an intelligence test in order to see if I could qualify.

With the courage of an Asimov, I promptly quailed. I had not taken an intelligence test for many years, and I didn't think I any longer remembered the answers. I therefore tried to get out of it.

'Isn't my life, my profession, my books, an obvious demonstration of my intelligence?' I demanded.

'No,' said Gloria sweetly. 'Here is the test. Here is a pencil. I will supervise.'

She stationed her husband (a large, muscular specimen) at the door to prevent my escape, and I took the test. Fortunately I passed and was made a member.

For several years, I attended meetings with vigorous assiduity. (That's just Mensa talk. I'm not sure what it means.) Then I stopped.

You see, I am what is called a prolific writer. I have had 334 books published (so far), and hundreds of short stories, and thousands of essays, and you may think these things all write themselves, but they don't. Just *copying* all that stuff would take me nine hours a day, seven days a week. Making them up in the first place takes me an additional hour every single day.

It all earns me a moderate living, but the other side of the coin is that I have no time for anything else – so I just quietly dropped my Mensa meetings and, being a frugal person, stopped paying my dues.

As time passed, I moved to New York in 1970, and in 1972, Victor Serebriakoff visited New York and demanded to meet me for some nefarious reason of his own. (He's never had an un-nefarious reason in his life.) I was not proof against the imperious summons. There I was staring at this five-foot-five fellow with a seven-foot-seven charisma.

'Why,' he demanded, 'have you allowed your Mensa membership to lapse?'

I tried to explain.

He dismissed the explanation with an impatient 'Tchah!' (which may be Russian for 'In your hat,' but I'm not sure). Then he said, 'Just renew your membership.'

I demurred (more Mensa talk).

'You might as well,' he said, with a Serebriakoffian snarl, 'because if you don't, I'll pay your dues for you and we'll list you as a member, anyway.'

With the typical pride of an Asimov, I said, 'Okay,' but my wife wouldn't let me accept his charity, and I joined up once more at my own expense.

Victor then revealed the base scheme that lay behind all this. He began a shrewd campaign to get me to come to Great Britain, even though all my instincts are against travel. He seized me by the throat and said, 'You will come or I will strangle you.'

I was unable to resist the subtlety of the approach so, in 1974, I made the trip. There I discovered the full depth of Mensa hospitality, the beauty of the English countryside, the charm of London, and most of all, *most* of all, the absolute excellence of Mensa people as an audience.

And as I was about to leave, Victor said to me, 'You are one of the two International Vice-Presidents of Mensa.'

With the typical penetration of an Asimov, I said, 'What?'

He repeated his remark, and I said I didn't know how to run for the post and that I didn't think the Mensans would vote for me.

'That's all right,' said Victor, with Serebriakoffian hauteur (we Mensa people speak French), 'this is a democratic organisation and I've just appointed you.'

I'm afraid to ask, actually, but I think I'm still International Vice-President, and in that capacity, I want to invite you all to read this book, which will tell you all that you can possibly want to know about Mensa. If you have any doubts, just stare into the eyes of Victor, whose picture graces the inside back-flap. Then you'll not only buy the book, but you will join Mensa. Buying this book is an unmistakable indication that you have the requisite intelligence.

Preface

This book is written to satisfy the growing curiosity about Mensa;
to explain what it is and what it is not, and to give an experienced
layman's account of the scientific background which made such
an unusual organisation possible.

The only qualification for membership in Mensa is the mental
ability to get a score in any standard test of general intelligence
which puts the applicant in the top two percent of the general
population. Mensa's simple, ostensible, purposes are to provide
opportunities for contact and interaction between intelligent
people everywhere, to investigate the opinions, attitudes and
problems of members, and of the intelligent generally, using the
methods of psychology and social science, and fostering intelligence for the benefit of humanity.

Founded in 1946, Mensa has, after a shaky beginning, spread
and developed with a strange dynamism which is all its own. It
now has members in every occupation and from every social class
in many countries in the Western and Third worlds. Mensa
frankly discriminates in favour of intelligence but does not
recognise distinctions of race, politics or religion. It is a multi-
disciplinary forum where intelligent people can surmount the
normal cultural, ethnic and social barriers. Better than average
mutual comprehension enables us to explore and sometimes
resolve our differences in an atmosphere which is typically
friendly, urbane and sophisticated.

Mensa is protean; its most visible feature, apart from the
obvious one, is its diversity. It recruits its members, not like other
societies from those who accept pre-established aims or tenets,

but by scientifically selecting those who are able to think for themselves. As I write in 1984 we have over 67,000 members in around 80 countries in all parts of the world.

An autodidact without much formal education, I am not a qualified psychologist nor indeed a scholar of any kind. However I have always been a spare time professional writer and since I first became the Secretary of Mensa in 1954 it has grown and flourished in such a disconcerting way that I feel that it may develop into a permanent institution. Someone has to be the scribe so I have taken it on.

It was in 1964 that I wrote the first book about Mensa. I was then in the full rush and scurry of organising Mensa's exciting growth. The impressions were fresh in my mind. This second book borrows extensively from the first one, *IQ, A Mensa Analysis and History*. At that time we had survived for fourteen years and reached a world membership of ten thousand.

Now, twenty years later in 1984, having been in the central leadership role for nearly all of that time, and having been 'kicked upstairs' to the honorific, non-executive post of World President, I have time to, and can, tell a fuller story with a wider perspective.

An organisation based on an assessment of human capacity rather than achievement is a natural Aunt Sally for critics and I look forward with complacent zest to the condescension of established academe and the mockery and simulated shock from procrustean egalitarians who cannot unmuddle the difference between equality of rights and clone-like equality of personality and ability. I feel that the persistent, steady, obstinate growth of Mensa despite these attitudes and the vicissitudes that I shall describe, needs an explanation if not an apologia. Since I have had such a hand in it, I am in a good position to tell the story. If what I say appears presumptuous or shows a lack of proper humility, then I ask my readers to blame me and not Mensa, because these faults are just those which are not evident in Mensa meetings and occasions. I on the other hand, am known for the view that self-deprecation is a frequent fault among the able and that humility is nothing to be proud of.

The mental climate of Mensa is sharp and critical. Intellectual arrogance is suffered less in our unstructured ranks than in most places. President or no, I find in Mensa that my place is that, back into which, I am often, firmly, put.

I must emphasise that I do not claim that this is an official history, researched in every particular. It is a story, my Mensa story. I inherited from my cockney Mother a story teller's embroidering memory. That is a memory which tries to catch the essence, the feel and the drama of events but may embroider a little to do it.

I used to complain of my mother's inaccuracy over detail, after she had kept a whole British war-time pub full of strangers entranced for an evening with her tales of simple family events. I am sure that I, in my turn, shall have critics who will run at the foot of the letter to dispute the details of my memory. To them I can only give my mother's invariable reply to me: 'Very well, the horse was grey, it was not black'!

I am as pleased as Punch to add this welcome to American readers to my Preface.

American Mensa is still, alas!, most of Mensa, to the credit of the Mensa workers all over these States and the envy and chagrin of all non-American Mensas. American Mensans are no more pleased with their predominance than are their overseas colleagues. American support for the International Board and for other National Mensa's is massive and continuous. So it is nice to report that the proportion of non-Americans in our world-wide membership is improving. With American help I am sure that Mensans will one day be both more widely and more evenly distributed around Planet Earth. That is the aim.

I have a curious, sometimes ridiculous story to tell and in one way it inevitably misrepresents. In a case like mine there has to be a war between the president, the enthusiast who loves Mensa and the writer who must tell the whole truth and be readable. If I had written 300 pages of fulsome Mensa propaganda, I would have neither been published nor read. I tell my tale as Oliver Cromwell wanted to be painted, 'warts and all'. With the first edition, the media have naturally shown most interest in the stories of the curious and dishonorable but completely untypical behaviour of a small minority of members. News (I might say 'olds') of what is good, typical, normal and pleasant, which is nearly all in Mensa, will stop no press.

I cannot win so I do not try. Here I am writer, which is my profession, before Honorary President, worker and advocate, which is my hobby. I tell a tale both to amuse and record.

Finally, Mensa is, collectively, uncommitted and impartial. Any book about it can only be the view of the individual writer. These pages do not represent Mensa ideas, policy, nor anything other than the personal views, thoughts, and perhaps fallible memories of,

Your unhumble servant,

VICTOR SEREBRIAKOFF

London 1985

MENSA

History: the beginning

Nineteen-forty-five was a year of historic happenings: the year World War II came to an end and the Nuclear Age began with two world-shaking explosions in Japan.

Roosevelt and Hitler both died that year and the victorious Churchill lost office in the biggest electoral upset of modern times. The political shape of the post-war world was settled at Yalta and seeds of Communist rule were sown in China. The United Nations and the Arab League were founded that year while power came to De Gaulle in France, and to Tito in Yugoslavia. Zionists began the fight to establish Israel.

It was a year when things happened. That was the enormous background.

There was that year a trivial happening in the foreground of my story in England. It had unexpected consequences.

An Englishman met an Australian on a train in Surrey. The meeting is worth recording only because it had consequences which were much greater than any reasonable judgement would have credited at the time. I tell how two ill-assorted men met on a train and what the extraordinary consequence was.

They could hardly have been more different in personality. They were complete strangers and on the balance of probabilities might have remained so.

Imagine the tattered, war-torn carriage of a rattling, neglected British train approaching the prosperous Surrey town of Godalming on a hot August day.

The younger man was slender, unobtrusive, had a receding chin and a reserved, very English upper class style and manner.

He was studying Hansard (the British Parliamentary Report) and, had he been reading *The Times*, Mensa might never have happened.

The older man was forty-nine, thick-set and sturdy. He was smartly and prosperously dressed. He sported that which was unusual to the point of eccentricity in those days: a full, well-tended, dark beard and moustache. He was above all things a noticeable man. His large, confident, protruding eyes turned masterfully this way and that as he subjected the carriage to his inspection. I am in no doubt that the quiet young Englishman was less than comfortable with these manners which may have had their origin more in the antipodal upbringing than in the English education of the Australian, Roland Berrill, the bearded starer and the future Founder of Mensa. For that is who it was.

Perhaps the English university student, Lancelot Lionel Ware, tucked his face even deeper behind the pages of Hansard until, in the end, it was they that caught the imperious eye of the unselfconscious Berrill.

'Is that Hansard that you are reading, young man?' Berrill's firm, pleasant voice revealed his English upper class schooling, not his Australian birth.

'Obviously.' The slight young man's accent was also confident and impeccably upper class. He read on. A firm English put-down.

There was a silent contest of wills and cultures. English traditional railway carriage reserve contended with confident colonial brashness and bonhomie.

Berrill persisted. He overcame Ware's reserve and the two Mensa pioneers began to talk as the worn-out train rattled serenely on in the August sunshine through the bomb-shattered London suburbs. The men exchanged addresses and, unthinking, parted. But Mensa had entered the realm of the possible. A very, very, unlikely association had become just slightly less improbable.

The beard was not, as we shall hear, the only eccentricity of Mr Roland Berrill, who was by that time a man of independent means. During the depression, some years earlier, he had been a man of almost no means, as dividends were passed in the best of investments. Although he had eaten his dinners and been called to the bar, he had never practised.

Ware, after taking his biology doctorate in London was preparing to go up to Oxford as a mature student, being one of those whose university career had been delayed by research work during the war. He secured a whole string of qualifications in science and the law, and became a successful barrister. When his father died Ware had found himself in charge of the education of his younger sister Elaine, who was ten years his junior. It was this family responsibility which started his interest in intelligence tests and set him experimenting with them. He tells me that he wanted to base his educational judgements about his sister on sound objective and scientific grounds.

Ware says he was surprised when, a little afterwards he got a letter from 'the man on the train' suggesting a meeting. At any rate they met, became friends, and started along the road that led to Mensa.

We have little idea of what happened in their meetings during the rest of 1945. The next meeting on the record, and an important one, was on 11 March 1946 in Oxford. It was at this meeting that Ware gave Berrill the Cattell Intelligence Test and informed the older man that he had a superior intelligence quotient. Berrill, Ware says, was deeply impressed and said that at last he understood the difficulties of mutual understanding that he had always had with other people.

It is easy to laugh at this sort of statement. However, I find that most Mensans, especially that majority like myself who are from more humble environments, will in moments of self-revelation, admit to some such thought. A black girl I met somewhere in America put it like this: 'When I joined Mensa I found out at last that what was different about me was all right.'

Now there is some dispute in Mensa about who it was who first thought of the idea of a high IQ society. Professor Sir Cyril Burt, Professor of Psychology at University College London and past President of Mensa seems to be under the impression that he sowed the seed by a suggestion he made in a broadcast. Sir Cyril made this claim in his introduction to my first book about Mensa in 1963. This was certainly the usual account which was repeated in many newspaper articles for the first twenty-two years. It remained uncontradicted until 1968 when, after a visit to Dr Ware, a new editor of the Mensa journal wrote an article in which Dr Ware was erroneously saluted as the founder, as he had agreed. The journal article was amended due to pressure from some older members, and Ware was given the title of Vice President.

My own view is that there certainly was a discussion about the formation of a High IQ Club at that meeting and I see no reason to doubt Ware's story that he thought of such an idea. Whether Berrill had heard and been influenced by Burt's ideas, as Burt claimed, we do not know, but from another source we know that Berrill's mind was adventuring in a direction which was not too dissimilar before the meeting. We know from Berrill's friend, K. P. Brown, and from my wife that Berrill himself credited Burt with the idea. I consulted his brother Adrian on the point and he says that he is under the impression that Berrill had met Burt before the war. A month before the meeting with Ware mentioned above, in a letter to his friend Jaques Schupbach, who shared Berrill's interest in phrenology, Berrill had been deploring that there was no form of recognition for 'Nature' as distinct from 'Nurture'. He even proposed that there should be a Gold Medal to be awarded to those who were 'phrenologically good'. I think that in an uninstructed way he was feeling his way towards the idea of selecting for what he saw as the heritable quality of intelligence. We shall see as my story develops that Berrill had a great talent for credulity and was a sucker for far-out and cranky beliefs. This proved to be an obstacle to Mensa development in the early days. Brown also tells me that Berrill set up quite a few little societies of one kind and another: apart from Mensa they proved to be ephemeral. So if, in April 1946, Ware came up with the suggestion of an intelligence test as a better and more respectable measure of human value than bump feeling, his message was falling on prepared soil.

Whenever the Burt idea appeared it was an important at least as an addition, from the point of view of establishing the society as a serious and scientifically sensible idea. Burt's broadcast suggestion, according to his own account and those of several reliable witnesses (none of whom remember the date), was that a group of people whose IQ score was high should be used as a panel which could be polled on questions of public interest.

Sir Cyril gave six broadcasts between September and November 1945 and the one which Berrill heard can have been any of these. If he did put out the idea in one of these it must have been as one of his customary ad lib additions because it does not appear in the scripts. There were also some Burt broadcasts after the formation of Mensa and one of these may be the one at which the idea was put out.

The first written proposal concerning the formation of the High IQ Club of which we have evidence is in a partial copy of a letter from Berrill to Ware in which Berrill is setting out details of a plan to recruit members, not by direct approach but by asking psychologists to notify the client and the Club when quotients over 155 are achieved in tests they conducted. This proved to be an impractical approach at that time. Berrill's letter finishes: 'The club would thus begin in obscurity, even in secrecy, which would avoid ridicule in the days of weakness.' At the end of the copy there is written in another hand: 'From Roland Berrill, Dr L. L. Ware, 22 April 1946.' If we could see the first two pages we should be wiser. Dr Ware's account is that this letter was a response to his own suggestion that the club should be set up.

The next relevant letter is from Berrill to his friend Jaques Schupbach (a civil servant) in which the latter is told that he is 'eligible to become a member of Mensa'. Berrill says confidently, 'I shall be starting in October'. And he did. The date of the letter was 29 July 1946.

To the indignation of some of the neighbours, there appeared, in October 1971 outside a small house in Oxford a blue plaque. It announced that it was at this address that Mensa was founded. This address, 12 St John Street, was the lodging house at which Ware stayed during term time and where his friend Berrill also took rooms in the summer of 1946. And it was from there, on 1 October 1946, that Mensa was founded by Roland Berrill. (I use the word 'founded' in its normal sense, that of 'established' or 'constituted on a permanent basis'.) What happened on that day was simply that Berrill set off to the printers with the copy that was to form the first Mensa literature.

Why Mensa? Originally Berrill decided the club was to be called The High IQ Club and it was to have a monthly journal called Mens (the Latin for 'mind'). However, Ware tells us that he warned Berrill that this might be confused with the journal *Men Only*.

On further thought, Berrill decided to use the name Mensa (Latin for 'table') for the club and the Mensa Magazine for the journal. Berrill's justification for this was that 'mensa' is the first Latin word one learns. His secondary connotation was that of a Round Table Society where no one has precedence (because all are selected by the same criterion). Berrill's brother Adrian tells me that the latin tag '*mens sana in corpore sano*' was also in Roland's mind.

I must be frank and give my impression of the aspects of Berrill's character and background which led him to devote so much of his time and his money to setting Mensa on track, but before I do that I must in fairness to present members point out that what Berrill, Burt, and Ware conceived then is very far from what Mensa is now. Within five years of its beginning Mensa was foundering, deserted by Berrill and Ware, both of whom were dissatisfied with it. But Berrill wrought better than he knew. The abandoned brain orphan nearly died. But not quite.

My impression of Berrill, which is supported by the accounts from early members, is that he was among that minority in England at the time who regretted the passing of an ancient aristocratic tradition. To preserve the great houses, under that tradition, everything had to go to the eldest son. Berrill was one of the disinherited, a second son and one from a family which had hoped he would be a daughter. He felt it keenly that he had not, like his elder brother, been to Balliol College. Dr Ware reports that Berrill selected himself for the post of unofficial rowing coach to the Balliol team and used to run along the towpath shouting less than welcome exhortations and advice.

K. P. Brown tells me that Berrill was envious of women who are encouraged to dress up and make the most of their appearance. One of the many fringe societies he joined or started was The

Men's Dress Reform Movement. Followers believed in more colour in men's clothes and objected to the uniformity of those days. Berrill was fascinated by the idea of dressing women and Brown thinks this arose from envy of his brightly clad younger sister, Joan, in childhood. This led to what Brown described as a 'Queen complex'. This certainly appeared in his set-up for Mensa.

As a 'focus of loyalty', in Mensa, he decreed that there was to be a queen under the title *Corps d'Esprit*. This 'personage' was to be selected on the grounds only of 'pulchritude'. We early members had to write effusive, submissive letters of great formality to this lady in order to be accepted into the exclusive ranks of this little 'Aristocracy of the Intellect', as Berrill called us. The turnover rate of Mensa queens was fairly high for reasons which will emerge.

The first lady that Berrill enthroned as 'Corps d'Esprit' was a friend of Elaine Ware, Dorothy Gee. There was a disconcerting abdication when Berrill explained the nature of the enrobing ceremony he planned. Having paid for the fine robes Berrill decreed that he should officiate personally in the ritual of investiture. That was reluctantly accepted. But things went wrong when he insisted that he should assist and supervise the prior undressing process as well. All was sweetly innocent fun by today's standards, but this was 1947.

Vera Davies, Vera the First, Mensa's second queen, created an initial problem. Berrill had decreed that members should refer to each other by their initials and hers were unspeakable in royal company. No problem. Berrill decreed a second name and Vera Rose Davies (VRD) was enthroned to reign over a growing band of Mensans.

One of the most frequent errors of understanding about human actions is the error of pure or single motivation. It hardly ever happens. Motivations are always, in human beings, mixed and never purely altruistic. Among Berrill's motivations evidently, perhaps unconsciously, was that of making his a little kingdom in which he could act out his daydreams of a return to the simple traditional certitudes of the primitive hunter-gatherer tribe with the face to face structure and single ruler. This is what the human animal was designed for by millions of years of slow evolution. This is the structure for which we never cease to hanker, the more so because we have forgotten how nasty, brutish and short was the life in such groups.

With scarcely a whimper of protest at that time after the war a tradition-ridden nation, England, was giving up the last vestiges of an ancient, ingrained aristocratic system (built from such a tribal base) by which special respect and deference had been willingly shown, by most people, to those from certain families and with certain styles, manners and traditions. It was all quietly, and without regret, going away. I believe that Berrill and Ware both saw themselves as part of this vanishing tradition and saw in Mensa a means and a justification to revise in some measure those ancient models and modes. At one of our occasional meetings after he had dropped out, Ware told me that the idea had been a good one but that he had been disappointed by the kind of people whom we admitted. At a snap poll at a meeting after he had rejoined, the chairman quizzed us on our self-perception of class membership. His was the only hand raised as one who classified himself as upper class.

Alas for human aspirations! The last thing that the reality Mensa could be said to represent is a return to such traditional conceptions. Mensa turned out to be the child of its age. Berrill's aristocratic phantasies as well as his ambition to provide an impartial panel which would be called upon to advise rulers and authorities caused only amused, tolerant smiles in the members who began to gather round the Table.

At the very beginning, it is true, the members that his idiosyncratic advertisements and brochures attracted were mainly of middle class or upper class origin. Indeed, the first few members included two future peers. Others, like my wife and I, were those of working class background who had, as one does in the permeable British system, passed quietly through the barriers. Today it is different. A majority of Mensans appear to have come from humble homes.

The growth of Mensa at first was discouragingly slow. Berrill worked hard, wrote to psychologists and advertised in prestigious academic and up-market journals. The results were negligible.

What recruitment there was came from personal approaches to friends and acquaintances of Berrill, with some from Ware and then from the first few members such as the Board of Trade official Schupbach, accountant, Brown, Spicer, a surveyor, the barrister, Galpin, Crompton an aspiring poet and Griffin who was a master at a boarding school.

The first evidence I have of contact between Berrill and Burt is in a long letter, evidently one of a series. It was dated 9 November 1946. With a great deal of superfluous detail Professor Burt sets out the mathematics which show, quite erroneously I found, that the selection of criterion chosen by Berrill, an IQ on the Cattell Intelligence Test for Superior Adults, of 155 was equivalent to a rating of 'one third per mille'. Only one in three thousand persons could qualify for Mensa! It was a bit of a let-down for me some years later when I learned how to check the calculations and found that the Professor had been careless and that the entire membership of Mensa had to be demoted to the 99th percentile or a paltry one in a hundred level. How was I to tell them? I plucked up the courage and spoke. They took it with phlegmatic stoicism. So we must blame Burt, not Berrill for the exaggerated claims that Berrill made in the early days in his advertisements. Incidentally, the ageing Burt's slip tends rather to support the 'carelessness' rather than the 'fraud' hypothesis concerning his bad science in reports of twin studies. This bad science was used for the assassination of Burt's character many years later.

The very first of many scores of thousands of Mensa publications appeared in April 1946, just a year after Berrill's letter setting out his plans. I do not know who designed the 'logo', as it would now be called, on the front cover. When I joined I found the masked cloaked figures and the pointed hats a bit disconcerting with too much echo of the racialist Ku Klux Klan. I do not, even remotely, think that any such idea was in Berrill's mind. He had no racialist tendencies and was as shocked as anyone at an early meeting when a member calmly proposed a motion that black persons should not be invited to join. Someone, it may have been Berrill, interrupted the long shocked silence by proposing the amendment that the words 'black people' in the motion should be amended to the form 'green people with yellow stripes'. In that form the motion was silently passed with one vote against and the rule would remain in Mensa today if those minutes had not been mislaid. Racism is one of the very few '-isms' that are hard to find in Mensa.

It was typical of Berrill, who edited the magazine, that he numbered it 'Old Series. Volume 1. No. 1'. He called it, 'the official organ of Mensa, a round table society.' He was obviously looking forward to the day when someone would be writing a history of what he was starting. His aim was to make things easy for his unknown future chronicler. Alas there is another 'Old Series. Volume 1. Number 1.', quite different, in my collection (the first issue of *The Mensa Quarterly*, issued later, when he found he could not maintain a monthly).

The very first issue had an Editorial mostly concerned with his plans for the magazine but the next two issues give the best idea there is of his ideas and intentions.

How did membership grow? The first correspondence on this was a letter to Jaques Schupbach from Berrill (2 November 46) saying, 'We have now about six members', and that treasurer Yorke Crompton had received his, the first cheque. These six must have been Berrill, Ware, Elaine Ware, Schupbach, Crompton and probably Dorothy Gee. Berrill says also that 'My friend Dr Ware's contacts have proved disappointing; or else they were merely slow with their correspondence'. He also says that he has had a favourable reply from Professor Burt, which places his approach to Burt in October or before. In February 1947 Berrill, writing a discouraged letter to Schupbach, claimed only fourteen members. He had discovered that professional psychologists, testing mostly recruits and schoolchildren, were not going to be a rich source of recruits, and is despairingly urging Jaques to tackle his friends and acquaintances. 'Life', Berrill sadly points out, 'is sometimes difficult to bear'.

In another letter to Schupbach on 5 March he grimly notes that every member, so far, is either a relative, friend or acquaintance of himself or Dr Ware. He has fixed his gaze on the difficult target of thirty members so that it will be worthwhile publishing a membership list and a periodical.

'Perhaps when we have a periodical, it will be easier. Mensa will exist. It is difficult to ask people to join an idea, to join a dream.'

In July, still short of the dreamed-of thirty, Berrill published the first membership list revealing that twenty-two human souls had been selected from the world's teeming millions and had taken a seat at this round table of 'aristocrats of the intellect'.

But later that year the fragile, improbable dream-like entity, Mensa, became at last more than an idea in a few heads. It materialised out of the mist of Berrill's dreams. The hoped-for thirty mark having been triumphantly passed in November and a new list boasting thirty-three names published, the plunge was taken and Mensa members began to meet socially. The most formal of these functions in 1947 was held on 6 December.

Fourteen members appeared at a dinner in a private room at the Jill-on-the-Green restaurant in Soho. The conversation was general, as always when Berrill was present. These points from the discussion came down to us:

1 Mensa opinion was not to be considered as more important than any other, particularly when specialist knowledge was involved.
2 Mensa members were likely to be more introverted than the average. (This guess was subsequently confirmed by a sample research.) Introverts often do not know what they want in life so opinion research results may be equivocal.
3 Official opinion poll researches reflect people's feelings more than their thoughts. Mensa polls may have the opposite tendency which would be good.
4 The declared aim was to recruit six hundred members and then close the door. With a sample this large the bias in polls would be eliminated.
5 Mensa need not be widely known to be effective. Discreetly working behind the scenes, it might be more influential than if it worked in the glare of publicity.

Berrill concluded the evening with a speech in which he compared Mensa to Milton; the commercial disinfectant fluid, not the poet. When Milton was advertised as having 101 uses, it did not sell. When it was advertised as the fluid in which to put false teeth at night, it sold in millions. Mensa had 101 uses too, but the best way to put it over was to appeal to public spirit with a hint of power behind it. He did not know how Mensa would develop but he wanted it to become viable without him.

As can be seen from his early writings about Mensa, Berrill's main dream was that this panel of highly intelligent people, scientifically and therefore objectively selected, would have advantages as an unbiased panel which could be consulted by the government and other authorities to improve their decision-making. The techniques of the opinion polls which were being developed at the time made this possible.

He actually did try, later, to make contact, for instance, with government ministers with this in mind. We are obviously unsurprised that his idiosyncratic approaches were brushed off and that the early members were embarrassed by them, rightly fearing that they would leave an impression of crankiness rather than wisdom.

Mensa never went far along that road after Berrill's days. However, a constantly recurring theme in my letters from new members is the thought that today, with our world-wide membership gradually climbing up towards a hundred thousand, there may be areas of opinion where it could be useful to compare the general average opinion with intelligent but otherwise random opinion. Where I think Berrill was wrong was in thinking that intelligent opinion is additive, that the opinion of an intelligent group must be more valid than that of an intelligent individual. Intelligence does not work like that. The views of the group have to interact and integrate before group outcome becomes better than solo outcome. Berrill's more important mistake was to expect that, on controversial questions, Mensa opinion would be more unanimous. Mensa is the living proof that, contrary to the adage, great minds (or at any rate bright minds), think unlike. The result of applying intelligence to an unsettled or controversial problem is the reverse. There are more and not fewer different opinions, less not more agreement. Berrill once said in a very revealing way, 'I have been shocked, again and again, by the way in which what seemed logical and obvious to me, proved quite otherwise to the majority of my acquaintances.'

There is no doubt that he expected, as he worked to build Mensa, that, at last, this would all come right. Everyone is intelligent. Berrill is intelligent. Everyone will agree with Berrill.

Alas! He found that on questions of opinion, that is on controversial questions, Mensa is simply more diverse and less conclusive. An important function of intelligence, where an answer is not yet known or knowable, is to throw up options, to propose choices, to explore the ground and produce hypotheses, schemes and plans for test by experiment, by trial and error, by judgemental or by democratic choice. Intelligence will find a logical track to a single answer when there is one to be found.

The Constitution, the rules of government for Mensa conceived by Berrill, were short, simple and completely impractical. He was at first, not unreasonably, as the man who did all the work and paid all the bills, an uncontested autocrat and it is doubtful Mensa would have got off the ground had he not been. No one opposed him because no one was sufficiently motivated. He went along, doing as he pleased, deciding everything, paying the bills and indulging his idiosyncratic whims and fancies with no correction and no reproof beyond the tolerant smiles or amused wry looks of his slowly growing band. 'Mensa', he said, 'aims at six hundred members and no more. It will be, and is now in our imagination, about the size of a battalion, . . . about the size of a clan; and being a clan it may have a clan's constitution, which is no constitution at all.'

Never much worried by the need for consistency he did decree a small written constitution. It put all power in the hands of 'The Secretary' (Berrill), and 'The Treasurer' (Berrill's choice). 'There will be no committees'. No mention was made of elections; they are not usual in clans. Disputes were to be settled by postal referenda. These were to be called at the request of any two members. Such innocent simplicity! If this were enforced today the subscriptions would have to be five thousand pounds a year so as to pay for twenty or thirty world-wide postal referenda a day. Mensa came to the day when it nearly died of constitution-eering. And as for elections, some of these were difficult to survive.

It was at this point that Berrill abandoned his hope that Mensa could be developed secretly, avoiding public attention. He began to put small advertisements in various places and these soon caused publicity in the press.

Publicity, he found, though often derisive, was the only way to extend Mensa beyond the friends of the small group, mostly bachelors who were its first activists.

This turned out to be a fundamental discovery. There is something about Mensa's pretensions that make it easy to get press reports. Mensa has survived and grown as it has learned to attract unpaid-for public attention via the media. It is only since 1980 that Mensa in Britain has begun to find effective ways to use large scale paid advertising for its development.

By April 1948 a Mensa dinner at the Trocadero drew 26 members to greet the newly-appointed Queen of Mensa the *Corps d'Esprit* V(R)D. Shy, petite Vera Davies was petrified by the experience. She spoke briefly in a soundless voice and with some agitation of spirit. Kenneth Brown tells of another dinner in 1948 when the queen-struck Berrill hired a large ornate room in which there had been set an enormous ormolu throne for the *Corps d'Esprit*. The tiny, modest, embarrassed Mensa Queen, Miss Davies, sat in misery in one small corner of her vast throne on a zebra skin provided by the dominant Berrill. Those present dutifully raised glasses in the Mensa royal toast with amusement, embarrassment or both, according to their nature.

Today, there is not much left of the Berrill panache and flavour in Mensa but he left three indelible marks on our traditions. The most important is the Annual Gathering which he started in November 1948. The second is a publication to which he gave the title, *Booklet of Common Interests and Unique Skills*. The third is the Monthly Dinner.

The first Annual Gathering was announced by Berrill in his normal imperial style.

'The Annual Gathering', he was gracious enough to inform us, 'is Residential. We all sleep under the same roof on the night of the first Saturday in November and take luncheon together on the Sunday. The roof chosen for Saturday 6 November 1948, is that of the Cumberland Hotel, Marble Arch, London, W1. Members are requested to take all meals in the hotel, and when using the dining rooms or any other public room, to go to the North West corner.'

Something was learned. Berrill's autocratic command was obeyed and many members turned up. The dining room was quite full. Members of Mensa seem to like having arrangements made for them and they do not want to be consulted over details. They like to be told what someone is willing to organise and then vote with their feet.

Those that attended were much impressed by open, free and contentious but urbane discussions and arguments. There was an intellectual intoxication in the air and everyone went away pleased. Perhaps that is why there has been no break in that tradition in the 36 years from that day until this. An annual residential national meeting is still a feature of all national Mensas. At one time or other of the year, we all sleep under one roof, as Berrill ordained.

The Annual Gathering, the AG as it is now called, has developed into an enormous jamboree with attendances in some places in America going as high as 1200. The popularity is deserved. They are well-organised, intellectual, social and gustatory feasts which leave many members, who are normally slightly starved of intellectually stimulating company, with a warm glow when they reluctantly and lovingly break up when the weekend is over.

That Berrill institution has even developed a smaller brother called a Regional Gathering (RG), which is spreading widely. American Mensa alone has several Regional Gatherings at various places all over the country every month. And today there are also a number of International Gatherings each year.

Berrill's *Booklet of Common Interests and Unique Skills*, under the more sober title *Mensa Register*, is published sporadically in most countries until growing numbers create the obvious financial problem. Registers get larger and more expensive faster than the willingness to pay for them. But when they are published with full details of the interests and skills of all members and with a cross reference system, they are an invaluable talent bank for members and others. Many useful ideas, inventions, companies, projects, marriages and associations have come into existence through this agency.

Berrill's third tradition, the formal monthly dinners, had very much their own flavour. He used to hate the kind of dinner which breaks up into competing chit-chat between table neighbours and always insisted that conversation must be general. To that end he took the chairman role with the rule, 'One at a time, all talk to all.' When a topic flagged, he had the habit, terrifying to shy new members, of suddenly turning his commanding exophthalmic eyes upon the innocent newcomer and commanding, 'propose a topic'. Obediently they did.

The true Berrill-style formal Black Tie Dinner died during the sad, long, years of the age of scruffy boiler suits, which is now mercifully passing. It has been revived amid loud cries of 'elitism' in London and several other places over the last five years. London's 'The President's Dinner' and the equally good 'Other Black Tie Dinner' each month are over-subscribed regularly. The trick is to get a table as equal in length and width as possible (round is ideal) to ignore fashion and insist on formal dress to give a sense of occasion, and to have a chairman who unobtrusively encourages the 'each to all' rule. There has to be a limit to numbers at table. Twenty-four is just possible; twelve is ideal.

Berrill's Mensa magazine started in April 1947 and was issued monthly only until that August. In that month there was both a *Mensa Magazine* and a *Mensa Quarterly*. Twenty-two issues of *The Mensa Quarterly* were published between then and June 1960 when I had become the editor and changed the name to *The Mensa Proceedings* (in the interests of accuracy about what had become an annual). Meanwhile another simple monthly, three-page, duplicated sheet, *The Mensa Correspondence*, appeared (edited by Basil Mager) in January 1959 and this has continued with various name changes to the present day.

This monthly magazine split as we grew into different national journals of which there are now about twenty. The modern British version *MENSA* is a glossy well printed periodical with full colour illustrations and a professional style. The *Mensa Bulletin* from American Mensa is another such descendant. It is a well produced 36-page journal with a circulation of 50,000.

All the national monthly Mensa journals include a section to keep all members in mind of Mensa's cosmopolitan nature. *The Mensa Journal International* comprises between four and eight pages of international articles and correspondence from an independent international editor. These go out monthly to members world-wide. The annual *Mensa Proceedings*, which was in the direct line from Berril's *Mensa Magazine*, died in June 1960.

There is another Berrill tradition which partially survives. Berrill suggested what he thought of as an inconspicuous sign which members could wear as a badge for recognition only by other members. Members should sew a small yellow button where it could be visible on their clothing. This impractical idea never caught on in that form but in the first issue of *The Mensa Correspondence* I reminded an enquirer of the idea and suggested that a small yellow-headed map pin would be more convenient. This did catch on and is still the practice among veteran members. But now there are Mensa ties, badges, bumper stickers, sweat shirts, scarves and many other such horrors. They have the name 'Mensa' in letters up to twenty centimetres high.

The oddest of these recognition symbols was (of course) also a Berrill scheme. Each member was to fit a glazed tile in the hearth at their home. The tiles, which Berrill sent us all in 1950, bore the dread symbol of the three conspiring Klansters and was of a size which fitted no known standard. Berrill must have paid a great deal to have them designed and made. He sent hundreds to members.

Berrill's idea was anonymity. These were secret signs to be seen and understood only by the observant eyes of the cognoscenti. Not one of these tiles, except the one he had, I am sure, was ever installed by the ungrateful recipients.

In 1949 the Second Annual Gathering was held and 60 members turned up. Berrill's friend Jaques Schupbach described these Gatherings. 'It is difficult to give an adequate idea of these two Gatherings. I think that most of those who attended will remember them with some sense of achievement. At the discussion we had at the Jill-on-the-Green restaurant we felt that Mensa was taking shape. At these two Annual Gatherings one could feel that Mensa had come into being, and showed a strange vitality and appetite for discussion on a wide range of topics continuing all day, far into the night, and throughout the following day, with little signs of flagging. It was an exhilarating experience, but accomplished with no appearance of effort, spontaneously and naturally.'

Between 1948 and 1950 Berrill continued assiduously recruiting, gradually gaining experience, publicity and members. I have his early scrapbook and it is, I am afraid, quite clear that the image projected was that of a cranky group. Berrill tended to project his own views in such a way that they seemed to be Mensan and, since he was deficient in normal scepticism, his views were none too popular with Mensa's intelligent members. Palmistry, phrenology, dress reform, astrology and later Dianetics were among the many unpopular (in Mensa) cults that he favoured.

The active founding group, apart from Elaine Ware, were largely bachelors. Berrill never married. Ware did, but not until he was well into his sixties. Kenneth Passmore Brown and Jaques Schupbach were life-long bachelors. If this is significant it might be that intelligent companionship is of more value to the single than to the married man.

What was to be a persistent phenomenon in Mensa throughout its history made its first appearance between 1948 and 1950, when some members gradually began to object to Berrill's oddities.

It was late in 1949 that, at the suggestion of my first wife Mary, I sent a letter which started my Mensa career and transformed my life. I was newly out of the army, not very long married, and the father of a baby boy. I was the manager of a sawmill for a large timber importer on the Thames in Essex.

Roland Berrill's prompt reply to my letter brought a 'preliminary' home IQ Test. If I did well enough on this I was to be summoned for further examination. I did the test and sent it back. Berrill's autocratic reply firmly announced that I had 'cleared the bar at the arbitrary height at which we have pegged it, with sufficient daylight to spare, that we can accept you on the preliminary test alone without more ado.'

Berrill gave full details of my score on every subtest and showed his arithmetic. Any professional psychologist would have been shocked at such a revelation of the hidden mysteries. Berrill's letter continued in high vein, 'It is a brilliant performance!'

I was, according to his brochure, now one of an 'aristocracy of the intellect', whose opinions and advice might be useful to the Powers That Be. He had 'great pleasure in enclosing my Certificate', and hoped that I 'would be willing to place my extremely rare gifts to the service of my country and of humanity'.

I subsequently learned that the dreaded supervised test was a bluff to discourage cheating.

I was immodestly pleased at Berrill's news and, though intrigued, I remained hard-headed enough to be underwhelmed and faintly suspicious of such effusiveness. But I was reassured by the fact that I had not been asked for any money. 'So far', I thought. I was happy to have the views of the British army psychologist confirmed. I was highly intelligent.

At that time Berrill thought, as I have said, that he was selecting at the level of one in 3,000. My immodesty was equal to the task of accepting this exaggerated assessment with complacency. I had in fact rung the bell with the highest possible score on that test.

I began to receive at about monthly intervals Berrill's well-presented but odd circulations written in curious but impeccable English. I filled in his 'Interrogatories' and began to correspond with him about my proposed postal debates.

In this way my story was typical. Those members of Mensa who become the activists, usually acquire the addiction in stages. Mensa grows on you. It did so even then.

I was curious and mildly amused by all this, but I lived with my new high intellectual status in irresponsible unconcern as I went about my busy affairs. Little, as they say in novels, did I dream how much the rest of my life would be affected by this tenuously established contact with a very peculiar new group.

My first really intoxicating injection of the Mensa drug did not occur until many months later after reading the curiously compelling, autocratic instruction in a later edition of the *Mensa Quarterly*. We were all to sleep under the same roof at the Charing Cross Hotel on the Saturday 4 November 1950. I was summoned to the Presence. Resist I could not.

The Hotel is by London's south east railway terminal at

Charing Cross. It is a West End spot under the stern single eye of Nelson on his column in Trafalgar Square.

I duly turned up with a mixture of curiosity and trepidation to introduce myself to the group in the north east corner of the lounge, according to Berrill's careful instructions. The first encounter of the tyro member with Mensa colleagues remains traumatic, even today. Mensans are recruited largely by post and every member that actually joins in our activities (usually a minority), has to pass this hurdle of anticipated embarrassment.

What is one to expect from such a concentrated group of advanced intelligences? Can one possibly be up to this high standard or will one encounter compassionate smiles of embarrassment whenever one opens one's foolish mouth?

The event was utterly other than the anticipation.

I knew Berrill at once, because his face was prominent in the publications he liberally supplied to members in various forms. He was an impressive, stocky man with a full beard and bold, well-trimmed moustache. Of middle height, with staring eyes, and dark brown hair he spoke confidently to the group around him. There was an inevitability about his domination of the conversation, if that is what it could be called.

Self-consciousness was impossible for the pleasant, very mixed, but largely middle and upper class group of men and women who were occupying the armchairs in the designated corner. How can you be self-conscious when there seems to be no chance to get a word in?

I cannot remember what we discussed, or perhaps I should say he pronounced, except that it was impressive and interesting. I can remember the style and manner of his speech which was absolutely splendid.

Berrill spoke impeccably perfect prose with a confidence, facility and unanswerability that seemed more appropriate to a pope on his St Peter's Square balcony than to a layman in a hotel lounge.

I have never met anyone with quite his extraordinary power of making highly implausible notions sound like the Word of God. I listened in wrapt fascination. Perhaps, after all, I was in a circle of Greater Minds which dwelt in a world of the intellect far beyond my ken. It was only afterwards when chatting with the others that I was reassured. All of them felt much like I did once out of the Presence.

Berrill was a splendid quoter. He had an endless fund of perfectly remembered quotations from most of the books that educated Englishmen read. He had perfect instant recall. He ·interlarded his fascinating conversation with apt and well-remembered quotations and was always ready to deal with that despicable animal, the counter-quoter.

Counter-quoters, those who tried the nasty trick of correcting, capping or continuing his quotations, had short shrift with Berrill. He was as adept at counter-counter-quoting, correcting, capping or continuing counter-quotes as he was at quoting itself.

'Very apt', he would come back at the counter-quoter, 'very apt indeed, but you will remember of course that a little further on in the play (book or whatever) the author also says . . .' and then Berrill would continue with a correction, reservation or flat contradiction of the counter-quote.

He acknowledged me when I introduced myself with a nod. We had had some correspondence and I think we discussed my postal debates scheme, that which later led to my first Mensa activity.

I remember only two other incidents from that stimulating and habit-forming weekend when I got hooked on the addictive drug, Mensa.

The first was being thrown out by the cleaners at five o'clock in the morning after an all-night argument with the persuasive Tim Lazarides (husband of the then reigning *Corps d'Esprit*) about order, disorder and entropy.

My other memory was meeting, and not particularly liking, a tall woman, very smartly dressed in black, her then unfashionably long dark hair in a neat bun. When my first wife Mary died, I was to fall in love with and marry this dark-haired woman. Win Rouse as she preferred to be called (rather than Winifred), made a strong impression as a fast-thinking and rather ruthlessly brilliant wit but I was not used to that remarkable kind of woman then. I do remember just one of her sallies. A girl called Lily Lobner was complaining that Freud's theories did not work with her. 'Unacceptable desires', said Lily, 'are supposed to be sublimated in one's dreams but last night I dreamed that my father and I were having an incestuous affair.' 'I can interpret that,' said Win, 'it means that you had a suppressed desire to have a boiled egg for your breakfast'.

That was my first experience of Mensa and I was hooked. I went home on the Sunday evening quite intoxicated by the intellectual effervescence. My brain was quite buzzing from the stimulation. I had not had a University education and had never been in such a large intellectual company before. The kind of conversation that I had, the freedom of expression and language, the fluidity of the exchange of ideas, the give and take, the willingness to listen and actually respond to what I said, was quite new for me in any largish group.

I began to attend Berrill's Monthly Dinners which at that time were held at Beguinot's restaurant in Soho. Those evenings were all of a piece with that early experience and I began to get to know Berrill and the members who came regularly. Win was one of them. Joseph and George Wilson, and Ralph Spicer were others.

Berrill was a man who ought to have been of the first rather than the second Elizabethan age. At these memorable dinners he was always, splendidly, the upper class autocrat. Waiters loved him the more for it. He was like royalty or the Pope, magnificently unselfconscious, unaware of the attention that he inevitably attracted.

At one dinner at the A La Brioche restaurant in Jermyn Street he began to complain of the service in an unsubdued fashion and soon the head waiter and several others were swarming round trying to pacify him. While we less extrovert Mensans shrank into our embarrassed collars, Berrill explained carefully and with detailed illustrations how a waiter should do his job. The experienced restaurant manager, who had by that time arrived; skilfully diverted Berrill from this topic, which was beginning to attract general attention by telling him that he would value his opinion on a very special wine.

By this time attention in the large dining room was general and the elegantly dressed people at other tables were turning our way. Berrill condescended to be mollified and a waiter dashed away to obtain the pacifying bottle. He returned carrying the bottle with the traditional reverent care which he had been trained to show. The manager himself, with due ceremony, poured the single glass of the precious fluid and set it before our Roland. There was a prolonged pause. The manager looked enquiringly at Berrill.

'Well! After this sad little claret surely I should have an olive to clear my palate if you want me to give a worthwhile opinion. A black one, if you please.'

'Immediately, sir.'

Another waiter hurried away. People at other tables were standing and staring frankly. There was tension in the air. The other Mensans at the table tried to look like pieces of furniture. The waiter speeded back with a single black olive on a silver tray.

Roland Berrill was unhurried. He took the olive, examined it while people at the nearby tables moved in to get a better view of the show. He masticated the olive for what seemed like an hour or two as general interest grew. Then he slowly deposited the stone on the proffered salver, took the glass, rolled the wine round, held it to the light, frowned and sipped.

The restaurant clientele was at a breath-holding standstill. There was a complete silence.

He sipped again, swizzled the wine round his mouth, paused, sipped again, considered the matter with time and care. Then he pronounced.

'It is a little sharp.'

At one public meeting he was handing down, from the platform, his proclamations about the world for our instruction when he became aware that the correct, respectful, assenting silence he required was defective. There was a pestering gadfly in the form of a young student member, Peter Rollings, who was actually interrupting from time to time with politely expressed, mild qualifications and contradictions. For a time Roland Berrill ignored the trivial distraction. Then he stopped and turned the full dreadful force of his severe gaze upon the irritating young man.

'Sir', he proclaimed, 'you have a neurotic tendency to disagree.'

Peter's reply was instantaneous.

'Sir. I disagree.'

We now have to turn back to Berrill's growing political troubles. As I have said, members began to raise objections to his eccentric, benevolent autocratic rule. In particular objection was made to his habit of exploiting and enjoying the publicity that Mensa was beginning to attract, to put forward his own odd views.

The critics' problem was that with an absurdly low subscription which did not pay for a fraction of the costs, Berrill, who largely paid the piper, was, by general apathetic consent, able to call the tune. The most expensive process, recruitment, was done without charge to the candidate, and since Mensa has to process at least ten applications to get one member, it depended entirely on the deep, generous Berrill pocket for survival. But dissenting voices are never far below the surface in Mensa and a group came to the Annual Gathering in 1950 to insist on the setting up of a commission to examine the defects of the existing Constitution and practice. The commission was led by a Dr Cyril Eastwood.

Its report in March 1951 was extraordinary in the extreme. It suggested that the affairs of the society should be administered by a council selected not by Berrill, not by the members, not by the *Corps d'Esprit*, but by chance, by drawing names out of a hat. This was to happen every six months (obviously to make quite sure that no one ever got any experience of what they were doing). Mensa was to be the first society in the world to be governed by random chance. Unbelievably the two hundred and forty-two members (47 women), accepted (by a 57 percent vote) this ridiculous recommendation in a ballot that was put to them.

The hat-picked council was predictably ineffective, few turned up and no one did anything. It seemed that Mensa was going to have to take desire and ability to serve into account like every other organisation. A great truth was established. High intelligence is a poor defence against collective stupidity.

It was at the Annual Gathering in 1951 that things came to a head. The first of innumerable Mensa struggles for power began. This first one ended most oddly.

Berrill was popular with most members but his critics wanted to curb his habit of promoting himself and his unusual ideas publicly. We can sympathise. To give an instance: in an article in the *News Review* he told the world that he had been guided by astrology when he started the society on his fiftieth birthday in 1946. (He actually started on the 1st and his birthday was the 6th.)

'You see', he seems to have told the grinning journalist, 'my Fourth House is very good. That indicates Inheritance. I shall have the Midas touch in my declining years. I cannot fail. I had the leisure and the money – and very few people have both. I concluded that Mensa was a job which should be done so I decided to do it.'

With trouble brewing, lobbying began at the 1951 Gathering and Joseph Wilson told me that there was a plot to oust Berrill, led by Dr Eastwood who would be standing as chairman against him with the plan to introduce democracy into Mensa. We were invited to support Berrill and, all unthinking, we did so. The result showed us how unpredictable Mensa was going to be. After a long but relatively polite debate in which Berrill was for once embarrassed and outclassed, Mensa's democratic vote was in favour of the autocrat and against democracy. Dr Eastwood, who had been given the chair by Berrill, and who had spoken well and sensibly, left it and swept out in evident disgust. Shortly afterwards the Council resigned *en bloc*.

After the vote we all felt a sense of exhilaration and cheered a great victory. But, looking back, all the ideas suggested by the Eastwood group have in fact been incorporated into the Mensa structure since. The Berrill notion of loose control, individual initiative, much ceremonial formality but no formal organisation or committees, seemed to have an anarchic appeal to the early members. Later events proved, as we shall see, that such methods were not viable and could not be sustained.

The 1951 meeting broke up in amused disorder and since we could see that Berrill was seriously upset and deeply discouraged by the hassle and the challenge, no one knew what would happen next.

What did happen was that Mensa lost the work, care and cash of its Founder and only activist and went into a long, almost fatal, decline. Such things have happened scores of times in the history of the society. Those who come forward to work effectively for Mensa are allowed to do so with some encouragement for a time. Then inevitably, after some successes, an out-group arises that contests the leadership of the active group. The active workers now find that as well as devoting all their spare time to the society they have to engage in a political struggle for the doubtful privilege of being allowed to go on doing so.

There being no great motivation they usually just stop. Then, often, the dissident group takes over. Sometimes this works out but more usually it is found that what the new clique is good at and interested in, is criticism *tout court*. As managers and organisers they usually turn out to be supine and their talent for complaint is used upon each other. Normally a period of squabbling decline sets in until some new set of active enthusiasts come forward. Oddly enough inactive and quarrelsome committees and groups do not attract opposition, only apathy. It is active and successful cliques who are given the label 'entrenched establishment', and are opposed by counter cliques.

It might be thought, of course, that if Dr Eastwood had been supported with his very reasonable demands for a democratic structure that all might have gone differently and the present day sort of Mensa might have arisen earlier.

This is doubtful because it was tried and did not work. Shortly after the 1951 meeting the dissident faction sent a circular to all members and we were asked to drop out of Mensa and join a new and democratic rival organisation which had been set up. This included Dr Eastwood and a dozen or so other members. However, the breakaway movement was still-born and nothing was heard of it after that first circular.

Berrill did not resign immediately but he began to sound very dissatisfied.

'The society,' he bitterly complained, 'lacks Cohesion. With our quarterly journal I sent a post card for return. But I only got 130 out of 239. That is bad. One must have Focus (that's me), Obligation (to send back the post card), and Obedience (the act of sending back the post card), the same as in the catholic church.'

When he got 199 postcards back out of 258 later he relented

and described it as 'a display of Conscientiousness, of Benevolence, and of Order that, when one remembers that a possession of these three virtues is not a condition precedent to membership of this society is extremely gratifying.'

But after the traumatic events of the 1951 meeting he returned to the miseries again. Via Darwin, Comic Verse and St Joan, in an editorial he finally came down to the shortcomings of the unresponsive members. 'Non- or delayed compliance', he irritably explained to us, referring to our refusal to send enough post cards to please him, 'must be due to psychological difficulties and not at all to circumstances'.

'First', the disobedient members are sadly told, 'to sign the card and lick on the stamp is in the nature of Work, as distinct from Sport or Play. Secondly, it is an expression of good will, of Kindness, of Benevolence, of Friendship, towards another adult male of the same genus. Thirdly it is a subordinate action. It is done from a sense of obligation. Fourthly it has something to do with politics and homo sapiens has no political sense whatever. He just does not care. How can he? The instinct is not there. Lastly, it is above all a gregarious or social action, its whole confessed purpose being to strengthen the group, as a group, like a herd of zebra, or a hive of bees, and that is precisely what homo sapiens does not want.' What a lot we learned about the whole human race from neglecting to send post cards!

Berrill never learned as a thousand Mensa enthusiasts who followed him never learn that whinging at unresponsive members is counter-productive. Members respond to that which touches their own interests. They cannot be infected or even persuaded by the enthusiasms of others. Mensa organisers must offer, members must choose. No grumbling if they do not choose what is offered. Offer something else, or seize a wonderful opportunity to be still.

In January 1952, after five and a half years of expenditure and effort, deeply disappointed with his creation, Mensa's generous, energetic, eccentric Founder, Roland Berrill, threw his hand in, resigned as Secretary and handed over the responsibility of Secretary to the late Joseph Wilson.

It was at that time that Berrill wrote the first among many

disappointed valedictories that have ended Mensa careers since. His was a good one and worth recording.

'Although I seem to have mastered the problem of Expansion, slow though our expansion was, I have found myself after five years of experiment, still baffled by the problem of Cohesion, and so decide to pass the problem to another mind.'

'The trouble with all these modern associations and societies,' the disconsolate Berrill went on, never worried about generalising from a single case, 'is that they are a pleasure to found, a pleasure to organise and a pleasure to join; but they are not a pleasure to belong to. Over the course of the last five years, I have employed every cohesive device that I could think of, and that my purse could buy – a superbly printed List of Members, the unique booklet of Common Interests and Unique Skills, a reminder card looking like a threat from The Black Hand, an expensive and beautiful periodical offering self-expression to the members, the Ornamental Tile, the Monthly Dinners in the West End of London and the Annual Gathering. Alas! Not one of these devices had had the effect desired.'

He complained that he had had, at great expense, to test 1,500 to gain a paltry 325 (a success rate that would cause elation or suspicion or both in any modern more rigorous Mensa). 'Less than half', Berrill went on, returning to the case against the unresponsiveness of Mensans, 'have been worth a damn, that is sufficiently loyal to perform their simple duties.'

Then with a last fierce complaint of the miserable 44 percent 'who bothered to reply', he concludes: 'Members will readily understand that there is a limit to the amount of discouragement that even the keenest organiser can endure.'

Wishing Joe Wilson, his successor, every success with his discarded duties, the disappointed man continued, 'A fresh mind may be able to think of something, a psychological device, some piece of emotional engineering, that will galvanise members and bring Mensa a new vigour and a new life.'

After 1952 he came more and more rarely to our meetings and eventually moved away from London to Eastbourne, where he took a flat.

Perhaps foreseeing his early death he contacted me a year or two later, out of the blue, and invited me down to a dinner. All his life he had been a man of ephemeral enthusiasms and he was deeply engaged in several of new crankeries about which he waxed enthusiastic over a good dinner which he had cooked and served himself. He had survived a stroke but was not well. There was a nurse in attendance but she was snapped at and kept in another room. After dinner he disappeared and returned with an enormous allegorical oil painting which he had commissioned and the painting of which, it seemed, he had closely supervised, brush stroke by brush stroke. He went into great detail for a long time explaining the symbolism and all the curious crowded figures in it. I was completely mystified.

Then quite suddenly, he said, 'And now you must rush to catch your train', took me to the door, thrust the enormous unwrapped painting into my arms as a gift, bid me farewell and sent me out into a rainstorm. I had brought no coat. I stood outside bewildered but lacked the courage to ring again and ask him to call a taxi. Eventually I set off, setting my large awkward burden down from time to time, trying hopelessly to flag down unresponsive taxis. Eventually I arrived on foot at the war-bombed, roofless station and waited in the rain, my enormous, curious, rain-soaked painting by my side, for the next train to London which was over an hour later. The painting was decisively unattractive but finally I managed to get a friend of Roland's to take it off my hands as a memento after his death. I never saw him again. Nor, mercifully, it.

Roland Berrill told us little about his early life but I have the story from his surviving younger brother Adrian, now eighty years old, and his nephew and one of the first few Mensa members, Mr Christopher Cruice Goodall. Cruice Goodall, who was Berrill's executor, was for many years the Managing Director of a large and successful company, Gordon and Gotch. Much of Berrill's income seems to have come from investments in that company.

There was a period during the depression, when some of Berrill's investments were passing dividends, when he became poor almost to the point of vagrancy. He seems never to have been gainfully employed apart from the period of his army service. He fought as an officer on the Somme in the first world war and later joined the Air Force with the rank of Flying Officer.

Both his relatives maintain that there is no question that it was Roland Berrill who was both the Founder and the 'fons et origo' of Mensa and I have a letter from Judge Galpin who was one of the earliest members to the same effect. Mr Cruice Goodall told me that Berrill knew Sir Cyril Burt much earlier than has been supposed since they met socially before 1945 when Ware and Berrill met. He says that he had been under the impression that the discussions about a possible high IQ club took place between the professor and Berrill much earlier than the Burt broadcast (which was probably in November 1946). This would mean that Dr Ware's suggestions to Berrill in July 1945 may have been falling on previously prepared ground. We cannot know for sure.

Adrian Berrill's story about his brother is revealing. He outlines the circumstances that formed the character of a very unusual man. Roland's elder brother, Bernard, was a profound influence. He was one of those public schoolboys of almost appalling excellence who fell in the idiotic slaughter of the first world war. Quoting his brother Adrian: 'The eldest son of our family, Bernard, was by any standards the real "golden lad". He was successful in practically everything he undertook, he became Captain of the school, Captain of the boating club (he stroked the school eight to unprecedented wins at Henley and the other regattas up and down the Thames); Colour Sergeant of the School Officers' Training Corps, Victor Ludorum as well as taking the academic prizes . . . When he went up to Oxford the Master of Balliol remarked to someone, "The school that produced this boy must be the finest school in England." '

When war broke out Bernard was desperate to get into the front line and was killed in action on St Patrick's Day 1915.

This was the elder brother whose achievements our poor Roland had to live with and up to. According to upper middle class tradition his parents would have preferred him to be a girl and he was not given the chances or the encouragement his triumphant elder brother had. So perhaps the weaknesses we find in Berrill have their root in this aspect of his early life.

What does Adrian tell us about his middle brother Roland? First he admits that there had been a prolonged rift between them but that now he felt closer to his late brother whose initiative had produced such a strange and unexpected result in the development of Mensa.

In an unfinished recent letter intended for Paul Griffin, a very early member and Berrill's friend, Adrian Berrill says of his brother, 'he was undoubtedly a strange character, highly intelligent but somewhat lacking in practical common sense. It is sad that, with his potential, he made so little of his life. His personal idiosyncrasies and egocentricities seemed always to prevent him from making a real success of anything. Mensa might be considered his only monument. It was a good idea as is proved by the fact that it not only survived and expanded but it has become generally recognised and, "member of Mensa", is now commonly used on the *curriculum vitae* by those applying for responsible jobs.'

'Over the years I and members of the family – especially my poor mother – suffered much social embarrassment and no little financial loss from what you (Griffin) aptly describe as his "outrageous gestures". Nevertheless I find it hard to be angry with him now, as I remember many kindnesses from him when we were young.'

Adrian Berrill then goes on to tell Paul Griffin of the early life of the man described around the family as 'Great Uncle Roly'.

'Roland was always known in the family by the childhood nickname "Pie" from the nursery rhyme "Roly poly pudding and pie". He was the second of a family of four and I was the youngest. My sister Joan came in between. Pie was seven years older than I was . . .'

'He was apparently a perfectly normal little boy and reputedly "a beautiful child" with his curly hair and cherubic face . . . When he was old enough he went to St John's, the junior school for Beaumont (a public school). Again he appears to have been a thoroughly normal, healthy and popular small boy and after a few years he was made Captain of the school. It was then that things started to happen, that must have led to profound effect on the rest of his life.'

Adrian describes how 'Pie' had a sudden inexplicable illness. After an exploratory operation on his stomach his condition became grave and there were sixty little boys at the school praying for the life of their popular Captain. Then, as unexpectedly as they started the symptoms abated and 'Pie' recovered. 'There is still', says Adrian, 'in the beautiful little chapel at St John's . . . a brass plate commemorating "the miraculous recovery of Roland Berrill".'

Pie appears to have been unhappy at public school because, his brother thinks, he was so much more intelligent than the others but not recognised for it. He was a sensitive boy, just having recovered from a serious illness, not allowed to do sports, among strangers in a strange place and having come from a little school where he had been popular and important. It was the little fish who had dominated the small pond finding himself with many rivals in the big pond. And, worse, one of those rivals was his own brother, the brilliantly successful and popular Bernard, two years his senior and one of the 'swells' of this very snobbish English public school. This particular trauma is one which affects many Mensans.

Before I leave the Berrill epoch I must recognise others in the pioneer phase.

I have the 1946 Mensa files of Brian Galpin, now Judge Brian Galpin, and of Paul Griffin. Galpin was very active and helpful during a period starting in 1946. Much correspondence shows that he played an active role in helping and comforting Berrill in the early discouraging days. In a recent letter to me he says that he always thought of Berrill himself as the *fons et origo* of Mensa.

Even more helpful to Berrill was Paul Griffin whose voluminous detailed files tell us a lot. Paul was a public schoolmaster at the time. The correspondence starts very formally in 1946 and extends to 1952, by which time it has become friendly. It contains many of Berrill's highly individualistic letters. Griffin played an important and so far unrecognised part because Berrill had evidently loaded a lot of the routine work on to his friend who seemed to have done it with quiet efficiency.

Berrill's letters are very emotional about Mensa. He is up in the air with optimism at one moment and very depressed the next. He is bitter about those early members who resigned or failed to respond. 'Good riddance!', he spitefully says of one. Another early helper was Yorke Crompton, the first of many treasurers.

To say that the next epoch in Mensa, that of Joseph Wilson, was placid would give too great an impression of activity and progress. Joe was the uniovular twin brother of George and the two, being the sons of the very rich and indulgent widow of a Glasgow shipbuilder, lived in a very nice apartment in the very fashionable and expensive district of Queen's Gate, Kensington, where the post-Berrill Mensa was to be forged.

Joseph and George were stocky lowland Scots, each having an educated but strong Glaswegian accent. They were much alike, greying early at under forty and dressed with great care and fashion. Both were gentlemen in the best sense of the word. They were deeply interested in and lived for the arts.

Utterly unambitious, kind, sensitive, perceptive, brilliantly intelligent and witty, Joe was one of those whose desire was to be, to experience, to know, rather than to do, to make things happen, to leave a mark. He taught me to love ballet, and, with his alert eyes ever on all that was good, introduced Win and me to many delightful artistic experiences which we never would have known without him.

In Mensa as the new Secretary he continued the traditions that Berrill had established. The London dinners continued and the tradition of the Annual Gathering was uninterrupted during the two Wilson years of Mensa. There was little further recruitment, the *Mensa Quarterly* faded to an occasional single sheet and the three hundred-odd members Berrill had accumulated so painfully began, gently and imperceptibly to fade away like the Cheshire cat until little but a small rump of monthly diners was left as the remaining smile.

Joe believed in Berrill's notion of dispersed responsibility and rejected any idea of central initiative or enterprise. He was a busy executive and all his spare time went to satisfy his passionate appetite for artistic experience. After hating his war service in the British Army, he was a dedicated anti-authoritarian and so not the undiscourageable, persistent zealot who would be needed to set Mensa rolling again.

To my own amazement it was I that turned out to be that. I proved that there is no limit to the amount of discouragement that a Mensa organiser can endure and still go persistently on.

In September 1950, a little before my thirty-eighth birthday, my daughter Judith slid into the world. Mary and I now had two babies; we loved them and were very happy.

However, tragically soon afterwards Mary found a neoplasm on her tongue and, being a nurse by profession, knew what it was. Cancer.

The next two years were an up-and-down agony of operations, repeatedly revived and repeatedly doomed hopes, as the torturing disease gradually turned my wife, into an emaciated, agonised wretch, sustained only by her supreme, cheerful, obstinate, uncomplaining courage and her love for myself and her babies. We both knew she was to die but we never once discussed it. At the end of July 1952 the end came in the London Hospital in Whitechapel, East London.

Serving as a lady almoner, or medical social worker there, was the reigning Queen of Mensa, Miss Winifred Ida Rouse, MA, by that time the *Corps d'Esprit* of our declining band.

The night Mary died I was awoken from the merciful sleep which had overtaken me by the nurse with the inevitable British cup of tea. 'I've brought your bad news.'

Then, worried about a widower with two young babies, she told me to wait for morning and see the lady almoner.

There were a dozen almoners but the one I saw next morning was a familiar figure, well dressed, always in black, well-groomed and well-manicured, a confident and sophisticated lady looking at me with cool compassion through her smart, high myopia spectacles. It was Win Rouse.

She received me kindly and presented a persona different from the brilliant Lady Sharpwit that I knew, and by now respected and liked as a fellow member at Mensa dinners. Professionally she hid her surprise when I responded to her professional concern with an invitation to the theatre.

What could she say to a distracted bereaved man but, 'yes'. I do not understand myself sometimes. I do not feel good about that. But it turned out to be the most rewarded of the many examples of erratic behaviour in my life.

One thing leads to another. VVS began a stormy friendship with WIR. Then they began an even more tempestuous love affair which thirty-two years later is still going on.

A year later WIR suddenly stopped replying to the numerous proposals made by the widower, VVS, by saying that she could not 'see her way clear'. One day she 'saw her way clear' and became WIS at a registry office in Grimsby.

The children stayed with their grandmother for a time but when we had room my family was reunited and Win became the good and beloved stepmother who brought up Mark, my policeman son and my small, pretty, redheaded daughter Judith.

An article of mine had been published in the July *Mensa Quarterly* in 1952 in which I said that membership and interest were waning. 'This is either a normal plateau on the growth curve, heralding a fresh onset of expansion', I wrote, optimistically promoting a sharp decline to level pegging, 'or it may be a symptom of the collapse of the attempt to form an association of this kind.'

Then, quietly ignoring this likely, if pessimistic possibility, I went on: 'Assuming it is possible and desirable for a society by its nature so divided to continue, I should like to initiate a discussion of Mensa's purposes and possibilities so that we may determine a technique for the future.'

In a long article which attracted not one reply I set out the principles which I was to apply with some success later.

I questioned the assumption that high intelligence was additive, had any special value in the sense that the distribution of opinion in a bright group was somehow 'better' than that in an average one. I said that the evidence from the few Mensa researches I had done was that the distribution of intelligent opinion on what were really undecided or controversial questions spread over more opinion positions. It was more diverse. It was not more valid, merely less conclusive. I wanted Mensa opinion to be compared with the opinion expressed by an ordinary opinion poll.

I wanted to externalise the observer to have Mensa research conducted by scientists familiar with the statistical disciplines and those of the field. Membership brought a subjective influence. I questioned the randomness of the Mensa sample as a fair representation of intelligent opinion generally. I scouted the idea that the Mensa opinion split on matters involving specialist knowledge would be particularly valuable. I thought that when looking at general matters involving value judgements, the possession of a good mind might make it possible to take more into account so that in ethics, moral philosophy, metaphysics, art, religion and any other subject where expert prior knowledge was not vital, a Mensa collective judgement analysis might be more valued.

Mensa seemed to have most success as a social club but insofar as we were successful in that way we undermined our value for the Burt purpose of acting as a random sample to be used for finding out the distribution of intelligent opinion. Leadership, group loyalty and even our intellectual interaction would skew our sample and make it invalid.

Organising Mensa was an entirely new kind of problem. Most societies assemble round accepted views and tenets and seek uniformity. Our aim was to collect an intelligent sample and to seek to preserve random diversity. That would make things difficult.

We had to find a structure which would allow us to expand and cohere but in contradiction we had to ensure and retain our representative randomness, our protean diversity.

With Berrill gone Mensa was at its nadir. Through the rest of 1952 and most of 1953 we subsided gently like a badly tied balloon. A quarterly gathering was held at the Charing Cross Hotel in April and without Berrill's peremptory summons only a few members turned up. My scheme for reorganisation was discussed but only a luke-warm pessimistic non-rejection was accorded. The *Mensa Quarterly* appeared in July reduced to two small sheets, most of which was occupied by an article in which someone tried to draw courage from the fact that 'it is almost impossible to kill a penguin', describing how the poor birds lie for days in the snow after being battered about the head most severely. The bedraggled, blood-stained birds, we were encouraged to hear, then get up and stagger away. The writer's bold *non-sequitur* was that Mensa too had this fierce latent will to live. He noted that our paid-up membership had dropped to 120.

There was a short piece from me and a *'cri du coeur'* from

Secretary Wilson pleading for someone to take over the job for which he said he was too busy.

And not much later I did.

2

History: the takeover

It happened at a Mensa Monthly Dinner at Beguinot's Restaurant sometime late in 1953. The crowd of sixteen or so that used to be at table in Berrill's days, had shrunk to a tiny circle: the Wilson brothers, Win, and I. The discussion turned to Mensa affairs and George Wilson pointed out that it had been the same four at the last few dinners. 'This is not a Mensa dinner,' he reasonably pointed out. 'We are just four friends who enjoy eating together.' Joe then reminded us that he had had no volunteer after his request to be relieved and that we ought to face the fact that Mensa had quietly expired.

I agreed but I paused, remembering the great thrill and joy it had been when I first went to the Annual Gathering three years before. 'It seems a pity', I foolishly said.

That was the turning point. I had taken up the defence and released Joe to be the pessimist. I began to outline things I thought could be done and my late friend turned them down, stressed the difficulties, pointed out the problems and ever and again said, 'But who will do the work?'

I was finally goaded into an offer: 'Let me have a try at a membership campaign'. Joe then suggested that I should do the work and assume, experimentally, the status of Joint Secretary with him.

The joint idea never worked at all and I was effectively the Secretary, Chief Executive and Principal Officer of Mensa from that moment, without the slightest objection from the handful of members who were still paying up by then. The financial responsibility was not too daunting. The Treasurer had declared in July that the entire assets of Mensa, which it was his responsibility to administer, amounted to twenty-five pounds sterling. I have tried my best to be a good custodian of this sum. Mensa's yearly cash turnover today is in excess of two and a half million pounds. But the transformation took a long time and I did get a lot of help, in the end a great deal of help.

I went home from the dinner asking myself why I had allowed myself take on this new responsibility on top of all the others I had.

But I pitched in. Tentatively at first, and then with more confidence. I scrapped the pretentious, idiosyncratic wording Berrill had used and tried a few small personal adverts in the more serious newspapers. I simply offered to test the intelligence of the applicant without saying too much about why. I remembered my motivation in my own application and guessed that people would be curious to know their IQ.

My applicants received a brochure which I had completely rewritten, leaving out the pretensions and simply referring to the social aspects and the Burt aim of research on opinions distribution among the intelligent. I dropped all mention of the possibility of being a Think Tank to advise the authorities and, remembering Berrill's mistake in muddling his own and Mensa opinion in public, emphasised strongly that Mensa was impartial, uncommitted, and disinterested. Mensa was to be an agora, a forum for the exploration of opinions, not a pressure group with its own opinions or collective aims. This has remained our hidden strength through the years.

These were the sort of words: 'Members and groups within Mensa have views but Mensa itself has none. Nothing is to be done in the name of Mensa that could alienate or exclude people of any shade of opinion; no political action is to be taken by the society beyond the publication of the range of members' views. Mensa has no political, religious or nationalist affiliations and does not recognise distinctions of social class or race.'

A steady flow of replies came in and I set to work to devise a system for dealing with it, getting out forms and devising procedures to simplify the work so that it could be delegated when, as must happen before long, I got fed up with it.

The response grew as I experimented with the adverts to maximise it. And the phase take-up grew as I tried variations with the brochure and presentation.

The committee, which is the progenitor of the whole of Mensa's present day organisational set-up, arose informally as I called together groups of the Mensa helpers to whom I was able to communicate my growing enthusiasm.

The Mensa problem has always been that we have to process a lot of applicants to get a few new members and the work was very heavy for me working on my own. I began to importune the trickle of new members and some of established ones, asking them for help with the work.

They all took it the same way. They explained that they were far too busy, that they were unconvinced about the value of Mensa or its prospects, and that they were unsuitable for the task I was trying to foist upon them. Having got that clear, a proportion of them took up the task I had allocated on a strictly temporary and provisional basis. They proceeded to perform it quickly, and efficiently without help, instruction or encouragement. They were Mensa members. Here was another hidden strength.

More aware of the motivating and progress-checking aspects of meetings than of their democratic and decision-making function, I then began to persuade the activists to come and talk things over at meetings at my flat or Joe Wilson's flat, at Ralph Spicer's house, at Sinclair Eustace's house and all over the place. Some of the names of these very early helpers come back: George Stickland, a very thin young man, like me from humble home, taught me statistics and helped with the opinion researches I was doing. Dr Robert Green, who has been a long-term friend. He was the first psychologist to help me with the testing problems. A Freudian therapist called James Hayes and a chemist called Alan Stableford helped. A man we called Bunny Arnold. There were many more. They came, worked hard for a bit and then lost interest. But they were all essential. It would not have happened without them.

The fluid, changing group gradually began to behave more like a committee, to have both the faults and the virtues of one.

I found myself at these meetings, as I did in all my other circles, in the position of the supplicant enthusiast in a game like a slow bowler in cricket against a stone-wall batsman. I would put forward my increasingly ambitious ideas, plans and suggestions and the rest of the group, which included Win, would patiently explain to me with great care that what I proposed was, apart from being evidence of criminal insanity, morally, legally, and practically unsound and objectionable. Then after a discussion they would say in some form, 'Very well then, go ahead, but on your head be it.' I was not to come crying to them when it all went wrong.

Of course it often did but we averaged out all right and we began, noticeably, to grow. I sometimes got over a hundred replies to my adverts and processing them and marking the tests was quite a chore.

Then, after an extremely negative response to the idea from the committee, I made the decision which really made large-scale development possible. Doubtfully, I started a procedure which would have prevented my own application. A demand for money. I started charging for the tests which at that early stage were still unsupervised. I saw that if we depended for all the recruitment activity only upon subscriptions we should be loading the acquired members with heavy and growing costs as we expanded. We had to make the unsuccessful candidates pay towards the advertising, publicity and organisation costs involved in testing and recruitment. In return, they could get an assessment of their intelligence quotient. *Quid pro quo.*

In effect I started a little mail order intelligence testing business which was to be viable in its own right. And it had a spin off, a by-product. Mensa.

Projects have to be viable on several levels. Mensa is commercially viable although it is a non-profit making organisation because, like commercial ones, it persuades its enquirers to pay for the adverts and publicity which attract enquiries.

To avoid any misunderstanding, neither I nor any elected official of Mensa since has ever had any pecuniary interest in Mensa. I never had any payment of any kind for my time and work. Often I was not able to recover my expenses. Thousands of other Mensa volunteers as we grew have given their effort altruistically. Mensa is run by hobbyists. We now have paid staff but they are not members.

Soon with the income that Mensa got from test fees and from the growing number of subscribers I was able to set up the first prototype selection agency, a team of helpers working in their own homes, to deal with the routine work of testing and recruitment. Thus the committee were released to help organise a social programme to keep our growing band happy.

I was not inactive on the research front. I was convinced that Mensa had to be seen to be more than just an intellectually snobbish version of a social club and in publicity, which was beginning to come, I emphasised the research role which, for lack of other volunteers I was doing largely myself, gradually learning the statistical techniques of opinion sampling.

During 1955 my motivation as regards Mensa was growing with its first small successes. I must have begun to taper off on my other spare time interests and devote more time to Mensa, there is little on the record. In that year's *Proceedings*, I said in my editorial: 'The Miracle continues. Mensa maintains its flickering existence. The Society has not for some years been any one person's main interest but it persistently refuses quite to die. The small group, all very busy people, who reluctantly find the time to keep this tiny candle alight feel under an almost mystic compulsion. "Just a little longer", we say to ourselves, perhaps someone will emerge able and ready to organise and utilise this tenuous but persistent entity. Perhaps one of the universities will become interested. Perhaps one enlightened journal will be found to sponsor us.'

In March 1956 I was talking of the 'end of the plateau on our growth curve' and a 'new lease of life' and my little scribbled notebooks which are the only record of the unminuted meetings, tell me that we were feeling out vigorously in all directions as we began to sense that we were touching a sensitive nerve somehow. At this time I was avoiding press publicity. Mensa has been a natural Aunt Sally for journalists in an egalitarian age and, before I got experience with the press, I ran into the same ridicule that Berrill had had in a few articles. So I tended to brush off reporters. But my notebook shows that I was constantly thinking up new schemes, approaching people, getting speakers, organising meetings and proposing research projects.

In my notes there is one small but vital scribble heralding the beginning of Mensa International. I had noted, 'General. Accept overseas members?' Knowing the vaunting secret dreams I have dared to have from the first I am sure I argued for the inclusion of foreigners, although Berrill's idea had been for a British club. I am equally sure there was argument against. At any rate there is, against my query, my affirmative tick and the phrase, 'Charge more'. This little inky note marks the birth of World Mensa. The decision had been made. It would come to be.

Another note, 'Quarterly Residential', heralded the start of another Mensa Institution. We planned and had the first weekend conference at a beautiful Quaker retreat at Charney Basset in Berkshire, the forerunner of Eric Hills' twenty-five year series of similar meetings and of course of the numerous Regional Gatherings in America and Mensa At Cambridge and many such.

In this forward-looking year for Mensa there was another bold departure: the first beginnings of the future Local Groups structure. At the Stork Hotel in Birmingham a group of London members went to meet Bernard Billings the World's very first Locsec, as horribly but traditionally we called the Local Secretary or organiser of a local group. We met modestly in the coffee bar downstairs, and, consuming our coffee and buns, laid plans for the very first Mensa Local Group. Bernard, a short, modest, amiable man, was a draughtsman in a motor firm. He was the first of many Locsecs.

Erika Omasta took on recruitment in 1956 and dealt with a growing stream of enquiries. But she was very conscientious and, like some helpers who were to follow, was unhappy with what she saw as the unplanned, unconsidered rush of our progress. She resigned because she thought we should consolidate and do more for the new members we were attracting. At the end of the year I reported Erika's good work and talked of 'A new lease of life'.

At the 1956 Annual Gathering the Committee actually reported to the members an innovation, the beginning of democracy. We were routinely confirmed in office, I would say 're-elected *en bloc*, had we been elected in the first case. We tried to get agreement to an increase in subscriptions from ten shillings (nowadays 50 pence) to one pound and failed. The decision was that members should have the option of paying ten bob or a pound but that there should be no distinction between the ten shillingers and the pounders. Almost all paid the higher rate.

In 1957 we were getting such good attendances at the monthly dinners that I called them twice each month. We used to get a big, excited, eagerly talking and laughing group round a long table at a German restaurant called Schmidt's in Charlotte Street. There was a steady flow of applications which I found I could generate by an increasing array of means. I wrote letters to newspapers and placed advertisements in the personal columns. I badgered members for recommendations and continued to get press publicity. All these means interacted to produce a constant flow of applications. Members began to come steadily. A handful of overseas names began to appear on the records.

As Secretary I reported, 'An almost embarrassingly large number of applications came in and the conversion rate seems to be somewhat better than the usual ten percent, so that a useful group has joined us.'

And later, 'A further series of vigorous membership campaigns conducted by Joan and Peter Needs has continued the brisk expansion of our society. Well over a thousand applications have been dealt with in the year ... We have at the time of going to press increased our membership by over a hundred during the last nine months.'

The next important step was in 1958. I made my first real breakthrough.

Dr (later Professor) Bob Green was, is, a short, aggressive but sweet-natured man with curly hair, a broken nose in a kindly wrinkled face, and a great gift for friendship. He had first come to my attention in the early days, as a casually dressed student member who upset Roland Berrill. Berrill arranged a meeting with a speaker from the Dianetics movement which was beginning then. This is the movement that developed Scientology.

With his magnificent talent for credulity, Berrill swallowed Dianetics. He introduced the speaker by telling us with calm certitude and awe that we were about to hear teachings that were more important than any since those of Jesus Christ. The young innocent who had been hampered with that build-up started with a confident but muddled farrago of meaningless jargon. Berrill paid wrapt attention while the rest of us were embarrassed. Remedy was left to the young student, Bob Green. With quiet, polite but very shrewd questions, Bob skilfully brought out the contradictions and quickly reduced Berrill's protégé to a gawping mumbling silence. The poor young Dianeticist dried up, stood silent, then wisely and incontinently fled the scene. Berrill was not pleased. (Parenthetically, Berrill retained his faith in Dianetics, he shaved off his splendid beard and moustache, complained about his previous ways and seemed a diminished man. He used to tell me miserably how much good it was doing him. 'I used', he dolefully complained, 'to be a Happy Charlie.' Dianetics certainly cured that but I could not see the benefit myself.)

By 1958 I had become friends with Bob who had taken a post lecturing at the Psychology Department of London University. Ever importuning on behalf of Mensa I asked Bob's help about two things. I was worried about the fact that we were admitting members on an unsupervised test and I wanted to see how the members we were accepting would score on a supervised one. Would he conduct a test session or two for this purpose? Would the College let him hold it on their premises? Yes they would. We actually called applicants to the 'Later supervised test' which from Berrill's time had been a bluff to discourage cheating. Bob checked two sessions of about thirty candidates. He found that almost all those we had accepted at the ninety-ninth percentile (the one percent level) on an unsupervised test scored at the ninety-eighth percentile, the two percent level on the supervised one. It was then that I fixed the final criterion of acceptance. I decided that it was impractical to to give all members a supervised test and thus reject a lot of members. I convinced the Committee we should continue as we were, accepting the real position and abandoning illusions. Ever afterwards Mensa accepted members at the one percent level on unsupervised test but at the two percent level on the supervised test. Later the supervised test became the only acceptable qualification.

But that, though important, was not the breakthrough. The

breakthrough came when poor Bob, who has always been amused at my activity and enthusiasm, foolishly and kindly, consented to my second request. Ever ready to exploit a friend to serve my ambitions for Mensa, I wanted replies from applicants to be addressed to him at his respected address at the University. I thought the address would give assurance about Mensa's bona fides (which were good but not widely known). 'How many letters do you get?' said the incautious Bob. 'Oh! A dozen or so a week.'

A week or two later he was on the mat before his furious professor because of the sacks of mail addressed to him that were coming in. My scheme had come off with a vengeance. Bob rang me in alarm and told me to stop the flood. I cancelled the advert and apologised. The professor was given a promise that there would be no repetition.

A week later Bob phoned again in a real frenzy because many more sacks of mail had arrived for him, a very junior lecturer. The newspaper had ignored my cancellation. The professor was livid, Bob was under a cloud for a time, and I was distressed at hurting my friend.

But I found myself gloating over 1400 applications. More important, my ambitious eyes were opened to hitherto unforeseen possibilities.

It was sometime round then that I made the first of a very large number of television appearances.

An upper class gentleman, the Honourable Anthony Wedgwood Benn was the compère of a regular feature in which he quizzed the leaders of the many odd and cranky societies that thrive so well in the obscurity of the muggy English air.

At our interview he was friendly and seemed to accept that it had been wrong to class me as a crank.

My first appearance on television brought a fair batch of applications in spite of the context. I gained experience. I learned for myself about the publicity. There is very good publicity, good publicity and bad publicity. Very good is when they do not knock you, good is when they *do* knock you and bad is when you do not get any publicity at all. Mensa has done very well by observing this principle.

In the *Mensa Proceedings* of 1958 my Editorial after the Bob

Green breakthrough is headed by the single word. 'Swamped'. 'Mensa's new dynamic continues', I wrote. 'We have had a year of almost embarrassingly rapid expansion and progress. A few small advertisements in *The Observer* (the fatal ones which embarrassed Bob Green), brought us an overwhelming rush of applications which almost swamped us. As we accept the last few members from this campaign we are trying to summon up enough courage to invite another deluge by inserting a new series of advertisements, but we really need more clerical help before we do.' I pointed out that Mensa was now active in two centres, London and Birmingham, and complained that we still lacked the initiative from someone to set up the third centre.

The Annual Gathering was larger now than any before with 60 members attending a really successful weekend like those of Berrill's time.

I had started a series called The Annual Lecture and Professor Philip Vernon gave the first in 1956. Professor Stanislav Andreski gave the second one in 1957, and Professor Sir Cyril Burt was to give the third one in 1958. It was on that occasion that I asked him to accept the role of Mensa President.

It was also in that year that I started the regular lecture-discussion meetings that are now known as Think-Ins. A group which is ideally between twenty and forty assemble in a room with fairly comfortable seats and decent surroundings to hear a shortish talk by a speaker of distinction on some topic which should be speculative or controversial. The talk is followed by a long discussion with plenty of contributions from the floor and the chairman trying to see that everybody gets a word in and that no one dominates the floor. 'And now someone who has not spoken before' is his cry. Members love the free-rein rambling and often excitable and contentious arguments that go on at Think-Ins. There is always a lot of teasing and laughter in a climate which manages to be both hard-hitting and critical but essentially urbane and friendly. It reminds me of the amicable contention in large families that I have known. When later I split away as the leader of Mensa International and a new British Committee took over, both the Think-In, and the Annual Lecture were discontinued, but largely due to a much loved American

London member Harry Schacter, Think-Ins were revived under the new name early in the seventies and have been increasingly successful ever since. (This year (1984) the Annual Lecture was revived with a masterly discourse by Professor Richard Gregory.)

In January 1959 Mensa solved another problem. Berrill had known that the society had to have a means of regular and frequent communication before it would be more than an idea, a dream, but his own attempt to sustain a monthly periodical foundered after three months.

Some time in 1959 a small quiet man, Basil Mager, a grey-haired teacher from the new sprawling subtobian brick town of Burgess Hill responded to my importunities by saying that he would not mind having a shot at producing the regular monthly magazine we needed so as to keep members informed of the growing list of meetings and activities. 'On an experimental basis for a month or two', he cautiously qualified. Promptly as promised, on January 1959 the periodical appeared. *The Mensa Correspondence* was a six-sided foolscap duplicated sheet which was the precursor of many monthly National Mensa Newsletters around the world today. Some are now large full colour magazines.

The first issue had a criticism by a very tall and beautiful American member called Valery Gerry of Michael Young's *The Rise Of The Meritocracy*, articles knocking radiaesthesia and telepathy, a long article by a German member about the problem of Berlin and Kruschev and the piece of my lightweight doggerel. Val Gerry joined the committee and helped me in New York later.

In the next issue I refer to a *very bad* article I had about me in *The People* which put me off journalists for a time.

In the fifth issue in June we begin to get the list of meetings that has been the main feature of the journal and its successors ever since. There were eight meetings in June.

Further, May 1959 was the historic month when I hit Berrill's original target of six hundred members. Berrill's tribe was, at last, thirteen years after, up to full strength.

In July there was a meeting of members at the arboretum in Sheffield Park. It was the very last Mensa occasion at which our Founder Roland Berrill appeared. He had grown his beard again but was very subdued.

A young trainee solicitor called Maurice Salzedo put a short note in the journal to explain that he had been asked to help organise a local group structure for our spreading band. Salzedo reported that the Birmingham and Bristol groups had faded but he had set up new ones in Leeds, Cambridge, Manchester and Brighton and had high hopes for other places. At the AG we had a number of distinguished speakers and Professor Sir Cyril Burt gave the Annual Lecture on the subject of 'The Gifted Child'.

In June 1960 I announced that Professor Sir Cyril Burt, quite an old man by that time, had consented to accept the honorary post of President of Mensa. As the world doyen in psychology at the time he brought us respectability, his support helped us to overcome the very natural suspicions of professional psychologists (later all over the world), and his many beautifully legible handwritten letters were for many years a source of comfort and advice to me in my growing task.

In a note in January 1960 I point out that I am in touch with the newly established American National Association for Gifted Children and that, together with an American who had joined here, A. A. Hyatt, they were working on the possibility of an American Branch of Mensa. In February 1960 a T. F. Sandeman from Melbourne wonders if he is the only antipodean M (as we were beginning to call ourselves). I told him there was another, a Michael McGuiness. This was the very first manifestation of the now flourishing Australian Mensa.

It was obviously because I was working from London that the Mensa infection began to spread abroad. Our little adverts were attracting interest from the millions of people who pass through London every year and so a gradually growing group of overseas members were being added to our rolls. The sort of people who can join are natural travellers; all travellers pass through London now and again. This was why we found ourselves in a world game.

My first really important television show was with that very distinguished broadcaster Alan Whicker, who then compèred a show called 'Tonight'. He took over my sitting room with an enormous team who spent an entire Sunday making an outrageous TV travesty of what we were. In my first real experience of TV the world's most powerful and peremptory autocracy. I got a really nasty knocking programme for my pains. However, as always, the publicity brought many enquiries and, of course, more attention from the press and other media. We were making a mark.

Through 1960 the *Mensa Correspondence* grew larger, featured more meetings, more regional groups and more activities of every kind. In May, Eric Hills, one who proved himself to be a Mensa stalwart, was asked by the Committee to take on the Residential Conferences which had been run by various people up till then. Edinburgh Mensa had started and that Universal and ubiquitous Mensa institution called the Pub Meeting had started and was being held several times a month. Steven Russell, the first treasurer who was a qualified accountant, had volunteered to help.

Joyce Mumford was a small pretty woman, a graduate and the wife of a cartographer. When she joined she had two very young children to look after and was soon to have a third. Joyce joined the Committee and, seeing and understanding the growing organisational problems, decisively took over the recruitment and office functions, working from her own home in Chessington, Surrey, which she turned into a Mensa office with a duplicating machine to produce the *Correspondence*.

Having done his stint Mager passed the editorship to Sinclair Eustace. Eustace was a friend, a maverick intellectual who was fluent in many languages and the author of the idea of The Mensa School, a school for gifted children, which he was ambitious to found. He was a bachelor and, like Berrill, an eccentric, whose life was a chain of new enthusiasms. He too was of the upper class and he had had a public school education. He was always starting new projects and societies and some of them attracted wide attention and survived. But Sinclair, like Roland Berrill, was a better starter than he was a runner. For a time he was a Mensa enthusiast and a hard worker for us. Then like so many who followed, having done a stint he passed to other things. In June 1960, things having gone wrong, Joyce Mumford having replicated herself (unexpectedly early) instead of the journal and Sinclair having tapered off, I found myself the involuntary editor again. My Mensa friend Bushy Eiloart had started a new offset print business and I took the work to him in the emergency. That was how the *Mensa Correspondence* climbed out of duplication into print. The first printed issue was for 5 July 1960 and the official Editor was my wife Win.

I had all the problems which are usual with organisations which try to develop with the help of volunteers. The pioneers or leaders of a growing group get overstretched and have to delegate. My volunteers were, it is true, usually competent, fast learners but like any other volunteers who take on heavy chores for the satisfaction they get out of it, they were sometimes less tolerant of difficulties and criticism than those who work for more tangible rewards.

Each new editor comes in with all the confident enthusiasm which arises from the combination of high intelligence and complete innocence of experience. Radical changes of style, size, format and content are the first step, then thinking about policy and searching for contributions. Then, just as the editor gets enough experience to do a tolerable job, he or she jibs at the heavy thankless task, the criticism and the accusations of censorship which come from an inevitable handful of members who feel that failure to publish their overlong, obscure, scruffy, hand-scribbled offerings proves that the editorial policy is rigid censorship. (There seems to be no problem with the writers of interesting, legible offerings that are crowded out.) The fed-up editor then often resigns with a scolding editorial to chasten critics and members alike and another keen volunteer comes along with another new broom to repeat the cycle. It is all good fun for the editors but if members want decent readable, consistent journals they will have, like everybody else, to pay professionals.

1960 was a vital year and the real beginning of Mensa as an international organisation. Also below the surface that year there were sown the seeds of many future quarrels and conflicts which were to liven the scene but be the brake on our progress.

In 1960 in America Mensa began to happen. A spore settled, lived precariously, began to thrive. The first overseas publicity was an article in *The Village Voice*, a Greenwich Village journal that would correspond to what is known as an 'alternative society' journal today. Since *The Village Voice* circulates widely in America, the result was a flood of enquiries from New York and many other states which fell on the mat of surprised Joyce Mumford in Chessington. One of these letters was from a New York graduate chemist, Peter Sturgeon. He had passed the test at the one percent level and became a member without a supervised test.

He wrote to Joyce Mumford and got the names of other New York members and, after writing to me, he took the initiative which started American Mensa. He called the very first Mensa meeting to be held outside England.

Further, in 1960, after much heartsearching and worry about the effect on our growth, the Committee decided to implement the new testing scheme I had worked out. I announced the introduction of the supervised test stage in recruitment which had been a bluff up until then. This involved finding qualified psychologists in many areas around the country and arranging for test sessions at regular intervals. There were problems and doubts. For fiscal reasons there had to be a largish group of second stage applicants at each test session. We had to hire a room, usually at the local university, and pay the psychologist out of the test fees. The fees had to be kept low if we were to get enough applicants.

This was a risky and difficult step but it had to be taken if Mensa was to gain acceptance and credence in the world of psychologists. After many false steps and mistakes we gradually evolved a system that worked and was fiscally sound. With local variants this evolved into the present selection system throughout Mensa as it grew and spread overseas.

I had much developed the configuration mentioned earlier which was fiscally viable as well as organisationally so. What was now possible was a business, capable of producing surplus resources which could be spent on publicity and advertising to attract more applicants. We had a chain reaction. I had the prototype of a mental testing organisation which functioned as a profitable business which often actually subsidised the members. It was a business that had an important by-product that was almost irrelevant to its own function. The by-product was Mensa, an ever growing and spreading network of intelligent humanity, brought together as an interacting group.

The British Annual Gathering that year was at the Russell Hotel, and the big newsbreak came this way. I had found the courage after my previous bad press to invite a young reporter, then of the *Sunday Times*, to come to the ice breaker party. His story changed the scene. Mensa was suddenly hot news. Over 180 members, trickled shyly into the Russell Hotel next day. They were even more bemused than normal Mensa first timers because of the intense media attention that greeted them.

One reporter spotted my little yellow map pin and that was his headline next day, 'YELLOW MAP PIN – SIGN OF GENIUS'. We had a good meeting and an amused crowd of new members at the AGM amiably shrugged consent to myself and the little group of unknown people, the 'committee' who were responsible for this exciting, amusing and promising confusion. 'Sure! Carry on!' was the attitude when we reported and asked for acceptance of what we were doing.

Applications flooded in and we grew and grew. In England Mensa was on the map – and there were repercussions elsewhere as well. The English-speaking world is in close touch and this first big publicity break in London was probably at least a partial trigger for the *New York Times* story on Mensa which broke on 18 December. It introduced Mensa and was followed by a WBCS radio show and a published letter from Peter Sturgeon. There was a flood of American enquiries. American Mensa was off and running.

By the end of 1960 Eric Hills, the new Local Groups Officer in the UK, was able to announce that he had 10 British groups meeting. But in the *Mensa Correspondence* Charles Strickland and one or two others had begun to talk about the need for a formal constitution. No-one mentioned Berrill's odd one-page effort which had been quietly forgotten. With around eight hundred members we had overshot his target of six hundred anyway.

We set up a sub-committee to work out a more suitable constitution for Mensa. It was headed by our Treasurer, Stephen Russell. It was a three-man committee and it revealed something we were going to have to get used to in Mensa: the difficulty of getting agreement on anything at all, especially Constitutions.

The three men were unable to agree on a single scheme so there were two detailed drafts which had to be put to a referendum of the members. Thus, back in 1960 were laid the fatal foundations of Mensa's favourite destructive blood sport, constitutioneering.

By February 1961 the *Mensa Correspondence*, still a duplicated sheet produced on a second-hand rotary machine at Chessington, was able to announce twenty-one meetings around Great Britain.

By September 1961 we had 1,550 members world-wide. And Mensa demonstrated its own quality by the results of the referendum ballot. Asked to choose between the two constitutions that had been produced by the three person committee, Mensa decided. Both constitutions were rejected. The majority of members preferred the British tradition of an unwritten constitution based on practice, case law and common law. But that perfectly democratic decision (401/548) led to prolonged, damaging quarrels and agitations by the minority who had been denied their way.

During the year Mensa grew vigorously both in Britain and America and Peter Sturgeon began, very reasonably, to complain to me about the long drawn-out process of recruitment via Chessington. It became obvious that a translatlantic recruitment procedure was not going to serve. Peter called for someone to go to New York and get things going in America and I realised that I might be able to contrive to do just that. I called a meeting. Tentatively I floated this outrageous idea.

The committee were becoming disturbed if not alarmed by the unexpected but traumatic successes that my increasing efforts were bringing. They were hesitant; there was a feeling that we had enough on our plate with what I had stirred up in England, that we should consolidate and concentrate on doing more for the many new members we already had in Britain. There were three views at the long contentious meeting. We ought to confine our attention to Britain and let other nations build up independent Mensa movements if they wanted to; we should accept overseas members but do nothing further to promote Mensa overseas; we should ride the tide while it was favourable. We did not know what our potential was but it looked bigger than we had thought possible. We should take courage, go forward and try, at least, to create a united international Mensa. This first attempt to unite a set of human beings with the sole common bond of intelligence should not falter because of our timidity. I managed to persuade the committee, by a narrow majority, to agree to fund a trip to America to satisfy Peter's urgent pleas and set up a recruitment centre.

By the time Peter got my news he had made contact with a new member, John Codella. John is the man who, more than any other, should have the credit for Mensa's immediate great expansion in America.

He had at that time just sold his interest in an extremely successful publicity company which he had built up at a fashionable address on Manhattan. He was an expert at the rapidly developing art of public relations and, relieved of the need to think about earning a living, the idea of Mensa appealed to him. He had the time and the enthusiasm and he took on the onerous, unpaid, and as it turned out, ill-rewarded task of building Mensa up in America. His influence was brief but decisive; it changed our ways and set us on the road to where we are. He showed us how to get the continuous public attention which is what Mensa then needed in order to survive.

In London on 15 August 1961 I got his first polite, formal letter offering help in the development of Mensa in America. Sensing the possible effectiveness of the man I replied with some enthusiasm, telling him in great detail of the organisational problems I anticipated. All through the summer I was in constant postal communication with John and Peter as we laid detailed plans for my visit which was to be early in November so that I could be back in time to report to the Annual General Meeting.

I insisted that John should advertise in good time so that there were candidates lined up, ready for me to interview. If the committee could be persuaded to take the further plunge we could then set up a testing and recruitment centre in New York. He advertised in *The New York Times* and by the time I arrived there were about thirty candidates willing to work from their own homes to make a replica of what we had organised in England.

My concept was a chain of what I called National Selection Agencies which were to be professional, separate from and partially independent of Mensa. The Mensa Selection agencies (MSAs) were to be confidential. Applicant's names would only be revealed to Mensa if they were successful. (I did not want candidates to fear that failure in the test could be revealed.) The first two agencies were to be BMSA and AMSA (for British, and American, Mensa Selection Agency). Agents and employees, if there were any, were not to be members. The MSA was to be the channel into Mensa but not part of it. Instructions on tests and the supervision thereof were to come from professional psychologists and were not to be subject to political control from Mensa authorities themselves. All this, as well as the cost of attracting applicants (clerical work, publicity, advertising), was to be paid for out of test fees that were to be charged at the two stages of testing. Members subscriptions were to be used exclusively for services to them.

The preliminary test phase was essential for two reasons. Firstly it generated a large proportion of the MSA income because a lot of people are curious to learn their IQ on a simple self-administered test at their home. Secondly the first test acts as a 'come on' which encourages many who would not be confident or motivated enough to make a long journey to a supervised test session. Those who got a good preliminary score were encouraged to proceed.

Mensa was to be set up on regional lines. The Committee was to see itself at first as two different committees. It would meet as the International Committee responsible for world-wide development and all testing and recruitment. It would also meet, with a different hat on, as simply the committee of British Mensa, which beside American Mensa, was to be just one of what was to be a growing chain of semi-autonomous national Mensas.

To stay within my tiny budget I had got a ticket on an ancient Iceland Airways prop-plane that wandered vaguely across the north of the world from Glasgow via refuelling stops in Reykjavik, Gander and some other icy places I do not remember. The journey took two wearisome days.

I was met by a party led by Peter Sturgeon and John Codella.

New York hit me like a blow. The two intensely alert, enthusiastic, talkative, young men took me over and began to instruct, explain, plan, guide, argue with and rush an exhausted bewildered Limey through the autumn afternoon to a welcoming party. I was rushed here and there, being interviewed by newspapers, radio, television, all arranged by the energetic and sapient John Codella. I met hundreds of people, was pursued by the press and given the fullest treatment.

But I had not quite forgotten the object of the exercise and all through the week I was talking to John and Peter and the ladies who had applied for the AMSA job. On the last day I had come to a decision and when John phoned me I told him I had got the right person.

'Don't decide yet', said John, 'I have one more lady I'd like you to talk to before you decide.'

Ten minutes talking to Margot Seitelman had disposed of my natural half loyalty to the other lady to whom I had almost promised the job. Margot was as obviously the woman as John was obviously the man we were going to have to depend on if this unlikely venture was to have a chance.

I left for England pleased and confident, my head buzzing with plans, ambitions and the certitude that Mensa was going to become a permanent and ubiquitous organisation.

Margot Seitelman took the job because, as a young mother of three, she could do it from her home without giving up her other career. And it is still from her home, despite the remarkable growth over the years of American Mensa, that she has continued to work. As the staff expanded she took on more apartments in the big apartment block in Brooklyn where she still lives. Today, 'Mensa, Brooklyn New York' is all the address you need if you want a letter to be in one of the sacks delivered to Margot's home every day.

America took to Mensa and the American 'branch' became bigger than the whole 'tree' and up till 1984 remains bigger than the rest of Mensa put together.

On 19 November the Annual Gathering heard of my American trip at the Russell Hotel and this time 250 members crowded in. A packed general meeting approved of what I described as a dangerous phase in the life cycle of the Mensa 'cell' as it went through its first mitosis and division.

'Clearly', I told my Mensa colleagues, whose numbers and keenness were both growing with the successes, 'Professor Burt's idea of a panel of people scientifically selected for high intelligence can have no connection with national boundaries. How do we cope with this from an organisational point of view?'

I went on to outline the structure I proposed for the formation of an international body: 'The duty of Mensa International will be to found and support Mensas in other countries in such a way as to preserve a linkage with a central body . . . Mensa International should not exert any influence on the activities of the National Mensa but should confine itself to ensuring the maintenance of Mensa's uncommitted stance and to keeping recruitment methods as nearly uniform as possible. It should also ensure its own financial stability and viability, and those of various national Mensas.'

The work continued and the enlarged committee gradually worked on the managerial structures we needed to keep Mensa together despite its sprawling and erratic growth. Joyce Mumford had given up running the British (and international) office from her home and I persuaded an energetic young woman, Mrs Hayes, who ran the clerical service and duplicating pool at the big wood company where I was a manager, to set up an operation in her home.

She ran this for some years with the help of spare-time neighbouring housewives in Rainham, Essex. It was an economical set-up, similar to the one Margot was setting up in her New York home.

The Rainham office continued until it grew out of Mrs Hayes's home and I passed the job to a Mr Reginald Candy, a retired business man who filled his large house in Eltham with a buzzing group of part-time lady clerks as the job grew.

An interesting thing about these early offices is that there seems to be no end to the stream of enquiries which, many, many years later, come to them from people reading ancient magazines in many places round the world. A recent letter was passed on to me. It was from a man in New York. He acknowledged a letter telling him he had succeeded in the preliminary test. He reported that he had been thinking it over and had decided that he would now like to take the supervised test. This was not a man who allows himself to be rushed into impulsive decisions. He had been turning the matter over in his careful mind for twenty-three years.

At the 1962 AGM I reported something else. Things were beginning to move in Europe, no doubt as a reflection of the publicity in London and New York.

It was in Holland that I accepted an offer from a retired naval officer to try to set up an MSA for Europe and he took this as an irrevocable franchise which he was to hold in perpetuity, regardless of results. This error proved to be damaging for a long time, but we overcame it.

By the time 1962 was out we had divided the Mensa Committee into British and International roles, we had taken Codella and Sturgeon on to the International Committee and Eric Hills was working out an International Constitution which would conform to the structure I suggested and to the successful practices which we had built up and modified through the years. There were already in outline three national Mensas to fit into the form we were building.

Peter Sturgeon came to the London AGM that November to report on the first results of the New York office. Already there were 641 American members and the independent American journal, *The American Activities Bulletin*, had been set going and was circulating to growing skein of members in every one of the United States. It went out as some pages inside the international journal which we sent to every member.

The British meeting was held at the Conway Hall and the Annual Lecture was by the very distinguished biologist, Sir Peter Medawar. It was a brilliant appreciation of the work of the British pioneer philosopher of science Professor W. Whewell.

At the, by then, traditional Marlow picnic at the Summer Solstice, that year I met Marianne Tanon, a French student, later Madame Seydoux, who went off back to France when she had finished her studies and founded French Mensa, which has continued, a little erratically to be sure, in its own light, humorous, Gallic way, ever since.

Austrian Mensa, always one of the most stable and reliable, started when a short dynamic young man who had been an officer in the British Army during the war joined Mensa from Austria and wrote to me from his office in Vienna where as a psychologist he ran a successful management selection operation serving Austrian industrialists. Dr Georg Fischhof is the Founder of Austrian Mensa. He was then and is now much more so, a famous man in his country and his work both in building up and supporting Austrian Mensa and in giving sensible and practical psychological guidance to International Mensa has been invaluable.

He started by doing successfully what Berrill had thought of, but failed to implement. He was testing the intelligence of candidates for jobs as part of his service and, whenever any candidate got a score over the threshold, he would issue an invitation to join. At various times we found it difficult to get supplies of tests because of the suspicions of the professional psychologists of our activities, but Georg broke through the problems and supplied us.

This might be the point to mention an underlying Mensa recruitment problem which I had to overcome then and which has dogged us ever since. It causes a sort of schizophrenia in suppliers of mental tests because of the conflict between the professional ethics and the desire to sell us very large numbers of test forms.

The preliminary stage, the self-supervised home test is not mandatory but is a fiscally valuable part of our procedure. It is also useful as a means to give confidence to many applicants who are mistakenly unsure of themselves. However, the psychology profession frowns on mental tests which are not administered personally by a skilled practitioner. It is thought also that any test sent through the post loses its validity because it is possible for the answers to become known to the public. From the Mensa point of view this does not matter since we only offer membership to those who have had a supervised test. In practice the problem has been solved by using a small number of rather obsolescent tests for the preliminary stage. The authors of these are usually pleased to have the royalties and prefer not to know about what would be seen as the misuse of the tests from the strictly professional point of view. My hope for the future is that we may be able to organise the computer supervision of tests in such a way as to satisfy all interests.

1963 saw the *Mensa Correspondence* and the *American Bulletin* go into letterpress form, and Sir Cyril Burt launched the Premises Fund which was set up to raise money for a permanent head-quarters in London. The fund proved abortive because of the lopsided way that Mensa grew.

On 15 June 1963 there was the first American Annual Gather-ing and it was a huge, unexpected and heartening success with 160 members at this first American transplant of Berrill's institu-tion. An American Mensa Committee was democratically accepted. In the same month was the very first meeting of Dutch Mensa in Holland. In October I announced a world membership of 2,623, and developments in France, Germany, Holland and America.

Toronto which was then part of 'North American Mensa' had also had meetings. Later Canadian Mensa preferred a separate identity and a separate National Mensa was formed.

The 1963 Annual Gathering in London at the Conway Hall included a Mensa Artists' exhibition and was shown on television. The Annual Lecturer was a fellow member of the Philosophy of Science Society, Sir Karl Popper.

Professor Popper's conditions when I asked him to lecture were stringent. He proclaimed himself to be so deeply allergic to tobacco smoke that he wanted a guarantee, not only that no one should smoke while he spoke but that there should have been no smoking for two days before in the lecture hall. He indicated that the faintest whiff of tobacco smoke would bring him to the ground in paroxysms.

I was his chairman and I sounded the warning by asking the audience earnestly not to steal the briefest whiff. To reinforce my words there were enormous 'NO SMOKING' notices at every hand, whose format had been specified by the great Professor himself.

Sir Karl was at his splendid best, he gave us an unforgettable two hours of the original, scene-changing wisdom which has had such a deep effect on Western science and philosophy. He answered with the expected brilliance many eager questions and he never even cleared his throat or coughed. Not once. Which was odd.

Why? Because an undisciplinable, anarchic Mensa lady was behind me on the platform, in a beautiful long black dress, eyeing the audience severely through a lorgnette. She was, either through inadvertence or from sheer mischief, chain-smoking behind the great man's unconscious back throughout the lecture. Should I intervene and draw attention or should I ignore her and hope that Karl would survive unspluttering? Wise, it turned out, was my masterly inactivity. The great man's professorial throat was not even cleared.

1964 was the last year of uncomplicated progress, but the seeds of trouble planted in earlier mistakes and over-confidence began to sprout and grow. Eric Hill's International Constitution was accepted by the overwhelming vote of the members and the international structure ratified. The first international election was held. The British membership was a little over 4,000. With an international panel of candidates I stood for election as the first International General Secretary, with Joe Wilson as the pioneer International Chairman in the first Mensa International Election. The Wilson/Serebriakoff panel of candidates was elected by a large majority against another American slate which immediately challenged the result and called for a second election. We decided that this was not justified. Growing opposition came from an ambitious American group who felt they might be able to take control. There was opposition from two contradictory directions.

A British group still wanted to challenge the new constitution on legal grounds because the original Berrill constitution had no provision for amendment. They wanted to govern the society from the Annual General Meeting in London.

The other group were simply ambitious to take over this big new toy from those they saw as the lucky incompetents who had stumbled upon the idea.

The reason for the 'slate' or 'panel' system was that we could see no way in which a mixed group from several countries could meet regularly as a committee inside a foreseeable budget. We had built up Mensa with a co-operating team and we thought members could select from a range of such teams who could offer themselves in the future. Even today this system has survived several fairly radical constitutional amendments and still seems to me to be right for Mensa.

Before that election, in June, Eric Hills and I were invited by new American chairman Codella to attend the second American Mensa Annual Gathering in New York. John wanted Eric to explain the new Constitution because of the objections that were being made in America where there was a demand for an American-type constitution. John Codella also wanted to create another big publicity success such as he had made from my first brief stop in New York. The trip was to be self-financing because publicity brings enquiries, brings cash.

He had done a very professional job again. He was there with Peter and Margot at the airport and they whisked us away in a car explaining all the way the constantly modified programme of radio, television, newspaper and magazine interviews they planned.

The magazine *Life* had allocated a very clever, pretty and witty young woman reporter to me full-time for four days. I myself could spare only a few days on that trip but Eric Hills did a more extended publicity tour of the East Coast with lots of radio and television exposure. My own exposure to publicity in New York was by far the most intensive I had ever had.

The *Life* article which followed was a four-page feature which, with all the other stories and broadcasts on Eric and me, brought in an even greater flood of enquiries to Margot's assembly of neighbouring wives who were brought in to help in the crisis.

In 1964 the membership of American Mensa hit 1,400 in June whilst we were in New York. Largely as a result of that trip and of the intense and well organised coping by Margot and John Codella when the flood of applications hit, the membership topped 4,400 by the next June. Already American Mensa was bigger than its parent, British Mensa.

But despite its obvious brilliant success and the surplus revenue it created for American Mensa, our tour marked the beginning of the anti-Codella drive in American Mensa. When it was successful the movement spread to Europe and became an anti-establishment and an anti-Serebriakoff movement.

It was what happened to Berrill all over again. It is during the 'up' phases of growth and development that opposition grows fierce and clamorous. In the bad times of decline, confusion and muddle the critics and politicians are strangely passive and full of strenuous and determined apathy.

June 1965 saw a Founder's Meeting in Frankfurt Germany. We had found a young psychologist, Dr Herbert Steiner, a friend of Georg Fischof, who got things going actively in Germany and became the German Founder. Marianne Seydoux and Rosemary Bertrand were there from France, Sam Naber from Holland, Sturgeon from America, Edouard Valencyns from Belgium and 'Hansi' Eberstark, the extraordinary linguist and calculating genius who represented Switzerland.

In America the Annual Gathering was an even bigger success with 275 members from 22 States at the Biltmore Hotel in New York. But the new American Committee had some members who were to participate in the contention that was soon to come.

'If you have a good formula stick to it' was the principle that Codella tried to follow. He began to plan to follow up the great success of the Serebriakoff publicity tours by having myself and my wife do a three week American tour in October. But by now there was real opposition in Britain and many thought that I was getting too much of the limelight. Surely American Mensa was big enough already? But after strong contention, the committee decided positively after a narrow postal vote. The trip was on.

The result was up to the wildest expectations and American Mensa got an even greater number of applications and another 3,000 members.

What was I on to? Why the unexpected success in several lands? John Codella was an extremely able publicist and Mensa was a new idea but new ideas usually have to fight for a hearing. And I had no Codella in London or Holland. I must be touching a sensitive nerve. I must be offering something, that somehow was wanted. Something was being said that people secretly wanted said, even if they laughed at it a little. I came to a conclusion upon which I have acted with some success ever since

For many centuries, ideas of the equality of man would have been considered ridiculous. But, in the last two hundred years we had had a brief age during which, in order to break the over-rigid mould of a stratified society, there had been the spread in all the advanced nations of a new egalitarian ethos. This was a sort of re-zeroing or datum setting. It was an operation to reset a status system which was no longer suited to the new sort of productive industrial society with its dependence on the widespread decentralisation of control and initiative.

What the unexpected attraction of the Mensa idea might be, I thought, was that it represented a partial counter-thrust to the over-egalitarian trend which was beginning, as all such trends do, to overshoot itself. Was the egalitarian pendulum swinging too far? Were intelligent observers beginning to feel safer seeing at least, though not yet accepting, a counter-trend movement, if only as a target for abuse.

I was in a world which had gained in long life, health and prosperity wherever it had implemented the amplification of intelligence which comes with modern scientific industrialism. Trying to feel what nerve it was I had touched in that world, I asked whether the idea of a scientifically and therefore objectively selected elite, not of wealth and privilege but of mental excellence rang a chord? At least it was not incompatible with the ideas of a centrally-planned socialist society which had so much attracted me in the confused times, the ideological wars and the industrial depressions through which I had lived. My Mensa experiences seemed to be a betrayal of all my former ideas; contrary to that which inspired the active work in politics and as a trade union leader in my earlier years.

The trip was extremely well-organised by the indefatigable Codella, everything slotted into place, and though we were rushed there was no waste of time. Many of the media people praised the organisation and echoed the words of the top reporter on the *Montreal Star*, Dusty Wineberg: 'Best damned publicity handout I ever did see.' This was the talent that a handful of Mensa politicians were so scornfully to drive away in a couple of years. That was what slowed the meteoric growth in America for some years.

Only in New York did we encounter anything but the kindly warmth that is America to the traveller. In a nasty political meeting there, the ordinary members were puzzled and shocked by the emerging ambitious Mensa politicians who were rude to Win and tried with little success to heckle me. I had learned my trade the hard way in my political and trade union youth.

After this extravaganza all over America, which John Codella told me brought more than 50,000 enquiries and 4,000 members, I went back to meet mounting troubles in Mensa in Britain. The political pot was beginning to boil and the pamphleteers were getting to work.

Mensa leaders in several places and times have had problems with litigious straw men.

These are men (or women) with few assets to risk on costs but the intelligence, dottiness, and zeal to bring and pursue self-represented legal actions against Mensa or its officials, either for the fun of it, or because of persecution mania (perhaps born of under-achiever's envy). A tiny handful of such people have been an extremely damaging plague in Mensa. We have things better arranged now as we are insured against this kind of thing.

The small but highly active political group that assembled was an international one. It was brought together by the growing Mensa internal communications system. All over Mensa, Local groups were being started by one local member appointed as the Local Secretary by the national centre, in accordance with the scheme set up by Maurice Salzedo and perfected by Eric Hills. Most of these groups produced a local newsletter of some kind and this was the media of communication of the pamphleteers. Lists of names and addresses of local groups secretaries and the editors of the many scores of little duplicated magazines that were beginning to proliferate were available to every member. Sending duplicated pamphlets and scandal-sheets to these key communicators was simple. The local editors were always fascinated to hear what seemed like inside scandals about the leading Mensa names they were beginning to recognise. Spicy gossip was eagerly reprinted by local editors who were always looking for interesting copy to fill their columns. They had no means of checking the facts, saw smoke and thought it meant fire.

In America particularly the local journals were subsidised by the National Committee because there were so many local groups that they could no longer be served by a single national journal. There was not the space to print details of all the meetings that were being called each month as the number of local chapters proliferated. The system was wide open to exploitation by the inventive and malicious scandal-monger. The group of political opportunists who pioneered this way of spreading distrust of the elected officers was small but its activists were zealous and dedicated and some of them were quite without scruples.

The limitation was that the conflict was mercifully confined to written abuse and mischief making. A vigorous and damaging war of letters and pamphlets went on which was as intriguing to all the participants as it was damaging to the society but there was no physical strife. Threats? Yes. Lawsuits? Some. Insulting letters? Lots! Press scandals? Yes. Knife fights? Broken pates? Bruises? Slapped faces? Tweaked noses? Pulled beards? Boringly, no sign! Even today, after nearly forty years with occasional bouts of happily vigorous, highly effective, well-directed and unrestrained mutual written abuse among a tiny minority, Mensa is still waiting with vanishing hope for the thrill of its first black eye. Mensa's production of jaw-jaw is fair for such societies. Its war-war output is abysmal. But the virulence of the poison in the pens and on the typewriter ribbons in the coming period was extreme. Those that do not want to get warm were advised, by Truman, to keep out of the kitchen. In 1965/7 the kitchen my colleagues and I were in became very very warm indeed. I stayed but my wiser colleagues paradoxically took the risk of spoiling the broth by *resigning* as cooks in such an overheated kitchen.

Another curious thing is that the abuse, libel and insults were not only non-violent but inaudible, entirely on paper. The member that would accuse one, in a letter, of having one's political opponents committed to a lunatic asylum, would in a face to face meeting be courteous if not charming. I speak of something that really happened.

So just as everything looked set for world-wide expansion at the external level, on the internal level things became extremely fraught and messy. As a result Mensa went into neutral gear for some years.

There were three characters at the centre of the opposition group in the bad days. They called themselves the Three Musketeers, and soon gathered a band of supporters, most of them deceived, round them as they began to make a mark. All three being only intermittently employed or unemployed and having the useful litigious man of straw status, they dedicated themselves to the task of discrediting the incumbents whoever they were and taking control of what the pioneer group were beginning to build up. Using the 'the repeated big lie' technique, the group were able to exploit the normal, 'no smoke without fire' reaction to scandal so that by a narrow margin they succeeded in showing that the 'Establishment' was not that well 'entrenched', and evicting it, whereupon their own nominees took over. But much mud had stuck to the Musketeers themselves so wisely they did not become candidates themselves.

Shall we call the Musketeers by their fictional names?

Porthos was an American, who at face-to-face contact was pleasant enough, plausible, even charming. He gave a surface impression of good manners and intelligence. They say that he flew into rages and was screamingly abusive but I never saw that in my few contacts with him. His effectiveness was largely due to this apparent decency on superficial acquaintance. It was difficult to convince people that this apparently pleasant young man could be guilty of the things of which his many victims accused him. So he was always able, in an organisation like Mensa, to find a new circle, when the old one found him out, who could see him as the victim he claimed to be.

He first appeared in an American group where, correspondents tell me, he met any opposition with fierce rages. He wrote letters of intemperate, abusive threats to anyone who thwarted him and circulated them widely. His grip on reality was not strong and his posture in life was that of a victim who was engaged in a fight for survival against powerful, relentless enemies for whom no punishment was too severe and against whom any methods were legitimate. It is probable that he was sincere and believed his own fantasies. His weakness was that his innocent front could never hold for long and all the associates he was able so easily to recruit found him out eventually and joined those he saw as the vicious enemies who constantly ringed him.

Athos was, in a way, an English version of the same sort of personality. Face to face he was more than personable, he was quite charming and had no difficulty in securing a long chain of jobs which never lasted. One of his false charges about me was that I had played some sinister part in his losing jobs. He had a flair for language and could write very well. This was useful for a dedicated mischief-maker. Again, he could always charm a new circle of supporters as soon as he disenchanted an old one. He would have made an effective confidence trickster since he had had a good middle class education and the style and manner of a gentleman.

Aramis was a shadowy figure from Kansas City whom I never met. I first heard of him because apparently he had, in the easy early enthusiastic days, been given the 'franchise', as it were, as Locsec in the town and had eventually been pushed aside by local members when his character had been revealed. A feud arose between two Mensa sects in Kansas City which rumbled on for years. He was a leader of a faction which opposed the recognised group. The Aramis faction published one of the scandal sheets called 'Skulduggery' in which I featured as a vicious and unscrupulous profiteer tyrant.

These were 'The Three' that saw themselves as the bold riders who were to bring down first Codella (and they made his life so uncomfortable with incessant attacks that he *did* wisely resign). Then it was, 'We Three Ride Again', against the Establishment. Later as they gained ground they were joined by a succession of other figures who came and went in a loose mutually quarrelling group that was in effect a political party with take-over aims. Their first political action was to set up and try to get recognition for a Special Interest Group.

While Mensa has no collective aims or purposes it does encourage those with various points of view, aims or interests to use Mensa to find others like them and form meeting and corresponding groups. The Musketeers asked for recognition of

'Special Interest Group for Reform in Mensa', and it became known as SIGRIM.

Mistakenly, I think, but understandably, the American Committee under Codella's leadership were reluctant to give credence and publicity to this group by granting them official recognition, and their refusal to 'recognise' SIGRIM constituted the first political cause by which they could attract the sympathy and attention of members in general. I began to receive protest letters about the autocratic methods of the American Committee and the illiberal way in which they were trying to suppress legitimate political opposition.

SIGRIM and their supporters nominated an opposition panel in the 1964 international election upon which Porthos appeared as a candidate for international office. One of the candidates wrote from the prestigious Hudson Institute. He complained that his acceptance of nomination had never been obtained. He had signed a document which he had thought was simply a record of the names and addresses of the people at a meeting. This panel put up a case against the international constitition attacking the panel system which had just been accepted. In the 1964 election, they got thirteen percent of the votes cast in a low poll. They raised an enormous rumpus afterwards on various grounds, demanding a new election because of imagined irregularities and those minor real ones which cannot possibly be avoided in a postal election involving many countries and people.

By the time I wrote my article, 'On having your head turned', after the success of the American tour in 1964, signs of opposition were growing as SIGRIM began to circularise members and groups all over the world and write endless letters of protest to all those who were active.

Athos began, with the agreement of the new British Committee, to publish a regular column in the monthly magazine and in this he began, systematically, to undermine reputations in various ways. A concern for the truth was something that never bothered Athos. He wanted his tales to be credible, spicy and interesting.

It was the convergence of two strands of opposition that became formidable to the new and rather isolated International Committee that I was trying to get going. One of them was legitimate and honest. It was simply a group of those who did not want or agree with my ambitious international expansion schemes and my strong desire for the one-head unity of Mensa. The group was English and its aims and methods were at all times decent, they were just an early version of the consolidators who are always with us opposing initiative and adventure. There must be balance between the expansionists and the consolidators in any institution.

The other group, SIGRIM and its associates, wanted to take over control of International Mensa and in 1967 they actually succeeded, in an oblique way, in doing so. The years between 1964 and 1967 were the worst.

As I have said Mensa was then a natural Aunt Sally for the press in an egalitarian age. I have to admit that I would not have expected that a society with our pretensions would have had to pass, even in its formative stages, through such a period on its learning curve. But Mensa did.

Having a good brain does not ensure good will and, as a fair sample of the intelligent people on earth, Mensa aims to contain, and does contain, its fair proportion of malicious and destructive people and bright psychopaths. Further we have a few members who suffer from emotional retardation despite their good intelligence. Our trouble is that when those of ill will are mentally able they are capable of more than normal mischief. Mensa, beginning to be a world wide group, was learning how to cope with that particular problem. Now we still suffer from the same symptoms but we can cope.

Now follows my own account, for myself and my friends, of what happened in Mensa. It was not meant for general publication at the time. I shall disguise some names for fear of litigious men of straw. It is an edited version of what I wrote in 1967, just before I and my panel of candidates were defeated, getting 35 percent of votes as opposed to 46 percent for the SIGRIM panel in a three-cornered election.

'Mensa has always had reformers, a minority who want to modify and improve us. Others would, very naturally, like to replace the present team of workers. That is as it should be in a democratic society.

But of late some of those who are ambitious to take over, seem to have decided that the incumbents are so firmly entrenched that there is no hope of replacing them by honourable democratic political means. They have resorted to extreme methods and I feel I should tell about them. If you are one of those who feel that legitimate politics includes announcing your opponent's death, challenging people to duels, sending poison-pen letters under false names to opponent's employers, starting untruthful press scandals which bring Mensa a bad name, making false accusations of dishonesty and fraud to the police and other authorities, and making physical threats to Mensa employees: if all this seems good thinking and fair boxing to you then the rest of what I write might bore you. If you feel that such actions are marginally uncivil or even unkind then read on, I have a sad and comic tale to tell you, one which I would not have expected to be possible of a society with our pretensions.

The tale I have to tell is surprising and amusing but is not concerned with important events. Who runs Mensa is, so far, hardly a vital question of world-shaking importance. The actions, though ill-intentioned, have caused little real harm.

It is the bizarre story of a group of Mensans who set out to take control but find themselves playing the buffoons in a grotesque farce. Their maliciousness proves itself to be so incompetent as to excite more laughter than indignation.

The actions of the 'reform' group SIGRIM are marked by untruthfulness, rudeness, muddle and internal quarrels, but above all by incompetence so extreme that there almost seems to be a self-defeating deliberate quality about it. They are, to a man, loudmouths giving themselves away to each other and to those they see as their common 'enemies': the elected officers and workers on committees. They all accuse each other, with justice, of being extremists and are so busy misinforming each other and everybody else that they finish by believing their own untruths as they come back to them in distorted form.

The actions of SIGRIM have severely damaged Mensa's credit, they have caused many resignations especially among the active workers they have harassed and there is no doubt that the recent pause in the growth of Mensa can be put at their door both because of the bad publicity and because they make life too hot for those volunteers who work for Mensa.

We may never have known the full extent of SIGRIM activity and of the damage that has been done if they had not fallen to quarrelling among themselves. Some of them, unable to stomach the methods of some others have at last 'let the cat out of the bag' and revealed an inside story that has been concealed.

A copy of one of their broadsheets in August contains a revealing quotation published by Porthos. Speaking of the International Committee he writes: 'There is very little that can be ruled out of order in overthrowing them.' Much of what I report can be better understood in the context of this revealing sentence.

The underlying policy of SIGRIM has been to subject the pioneer workers and the elected officers, no matter who they are, one by one, on a pre-arranged rota, to an unremitting campaign of harassment, of untruthful and libellous attacks so as to force their resignation.

Few people who have established a good position in life can afford to hold out against such a campaign. Such tactics, however, are safe for the misfits and under-achievers who are the strike force of SIGRIM. They have little to lose and much to gain in this kind of contest. The remaining rump of the attacked incumbents is weakened by the consequent resignations: they *do* become less efficient and make some legitimate errors for which they can be fairly criticised. The voluntary workers who have to endure such harassment while they give their spare time to build up Mensa have to ask themselves why they should put up with it. The obvious answer is that they should not. And they resign, thus creating a vacuum at the top. The 'reformers' find it easy to move into key positions and some of them have done so in America.

The most effective and able Mensa builder in North America and the first American Chairman, John Codella, with virtually all the American pioneer group, have been driven to resignation in this way by this long campaign of energetic and unscrupulous harassment. Codella, and many other American Mensa pioneers have folded their tents and departed from these undignified scuffles and somewhat crazed behaviour.

On a personal level I do not complain. The underlying, almost deliberate, incompetence of the actions intended to harm me has prevented any real damage beyond the fact that in my obstinate persistence and refusal to give up I have had to waste a lot of time on the sterile and damaging nonsense which I shall describe.

My first contact with the SIGRIM character Athos was an idiosyncratic letter in which he offered to take over responsibility for publicity in Mensa. He left me kicking my heels in the pub where I agreed to meet him to discuss his offer. No show then, but much published criticism because I had failed to accept his offer. His next action was a nomination submitted to me as Secretary in which he nominated himself for all eight of the positions on the British Committee. I replied as one does to an arcane legpull only to have a long, serious letter in which he made a case that his nomination was valid and must be accepted. He was elected on an unopposed panel in 1964 but was bottom of the poll at the next election. Athos is the British end of SIGRIM. His skill is in innuendo and reasonably credible but false acccusations. Fiscal irresponsibility, threatening opponents with violence, undermining the confidence of employers in opponents and bringing lawsuits against them are all accusations which, without the remotest justification, flow easily from the multicoloured pens in the neat italic script of the inventive Athos.

Porthos hit the national headlines in America when he challenged another member to a duel over a girl and told the press. He could be called 'The Threatener'. To me he wrote, 'There are enough people who are thoroughly dissatisfied to make a mess of things if you don't start dealing with them directly.' To Jules Singer (who succeeded Codella as Chairman in America) he wrote, '. . . if you continue as Chairman I intend you to realise that what Codella got was sheer joy compared with what can be done . . .' He published an article in a scandal sheet called 'The Death of John Codella' which did not add to the peace of mind of John's family. This was the beginning of a planned campaign of harassment which was revealed when correspondence about it was leaked by the associate I mentioned who could not stomach his extreme methods. Thus John, that most effective worker, was accused unjustly of making money out of Mensa, of censorship, or stealing from Mensa funds and of anything else that came into the accuser's mind. John stoically took this nonsense for a time and then gave up and resigned with effect that can easily be seen in the recruitment and surplus cash figures in American Mensa.

Next the attack switched to the other members on the pioneer American Committee who have all been under similar attack and all have resigned. Even one member of their own group, Bob Sokol, resigned after threats of violence, as was revealed in the letter which circulated in the SIGRIM group that was published by the one who became disenchanted and gave the game away.

It was at this time that the internal Mensa disputes hit the national headlines in Britain and America. The SIGRIM group discovered that it was easy to attract publicity in the Mensa context that they could never get in any other way. The good news is that the press are unduly interested in Mensa. The bad news is also that the press are unduly interested in Mensa. They are delighted to find, in the action of a few of our oddballs, a fair case to ridicule what they can present as pretentiousness. Some reporters were quick to believe and publish imaginative tales by Porthos and Athos of fierce internal disputes within a society which seemed to be claiming superiority. To the central group in SIGRIM it was wonderful to see *their* names in print for a change. The damage to Mensa was no worry. I was astonished that quite reputable newspapers did nothing to check what were highly unlikely tales before they were published. I conducted a long campaign later with one of them which ended in a full retraction and my becoming friends with a top columnist who gave us a lot of good publicity afterwards.

In June 1966 there were reports of a fracas at the American AG resulting from SIGRIM floor motions for amendments to the International Constitution and which got bad, nation-wide publicity in America. Then there came in England what remains my worst moment in a long career at the hectic centre of things in Mensa.

My own and Mensa's low point came about like this. It was the British Annual Gathering at the French Institute in Kensington.

The now separate British Mensa Committee was to have Arthur Koestler as the Annual Lecturer on the Sunday. British members of SIGRIM led by Athos had moved a motion of no confidence in the depleted International Committee on which I was the leader and General Secretary. My team consisted of a few British, some Americans and many other national representatives. The working team had been reduced by the harassment resignations to the point that I was the only one in England who could be present to speak for it.

On the morning of the Saturday of the Annual General Meeting my heart sank as I read my copy of *The Times*. 'EGG-HEADS HEADING FOR TROUBLE. AMERICANS MAY JOIN IN SCRAP.'

Athos had convinced a *Times* reporter of the credibility of an inventive story from Porthos that 'an aircraft load of American members', would fly in for 'the showdown'.

Athos publicly castigated the IGC for 'financial profligacy' and 'administrative incompetence' and evidently unsuccessful, 'attempts to gag valid criticism'.

They quoted me as saying that grievances would be aired and that I looked forward to the battle with zest. I was lying. I looked forward to the rumpus and bad publicity for the strange society I had tried to build up as one looks forward to 'dying for days over the small fire'. The British Committee banned the press but there were reporters everywhere taking down all that the various contending groups had to say outside the meeting.

There was, of course, no truth in the tale about the American contingent nor in the other arguments that were produced by Athos and others. I was the sole speaker for the International Committee and I did not do well. A crowded, confused AGM after a press scandal is no place to deal with confidently stated untruths such as the IGC had a serious deficit and had raided a non-existent trust fund. The members did not know till the next accounts were published that there was a comfortable surplus and no such fund.

I have never felt more alone in my life as I stood there trying to answer a dozen ridiculous untruthful charges which were sprung upon me.

Unfortunately the honest British faction joined in the attack on the IGC and the motion of 'no confidence' was passed. That, I am sure, was part of the reason why my faction lost the next election. The British AG had the prestige of the Mensa founding country and, although there were subsequent motions of confidence from the Swiss, American and Canadian AGMs when the facts came out, the damage was done.

A final blow on that rotten day was that Arthur Koestler, put off by the bad publicity, cancelled his lecture causing further dismay to the British Committee.

I staggered away from this meeting and tried not to read the many garbled press reports. In a moment of weakness I confess I did feel that I had been subjected to a real injustice. After years of unpaid, enthusiastic and successful work I had to endure a severe and unjustified public humiliation. But remembering the undue adulation I had had from many kindly Mensa groups around the world I suppose this undue disgrace left me with an undue credit balance of regard. The advice from Win (who resigned from Mensa in disgust), and all my friends, was to follow Codella and the others and give up the struggle.

But I took the advice of Bernard Shaw, 'Never resign', and with foolish obstinacy which I have never regretted, I simply prepared for the next battle which I lost. The war, in the oddest way, I eventually won.

The motion by one national branch upon the International Committee was not binding, of course. So when the triumphant SIGRIM faction found out to their surprise that I intended to soldier on and ignore the letters they sent demanding my resignation, they redoubled the harassment.

We were coming up to the next IGC election so the press campaign of scandals intensified. A *Sunday Times* article early in 1967, 'VIOLENCE THREAT IN MENSA FEUD', arose from Athos who claimed that he was phoned by the representative of a 'dreary clutch of bully boys' and threatened with violence if he did not resign. The newspaper also quoted the editor of the Mensa journal who called Athos 'An oily tongued rascal', in his resignation Editorial mentioned later.

There was much newspaper talk of the two factions in Mensa

and the feud between them but at that time the 'faction' in British Mensa was myself and a tiny bunch of personal friends. I would have been glad of even a 'dreary clutch of bully boys' on my side if they had existed anywhere but in poor Athos's imagination, over-excited as it was by his successes.

A nation-wide television programme, 'Panorama', featured Athos, Peter Goodman, the *Mensa Journal* editor, Eric Hills and the new British Chairman, Bill Lovett, and myself after this 'violence threat' publicity. There was an innocuous exchange which bore out my theory that even the Mensans with the most vitriolic pens tend to be polite to other Mensa faces. We were truthfully told by the perceptive Kenneth Robinson that we were like a 'lot of old ladies quarrelling over their teacups'. The only unboring part was when Goodman was asked why he called Athos an, 'oily tongued rascal'. He replied with admirable simplicity, 'because he is'. Athos wisely said nothing to this or about anything much on the programme. Afterwards, at a grisly party on BBC whisky in the green room, he calmly told me that Porthos and Aramis were planning to send damaging letters to the company of which I was by that time a director. This was to be part of the harassment campaign if I would not resign. He said that it was all the plan of an American Sigrimite and that he was mad.

I had heard something like this already from a young member. He told Win of a plot to send my firm a letter *denying*, 'the rumour' that my son was a juvenile delinquent and that my thirteen year old daughter had had two abortions. These letters were not sent as far as I know. To prepare them I had to tell my children of this threat. My son, now a policeman, took it phlegmatically since he is about as undelinquent as one could imagine, but my daughter was very upset. 'What a lot of liars', she cried, 'I'm nearly fifteen!' Denying the false rumour was of course just telling the truth. Who can be blamed for that? But poison pen letters were sent and some of them had just that form predicted, creating suspicion by denying accusations.

I was refusing all the rather more friendly overtures from the over-confident SIGRIM faction that I was receiving and persistently refusing to resign or, 'deal with them direct'. Their problem was that although a lot of people were afraid of them and their

methods, they had so smirched their own reputations that they
had no hope of being actually elected. They hoped to dominate
those that were. It was this weakness that led to their total defeat
in the end.

In March 1967 my employer sent for me and silently dropped
in front of me an airmail letter from America. It purported to
come from a member. It accused me of stealing money from my
firm and from Mensa and covering up my defalcations. It was the
first of five similar letters, all based on internal evidence from the
same source.

I had been with my firm for many years and had a good
reputation. But a Chairman has his responsibilities and I was
subjected to some questioning before he confirmed his immediate reaction of angry rejection of such a malicious libel. He wrote
a supportive letter to the addresses given on that and the other
four such letters saying that dishonesty was not something of
which any one who had known me for any time could possibly
suspect me. The letters all came back from the false addresses
that had been given. The purported writers were not to be traced
on the American Mensa files.

As the new few letters arrived over a period of a couple of
weeks, some affirming and some denying the 'rumours' about my
'malfeasances', the Chairman sent for me each time and, holding
the letter by one corner with a handkerchief, with his face averted
and his nose held, dropped them in front of me announcing,
'another letter from your fan club'.

Friends in America that I told about it wrote to say that only a
certain SIGRIM member could have done such a thing. But
when we got the facts later we discovered that Athos and maybe
some others were in the plot. Certainly it was Athos who supplied
my firm's address and some of the wordings, as was made clear by
the revelation of Andy Di Cyan of Chicago Mensa.

During that hectic period in the run up to the 1967 international election the harassment continued and I found that I had no
time to continue the development of Mensa. I was up to my neck
in counteracting the problems that were being arranged for me,
trying to get together a panel of sufficiently tough-minded candidates and running an election campaign. To add to my troubles a

report was made to the Fraud Squad in England by the SIGRIM faction and another to the Board of Trade. In New York there were similar attempts to cause official suspicion. It took all my time to deal with them. However there was no evidence to support the accusations and the malice was patent and demonstrable. There was an abrupt cessation of this kind of attack when enquiries bounced back in the faces of the instigators.

Chicago Mensa has, since the start, published a magazine called *Chime* (CHIcago MEnsa) and at the time the Editor was a very serious young man called Andy Di Cyan with whom I had been having a fairly acrimonious but decent correspondence. He co-operated and sympathised with the SIGRIM group and attacked me largely for the fault of 'supporting Codella', who had become the butt of many emotionally anti-establishment members in America. Let it be said in fairness that Codella had not always handled the many opposition factions very well and, being an entrepreneurial type, was inclined to be autocratic. He made enemies, not all of them among the crazy fringe I have been describing. Mensa needs its Codellas. It has to get used to ways of using them without being used by them.

Mensa owes much to the honesty and decency of Andy Di Cyan because it was he who had the courage that undoubtedly was needed to blow the whistle on the Three Musketeers when he repudiated them as associates.

REFORM YES! DISHONOUR NEVER! was the title of Andy's article in Chime in which he attacked Porthos for discrediting the reform movement in his methods.

He accused the SIGRIM members of being responsible for the poison-pen letters to my company and revealed his evidence in the form of a long rambling letter which had been circulating among the central SIGRIM group with each recipient adding his own comments, copying and passing on. Athos had clearly been the source of the address of my firm and in his own unmistakably oblique style gave instructions about the actions which he had himself foretold.

Athos started the letter by saying that his suspicions as to how he had lost his last two jobs were deepening into certainty but he disapproved of others suffering in the same way so he asked

Aramis 'NOT to send anonymous letters to the Chairman of the Board of Directors and to the Chief Accountant (each letter being marked 'Private and Confidential'), and here the name and address of my firm is given, 'concerning one of the directors of the company (though God knows he deserves it)'.

Later in this long rambling letter another SIGRIM member is reported to have passed on a suggestion that he should write a letter to my firm denying my daughter's abortions, my son's delinquency and my own embezzlements.

Athos goes on: 'Now it is obvious that Porthos wouldn't dream of sending anonymous letters to VS' employers, he says as much in his letter of 11 February. There can be no harm in letting him have the address, can there?'

Another passage from the letter purporting to be from Aramis says, 'April is get Heald month, May is get Vic, and June is get Sokol month'. This planned harassment programme was carried out. There is much more in the same vein.

The next big upset was about the article by Peter Goodman who, as editor, had suffered threats to himself and his invalid wife when he had refused publicity to unsubstantiated charges by SIGRIM writers against the International Committee. The blistering valedictory editorial he courageously wrote against them when he resigned exposed their methods but the SIGRIM faction seem to have managed to stop its publication in the American edition, something I found out only when researching this book.

I did my best to circulate news of the Di Cyan revelations but, although I had assembled a panel of candidates, I was very much isolated and very reluctant to risk more general publicity for the antics of a tiny untypical minority of loony fringe members. Goodman's exposure of SIGRIM appeared in January 1967, only in England.

With the bad publicity and faction fights on the American Committee there was a feeling among the increasing group of Canadian members that Mensa Canada should separate from North American Mensa. In June 1967 Mensa Canada was formed and recognised by the IGC, which was now meeting in its emaciated form every six weeks and doing most of its work by correspondence with its many overseas members. At this time we had 15,000 members worldwide and we had active operations in the UK, USA, Canada, France, Switzerland, Italy, Austria, New Zealand, Australia, Malta, Holland, Belgium, Sweden, Finland and India. We were planning operations in Greece and Israel and many other places but little could be done to help these developments because of the problems described. All these Mensa units had representation on the IGC on the basis of one vote per country regardless of membership.

We had no money to bring the committee together and I was trying to run all this from my small home study in the evenings and weekends. I communicated with my committee by post. My tools were a hand-held dictating machine, a telephone and a great deal of unjustified confidence and chutzpah. I worked with a series of part-time secretaries working from their own homes from tapes I dictated. I sometimes reflect with utter astonishment on what can be done in the western world by a person or small group if they are cheeky enough, have an interesting new idea and are ready to learn the ropes. It will be seen that my troubles arose when others found that they could challenge me at the same game used destructively.

Low point though it was, 1967 was not entirely a bad year for Mensa. There was an excellent meeting of European Mensa pioneers in Lugano where the little harassed London group of Mensa internationalists were able to renew their sense of the real value of Mensa. In this beautiful old town we heard from Marianne Seydoux that French Mensa, after a period in the doldrums, was reviving rapidly after some good publicity, Swiss Mensa was prospering and so were Austrian and Dutch Mensa. All the British/American troubles seemed not to have affected the Continent and I came away with a lifted heart. The best news of all about Lugano was the acceptance of what has been called the Third Aim of Mensa, which was later that year accepted by the whole society in a referendum.

For several days in the hurly burly of press attention and the scores of people who wanted to talk to me in Lugano, I had noticed a tiny little priest whose round not-too-well-shaven face was like that of a saintly cherub with its beaming goodwill. He made several attempts to engage me in conversation but my Italian is rudimentary and his English, at the time, was much the same. He failed to capture my attention in the competitive group that surrounded me most of the time. But eventually Don Calogera La Placa managed to attract, then hold, and then rivet my attention when we began to talk in French. He was one of the two or three members we had in Sicily and, as it turned out, one of those many folk around the world with whom I was corresponding. What he had done was remarkable and admirable. He was a priest in a rigidly traditional inward-looking, almost medieval culture in a small unprosperous mountain town in Sicily. He had decided that what was needed in order to bring his poor island into the prosperity of the modern world was a move to locate and educate bright underprivileged children, to build up the cadre of trained talent that was essential to a modern society. Educated within the stifling bigotry of the local culture, he had sufficiently emancipated himself by a painstaking reading which included my own books.

He conceived the idea of a school for underprivileged able children in Sicily which he later managed to found. Further he persuaded me that Mensa should take upon itself the aim of fostering giftedness (rather than just collecting it) for the general benefit of humanity.

Don Calogera is a natural orator, one of the most effective I have heard. He was so effective that an understanding of the language he spoke did not seem to be essential. I gave him a spot at the IGC meeting in Lugano and he managed by the sheer power of personal magnetism and charisma, with only a hesitant translation of his words by a local linguist, to persuade the meeting to accept his proposed amendment to our constitution. This became the Third Aim when it was accepted by a referendum.

At the American AG in June a 'no confidence' motion against the IGC was rejected.

At this point I must explain the split in the pioneers which contributed to the problems. There had been set up a small group of six to go into the objections of the small British group who opposed the new International Constitution which had been devised by Eric Hills and accepted by an overwhelming vote. It had been skilfully devised to enshrine and preserve the practices which had enabled us to develop until then. It was a clever document which was loose enough to be practical yet did not give too much scope to what are called 'barrack room lawyers' in England. It ensured democracy and an underlying sound practice.

It lasted until 1980. Eric Hills himself, Brian Locke and a few others, were on the 1966 commission and when they produced their draft it was at odds with what I myself and the rest of the IGC majority thought was essential to preserve the international unity of Mensa. It reduced the role, importance and finances of the International Committee and delegated most functions to the National Committees leaving the IGC with only a loose co-ordinating role. It was against everything I had been working for and frankly I did not like it at all. It upset my friend and colleague, Eric Hills, when I raised objections and we decided to put our different views to the membership. His was the really influential voice against me at the dreadful London meeting I have described. The majority of the International Committee supported my view and in the subsequent referendum after arguments in the *International Journal* it prevailed so that it was Eric Hills' first Constitution rather than his group's second version which took us through the next seventeen years when it was replaced by the one now in force.

The arguments over 'Motion Two' which would have accepted the new idea, took up a lot of time and attention during that year. There was a big problem and scandal over the International Committee Election.

An already very fraught, confused situation was made worse by a last minute telegram from the American Committee which by now had turned against the International Committee but represented the large majority of members. They demanded a delay in the date for the submission of nominations. My committee thought it wise to grant this unusual request and we appointed the British Electoral Reform Society to conduct the election and count the votes, because we had every reason to be confident that anything we did would be likely to be challenged by SIGRIM.

On the nomination day Athos arrived at the very last minute with his SIGRIM nomination and there was a third beside the Wilson/Serebriakoff nomination which I had managed to assemble.

The ballots were sent out, not easy to arrange in Mensa, now world wide, and the votes came in to the Electoral Reform Society. But SIGRIM were on the offensive in an undifferentiated way and now the Director of the Electoral Reform Society began to come under fire from the SIGRIM faction. SIGRIM evidently felt that insulting strictures, warnings and threats to the Electoral Reform Society were essential to ensure that they had any chance. These had a counter-productive effect. The poor Director, Frank Brittan, though a tough political veteran who often worked for the fractious factions of the British Trade Union Movement, said he had never known the like. He was so disturbed and upset that he went off sick and this delayed the count. There was a long, tense, stressful delay with all parties in the Mensa world screaming at me. I put all the pressure I could on the society but time went on and the letters and telegrams from the SIGRIM group became frantic as they sensed victory and felt, not altogether unreasonably, that they were being gerrymandered. Frank Brittan was extremely scathing to the press about the phone calls and letters he had received from the tiny group of Mensa loonies, and of course poor old Mensa had to take a lot more stick from the delighted media. Athos rushed eagerly in to cause another scandal which led to the piece in the *Sunday Times* of which I have told.

As I have explained the SIGRIM panel had not dared to feature any of their own, by now notorious, names on the nominations, so Athos had got together a large group of members, many from his own town, and the panel put forward consisted of perfectly respectable people, many of whom had little or no idea of the inside story about the SIGRIM group who were sponsoring them. Some of them have proved to be Mensa stalwarts since. This was the Mayne/Frisch panel and they won the election with 2,212 votes. The Wilson/Serebriakoff panel got 1,660, while the third 'Reconstruction' slate got 876 votes. I had not expected this defeat and was deeply downcast. I was extremely (and it turned out wrongly) worried about what would happen to Mensa with SIGRIM nominees in charge. What monster, I asked myself, had I created? I felt like the sorcerer's apprentice. My monster proved to be an inactive mouse.

3

History: the comeback

I had no fears about Alan Mayne, the new international chairman, a very early member from the Berrill days and a decent man, but I wondered how he would cope with his uninhibited sponsors. I met him with one or two of the other new incumbents and I passed over the files and tried to help them with the big job that they had unexpectedly taken on.

The election result which was announced in March 1968 marked the end of the low point in Mensa development.

Having won their famous victory SIGRIM vanished like a puff of smoke. There were no more scandal sheets, press scandals, meetings, protests or threats from that source. Nothing!

The Musketeers and the individual members were to remain and engage in even fiercer battles with each other, with National Mensa Committees and officers. There were to be new internal scandals and problems with and between its members but the organisation SIGRIM died on the spot in the moment of its triumph.

Athos became the Editor of the *International Journal* for a time. By November that year there was severe criticism of his editorship at the British AG. His first issue gave a flattering profile of Porthos and we saw some well posed pictures of himself at his best. But the troubles were over at least in the UK. Nothing constructive was happening but no actual harm was being done at the international level, except much wasteful spending.

Having reached a nadir Mensa began the slow healing process and thus proved its real viability and the fact that there was a pool of loyalty among our members despite the absurd public antics of

Mensa's inevitable, but minuscule, intelligent, able and zealous loony fringe.

The International Committee obtains its funds by drawing a proportion of the subscription of every member. In spite of Athos's *canards* a fair reserve had been built up in its coffers. The new Committee began to deplete these by meeting alternately in London and New York and, for the first time, there was a good deal of transatlantic travel chargeable to Mensa for attendance. I was asked to hold the proxy vote of two continental Mensas and amazed and embarrassed the new IGC by turning up at the London meetings. The newly elected panel, many of whom had no committee experience in Mensa, had got their ideas of me from those who had nominated them. The brazen presence of this arch villain, as I had been depicted, was an unexpected shock to some of the quite genuine people who were having to cope with a set of unfamiliar problems.

I enjoyed my new role in a perverse way. I had all the facts and precedents at my fingertips and I was extremely unpopular as I attacked impractical ideas and made suggestions that they would have liked to, but dared not, oppose. I had the time of my life with Athos because, unlike him, I was quite happy to make uninhibited, face-to-face attacks. I was now doing the harassing and he was trying to do the constructive defending. I flatter myself that I was better at the role switch than he.

At the first couple of meetings his new colleagues defended him and tried to controvert my detailed attacks, but later they heard me with embarrassed silence. Eventually they began to placate me and ask me to help. Within a few meetings I, who had been castigated for embezzlement and profligacy, was asked to take on the sensitive role of Publicity Officer for Mensa International. I soon found myself more influential with a committee that had beaten mine in the election than I had been with my own team.

The underlying secret in Mensa, as perhaps in all voluntary organisations, is that while politicians, place-seekers and outcries come and go, it is always the beavers which run the show. Anyone with patience and persistence and a willingness to take responsibility and work systematically will have no difficulty in rising in the hierarchy to the level at which their time and patience lasts. The next few years were calm after the storm in Mensa; no motion or progress of any kind whatever.

British Mensa subsided slowly from the peak of about 3,500. American Mensa remained fairly static during a period when Sander Rubin, as the new American Chairman, did his best to repair the ravages of the SIGRIM episode and deal with the rump of the faction who had penetrated the Committee and were now causing other troubles. He did a fair job at a difficult time.

At the AG in Tarrytown there were 225 members. American membership halted the previous year's downward drift and held at about 11,000.

In 1969 it was clear that the British were disenchanted with Athos and his idiosyncratic work as editor, and the American Committee were being accused by his faction of censoring the *International Journal* he edited.

Karl Ross, a Mensa stalwart who edited the American *Mensa Bulletin* for many years, appeared as assistant editor that year. In Britain a young student just down from the Machine Intelligence Unit at Edinburgh University became the British Mensa Secretary. Dr Nigel Searle became Assistant International General Secretary later. Sir Clive Sinclair was then a thin young red-headed journalist whom I met as member and with whom I was much impressed because of his lightning wit and penetratingly swift mental grasp. I tried to talk the youth out of his enthusiasm for the transistor as a substitute for the well developed thermionic valve but he swept my sensible arguments aside and I must admit has managed to make the things work somehow. Today his company, Sinclair Research Limited, has sold more computers than any other in the world. Nigel met Clive through Young Mensa contacts and today he runs Sinclair Research while Clive plans innovative industrial triumphs.

Clive has been British Mensa Chairman for five years, during which we have gained about 11,000 members. Clive has said that his take-off and later success as a world-famous innovative industrial pioneer was much aided by many Mensa contacts when he was a young unknown.

Mensa has only this answer to those who repeatedly ask, 'But what do you do with all those brains? What of general benefit do you achieve?' Our answer is that brains do not work *en masse* but in teams. Mensa has helped its members to build countless fine and effective teams but its apologists and chroniclers do not even know about most of them and certainly would not claim credit for them. But instead we have to bear blame and discredit for the frenzied loonies from those who love to laugh at what they erroneously see as our pretentiousness. Seventy thousand people cannot be made into a team, army or pressure group. But Mensa can be and is the substrate upon which excellent competitive teams grow and thrive.

In December that year I revived a special kind of lecture discussion which has been growing even more popular as a Mensa event. A distinguished speaker makes a speech on some speculative or controversial topic and this is followed by an hour and a half of discussion to which everyone is encouraged to contribute. The best of these are marvellous with lots of wit and clever joking, as well as serious, thoughtful talk. Even the worst are not bad. Mensa produces good talk.

It was in June 1969 that a British member, Peter Devenish, won a competition for the design of the Mensa Logo. This insignia has been accepted as the Mensa sign and replaced Berrill's Ku Klux Klan figures. For those who are unable to comprehend some of

the increasingly divergent variants, the original idea was a representation of the world on a table where the top and legs are shown so that they form the 'M' of Mensa. I am prepared to concede that it is an improvement on Berrill's idea.

Peter's design can now be seen everywhere, on badges, stickers, pins, car stickers, beer mats, matches, pens, flags, tee-shirts and tattoos!

One stunt during Athos's brief reign as International Editor was his attempt to rewrite Mensa history.

Dr L. L. Ware, Berrill's friend who had dropped out of Mensa seventeen years before, was approached by Athos and, as a result, there was a motion of the IGC in New York that Dr Ware should be recognised as the true founder, on the basis of his telling Athos that he had suggested the idea to Berrill. Athos was about to publish an article claiming that Dr Ware, not Berrill, was the founder. Word got out and some of the early members approached me with profound objections to what they saw as a failure to give credit to Berrill's major contribution. I was asked to see Dr Ware and he told me that he had made no claim to be the sole founder as Athos had said. He would give his account in an article which was eventually published. The headline was altered and Ware was featured as one of the founding pair. Soon afterwards there was a dinner party at which he was installed as a Honorary Vice President, in recognition of his initial contribution.

In July 1969 Eric Hills was honoured by being appointed to a new role, that of International Ombudsman which in Mensa is rather like being Lord Chief Justice. He has served in that difficult role with exemplary perseverance, patience and trust ever since. Here is another real Mensa stalwart. His courage and fairness made him the only man who ever ever induced the worst of Mensa-damaging loonies actually to apologise. It was Eric Hills who was given the dreadful and dangerous task of judging Porthos when, true to his nature if to nothing else, his continued mischief brought him into conflict with those whom his activities had brought to power.

Despite the bad things that were happening at this time there were some excellent developments, not much noticed at the time, which were to be of major importance much later. There was a new generation of Mensans who had joined in early youth. They got together in Young Mensa at a period when, in my opinion, it was more active and effective than the British Committee. The circle included many who are now famous in the computer world particularly. Some of this group are the really motivated driving force of Mensa in Britain today.

In late 1969 the by now much criticised Athos gave up as editor and handed over to George and Rosemary Atherton. Dr Atherton proved to be another Mensa stalwart at the international level. He was a tower of calm strength over many hard years during which he carried the torch of the *International Journal* with efficiency and credit. Looking back he was one of the best editors.

By 1970 the new International Committee, which was characterised by an unwise and unmasterly inactivity, was breaking up.

Nominations were called for the new International election and I made up my mind to stand again. I agreed with Bob Van Den Bosch that we would put up a joint slate called, 'The Unity Slate' which would try to heal Mensa's wounds.

During this period Porthos had turned back to America in his eager quest for attention and persecution. He protested in all possible ways on all possible occasions to all possible persons and committees. He eventually appealed in long rambling detailed letters to the International Ombudsman for justice, with the usual threats as to what would happen if he did not get it. Hills' published judgement was a round, complete and unreserved condemnation of Porthos himself and all his works. Porthos was ordered to apologise to those he had traduced and his membership was suspended for one year. To everyone's astonishment Porthos meekly complied. But it was not the last of Porthos: he continued his activities on much the same lines later in America and much later, after much heart searching, had to be expelled from Mensa by the American Committee.

Athos, who was not prosperous, eventually lapsed when well-wishers stopped paying his subscription. There is an option in Mensa by which those who cannot afford the subscriptions can be let off if they write and ask. He did not take this option, and for some reason no one urged him to do so. Later we heard newspaper stories of other scandals he was involved with in his own town and then he was quiet for several years before he died after a long illness some years ago. Aramis disappeared and has not been heard of for a long time.

That was how Mensa coped with its own special kind of problem in those formative days. We cope rather better these days. Because they are always changing leadership, collectivities like Mensa learn slowly, but in the end they learn. The malicious disrupter problem is an interesting and recurring one and it seems to arise from the fact that, as Professor Terman discovered in the great survey of which I shall write, most intelligent people are reasonable, polite, constructive and above average in accepted social behaviour. When they encounter inexplicable and motiveless mischief and malice in other people like themselves, they are slow to believe it or to accept that it may have no reasonable or logical cause. Time after time 'peace makers' come forward saying that if only the destructive few could be treated with better tact and understanding they could be brought to see reason and behave more normally. Time after time, challenged to try this, they have come surprisingly unstuck.

I believe that what motivates malice in bright humans is often under-achievers' envy. When you can out-think those who do better, you are more bitter and spiteful than when you cannot. Intelligence helps towards, but does not ensure, success. Many other qualities are required and lack of them is the bitter problem. In other cases there is the built-in failure trend in some of the very bright. Perhaps it is an introjection of early peer-group envy/hatred which poisons effort and reinforces under-achievement.

In October my book *How Intelligent Are You?* was published. It was a layman's popular account of IQ testing and it contained roughly standardised tests such as intelligence tests. I arranged for a feature in the *Daily Mirror*, and this proved to be another breakthrough which started a new very successful recruiting method that was to be developed into an important recruitment aid. *The Daily Mirror* is a popular tabloid newspaper and it has a very large circulation. For Mensa I had always, until then, aimed for publicity in the more serious newspapers like *The Times*.

This was an experiment with an admitted spin-off advantage to me as an author. I spent several nights at the *Daily Mirror* offices with the Features Editor and they ran a competition every day for a week with IQ type questions from my book. My aim was to make Mensa more representative and I wanted to reach the people like myself from underprivileged backgrounds who might be unaware of how bright they were. My title that attracted the *Mirror* editor was, 'ARE YOU A SECRET SUPERBRAIN?'

The deal was that British Mensa should have the reply coupons and a chance to use them for recruitment. At the end of the week the newspaper handed me eight mail bags with forty-seven thousand replies. There was near panic in our little office. A timely initiative by a Young Mensan started a major exercise in a clubroom over a London pub as he organised volunteers from Young Mensa.

Despite this spontaneous help the British Mensa office then was not able to cope with such a rush and the subsequent gain of members in the UK was not all that it should have been. But big gains were made, the downward trend was checked for a time and an important lesson was learned.

My 1970 Superbrain scheme was the model for much later development effort. It was repeated in numerous variations in British Mensa and still continues.

The greatest single explanation of British Mensa's recent very rapid growth has been the development and perfection of this and similar techniques. Other Mensas including American Mensa developed similar techniques and they were often very successful indeed. Apparently there are potential Mensans among the readers of all types of newspapers and they love to send in answers to published quizzes. What matters, it emerges, is more the circulation than the intellectual image of the journal.

I asked National Mensa Chairmen to let me have the local Mensa History and one of the few replies came from Ruth

Whittle of Australian Mensa. She and her husband have been the staunchest Mensans and since they became active in 1964 they have never faltered in their work and support.

At that time the world membership was 3,600, mostly in Britain. There were about 20 Australian members, some recruited from London and some who had emigrated from the UK.

Dr Tom Sandemen and Jeff Whittle met to discuss Mensa and, like the French founder Marianne Seydoux, firmly decided that nothing could or should be done about an Australian national branch. However a British member, Marjorie Meakins, had met me and asked me to speak to the girls at the private girls' school in Hertfordshire where she was headmistress. When she told me of her plan to emigrate I arranged with the Committee that she should be given an enormous grant and full instructions and authority to set up the Australian Branch. So, with twenty-five good British pound notes, she set out to establish the Mensa flag in the Antipodes. I told her to send back any surplus cash after she had succeeded but Australian Mensa has retained the whole of this great sum ever since. When American Mensa borrowed a thousand pounds when I went there, they returned it within a year.

Marjorie arrived in Melbourne with her three teenage children. She contacted the Whittles and Sandemen. Then, learning from the London successes a few years before, she soon got a spot on the TV programme, 'People '64'.

Following favourable exposure Marjorie, who could claim to be the founder of Australian Mensa, began advertising and recruiting members adapting the methods I had tried to explain in London. Most of the early members were expatriates but soon there were some 'real Australians'.

Activities began in the usual way with meetings in private houses that seem, according to Ruth, to have been after the think-in format, especially when they ran out of Mensan speakers and began to invite outside talent.

Marjorie ran things for about a year but the Australian Mensa problem is a difficult one because of the wide dispersal of a small population. The separate States had to set up their own systems and there was a long succession of changing incumbents each of

whom carried the Mensa torch through a year or two in the
pattern I have described. They have not yet reached the take-off
point when a professional staff can be engaged.

For many years the unifying element in a large continent has
been the Australian Mensa journal TABLEAUS (TABLE/AUS
tralia). It has always been lively and readable. Over the years until
1984 they have attracted 20,000 enquiries and enrolled 2,200
members of which they retain about 700 today. Mensa has a membership turnover problem everywhere because one motivation
for application is that of getting an economical IQ test. So there
are some who drop out after one year. This applies especially
in Australia where many new members are isolated from other
members and cannot get the benefit of meeting our network.

Sydney Jackson is a world expert on parachutes. He has to
make frequent business trips to Australia and he was a vital
personal link between the IGC and the Australian membership.
He was particularly helpful when Australian Mensa was having its
own version of the sort of troubles described above. A sincere and
obsessively persistent member of the litigious men of straw type
repeatedly found faults in the polling procedures (always easy to
do in view of the problems described). He managed to persuade
Mensa's bank to freeze all funds pending the outcome of some
obscure proposed litigation. Between 1970 and 1973 Australian
Mensa was at a standstill. I got many long emotional letters from
the complainer of which I could make little sense. It was Sydney
Jackson, who, on one of his business trips, made a stop at the
remote town and managed, in a face-to-face talk, to resolve the
matter.

Another responsive National Chairman was Udo Schultz, the
present chairman of German Mensa.

My first attempts in Germany had been with the help of a
popular author, Baron Soltikow. These came to nothing and the
real German Mensa beginning was, as I said, when my friend
Georg Fishhof introduced Dr Steiner. Steiner was a psychologist. He was extremely active and efficient during the short period
he remained interested. Mensa in Germany did well until he gave
up a year or two later. There was then a troubled and unprogres-
sive period under less active and less effective chairmen and
committees. At one point there was a story of a financial mess

which the IGC decided it must clear up for the good of the Mensa name. We were advised by the local members who remained loyal, to disband the German branch and set them up as international members. In fact the financial problems were easily sorted out by this new active group with the help of a British resident, Julian Parr, and no IGC support was needed. Since then there have been increasingly successful efforts towards a fresh start which were helped by an international meeting, with well known names such as Clive Sinclair, in Cologne. Another large and well publicised meeting this year just over the border at Kerkrade, Holland, may prove to have helped.

The new start was in 1981 and by the end of that year we had 72 paid-up German members and recruiting was going on effectively again.

Udo thinks that a psychological difficulty in the modern German climate is a suspicion of anything which smacks of the utterly disavowed 'herrenvolk' notion which the uncharitable, mistakenly, think they see in mental tests and Mensa.

It is not that German Mensa has had no publicity. There has been plenty but until recently it has been negative. But Mensa is news whether the media like it or not and the journalist cannot go on telling the same old story. If only to introduce novelty someone will, in the end, try another tack.

Quoting Udo, 'Painfully slowly members who were lucky enough to know newspaper people personally, managed to get fair reports into the press ... After a few articles had successfully been launched things looked somewhat brighter ... Right from the start close bonds existed between Mensa in Southern Germany and Mensa Austria, followed by frequent contacts and co-operation with Mensa in Britain, the Netherlands and Scandinavia. By the end of March 1984 membership had risen to 149, which means an increase of nearly fifty percent in one year.'

Greatly increased and more favourable recent publicity has made the German picture brighter and I hope to see in the next few years the true continental take-off we have never seemed to get before, from a base in Germanophone Europe.

Another chairman's story comes in from Philip Poole who for years has chaired the National Mensa which holds the world's Mensa penetration record. It is Channel Islands Mensa. Penetration is the Mensans per million of local population. Channel Islands has 130,000 people and they have 150 Mensans. That is 1,154 per million against the UK (second) with 205 and USA (third) with 178 per million. The Channel Islands are not, as many think, a part of the United Kingdom, and during a period of problems in British Mensa they chose to break away and were recognised by the IGC as a separate national Mensa.

It all started when Philip Anley, an estate agent in Jersey, joined and later became the CI Locsec. When he left and handed over to Philip Poole there were eight members. Philip was one of the enthusiasts we need everywhere but do not always find. He pitched in with successful publicity stunts and Superbrain competitions such as I have described and by 1972 had got the membership up to 70 so that there was quite a lot of Mensa activity on the group of islands. British Mensa had got into difficulties and raised the subscriptions at the same time as they reduced the publication which was all that the islands got from British Mensa. To publish a better magazine and continue activity Philip led a breakaway which was not resisted. With Philip's irrepressible enthusiasm and drive CI Mensa continued to grow on these small scattered Islands faster, relatively, than anywhere else. CI Mensa was strong enough by 1978 to host one of the best Mensa International Congresses I remember, with representation from about twenty countries. Philip was very active on the IGC also as a National Representative until the recent constitutional changes deprived International Mensa of his Mensa promoting talents.

These are just a few typical samples of the various National Mensa beginnings.

There were so many false starts in other countries that I could not record them. I was involved in it in my spare time for most of thirty years and most of the hundreds of abortive and mistaken efforts have gone from my mind.

I would get a letter or a call from a sole member in a far off country, for example Bolivia. I would give or send exemplary documentation and instructions and tell the enthusiast how to contact psychologists and get publicity. The IGC would make a small seed money grant if the case seemed promising and we would give all the support we could in view of distance and communications difficulties. Sometimes these seeds would germinate and a new Mensa would grow, sometimes we would get a small beginning which would fade after a year or two, more often we would hear little more. But sometimes, the seed germinates and the needed enthusiasts come forward to nurture it. If they manage to set up such a system whereby they are successively replaced when, inevitably, they tire of routine chores, then we add one more to the gradually growing list of National Mensas around the world. If that Mensa gets big enough to risk setting up a professional staff then, if it works out, we get a new large, stable, permanent Mensa.

The work of Mensa-building is challenging and interesting at first but once the effective methods for a region are worked out it becomes a matter of mechanical persistence in routine chores and that is no longer fun for the unpaid Mensan enthusiast. It is only when that less challenging part of the work is professionalised that Mensa really thrives.

Indian Mensa was started and sustained by a Calcutta student, Amitananda Das, but when he became too occupied with his studies the centre was transferred to a Bombay group connected with Dnyna Prabodhinee, a wonderful multi-caste school for gifted children founded and run by Dr V. V. Pendse. Indian Mensa was also chaired by a wealthy benevolent industrialist who helped the school, Mr P. V. Schroff. An Indian who lives in Germany, Sushil Bilaney has also been very helpful.

Recently, Indian Mensa was disclaimed by the new IBD because it has been unable to meet the minimum standards that the International Board insist upon. The Mensa problem in the poorer countries is that there are so few enthusiasts with the time, and there is so little cash available for testing, subscriptions and postal communications which are slow and difficult. We have to find ways of making Mensa into less of a luxury product for the richer countries before we can be satisfied.

Finnish Mensa has developed steadily since the late sixties and I have helped with visits and publicity because my past work as Managing Director of an innovative wood technology company took me frequently to all the Scandinavian countries.

Scandinavian Mensa, which includes Norway and Sweden, also started after numerous attempts when I found a very effective Norwegian Mensa enthusiast in the late Henrik Sellaeg. Henrik was an Oslo banker member who I contacted on a business trip. Henrik was a hard and effective worker and he beat the tough problems of developing Mensa in a small country with a scattered population.

As in Sweden the problem is the tendency for the press to deride and attack anything that can be labelled elitist. Although the Scandinavian countries have excellent traditions for finding, teaming up and using the talents of their ablest people, they have recently been affected by egalitarian, centralist, socialist ethos. Mensa has an uphill struggle in such countries until our real protean nature, our all-class origin and neutral political stance is perceived. Henrik's initiative was cleverly designed and successful and Norwegian Mensa became the recruiting base and merged with the smaller group in Sweden.

A very early Swedish Mensa set going by the expatriate American Jay Albrecht in the late fifties had disappeared completely and many personal efforts during business trips had proved abortive. Today things are going well and I expect Scandinavian Mensa to grow and thrive as Finnish Mensa has done.

Many attempts to form Mensa groups on the South American continent have failed or survived only briefly. We still await the pioneer there who can solve the local problems. Possibly Spanish American members can help American Mensa to find a way to sow the seed in better soil there. There are quite a large number of isolated members scattered around that continent.

The Far East there are large thriving groups in such world culture centres as Singapore and Hong Kong. All these have been going very well recently. Japan has a few hundred members but there was a severe communication problem as soon as the membership grew beyond the expatriate western group. This seems to be the inevitable starting point for countries and cultures with non-European languages.

Swiss Mensa was started by a multilingual Swiss, Alan Henderson, and nurtured by the mental arithmetic wizard and linguist, Dr Hans Eberstark, but it has never really developed strongly. It seems to remain stable with a membership a little below one hundred.

Israeli Mensa was set up after endless correspondence with London and holiday visits by myself and several other London Mensa workers at various times. It has a definite but precarious existence and awaits the real enthusiast who is also a communicator of enthusiasm who will one day galvanise it.

New Zealand Mensa is one of those Mensas with a really effective and innovative central group. For some years past it has held an honoured high place in the Mensa penetration stakes. Barbara Thompson, their latest chairman, is a professional airline pilot and an innovative organiser as well. Her mobility must be very useful in the work for Mensa that she is doing so well.

Holland and Belgium are two countries in which we have had the same serious problem of division. Perhaps the surprising thing is that we have not had the problem elsewhere. We have never had the finance for the enormous expense of protecting the Mensa name everywhere on earth. In both these countries the founder, having started with Mensa finance and support a genuine Mensa branch, got in first with a registration of the name on their own behalf. Without consent from the international body they both set up and registered with the national authorities organisations called 'Mensa' which were constitutionally under their personal, life-long control. This pre-empted the registration by the International Society of its democratic constitution and made it possible for these breakaway groups to prevent us using the name 'Mensa' in the two countries.

In both cases the unofficial undemocratic constitution was rejected by the IGC and that caused a split, with some members staying with the national founder and others setting up a new official and recognised branch. Mensa's apparent dual existence continued in both countries with each faction hampering and inhibiting the growth of the other and causing unhappy publicity. Attempts at legal action organised by Vice President Dr Ware in the seventies to prevent this 'passing off', were costly and ineffectual and we had to live with the split-personality Mensas for many years.

In the long run united International Mensa prevailed in both cases. In Holland there was a great celebration a year or two ago when, after some correspondence between the factions which I was able to initiate, they reunited leaving the original founder, the now ageing Commander Naber, with just a tiny rump of his old friends in the unofficial branch.

In Belgium, I understand, the breakaway Mensa has faded and almost disappeared while the official branch, led by a dynamic young man, Bernard Senault, is prospering.

Behind the Iron Curtain we have had a series of false dawns. Hearing of Mensa, a stream of people, mostly academics, write in and join under the special arrangements for countries where we have no possibility of supervised testing. They get a provisional membership. They write enthusiastically and some of them suggest setting up a branch. They often seem to be unaware that there might be official objections. We always warn them and they often contradict us. Then after a time, short or long, the chink in the iron curtain seems to clang shut and everything goes very quiet. We hear no more from that quarter and our letters remain unanswered.

A beautiful Polish woman became a member at one time. We were established in Poland. But it did not last. Dr Alan Henderson, at that time an International Development Officer, telegraphed to me with this mixed news.

'VICTOR STOP HAVE ABOLISHED POLISH MENSA BY MARRYING HER STOP'.

So Polish Mensa went to live with Alan in Basel but all too soon, sadly, the Polish Mensa divorced the disconsolate Alan. Learning the lesson, Mensa has discouraged marriages between National Branches and individuals since then.

Mensa always has a few 'Ostbloc' members but never many, never for very long. I yearn to see more informed and intelligent interchange across this dangerous ideological and philosophical divide and hope one day to welcome many members from the Marxist-ruled parts of the world. So long as we remain uncommitted and impartial this could not be bad but if it were otherwise there would be no sense and much danger in it. I would hate to see a Mensa dominated by any ideology or faction.

Italy is a country where Mensa has had several promising starts which have faded. The first I started myself on a holiday visit in 1966. I had found and inspired an enthusiastic and effective Italian American called Victor Viglino. After correspondence I arranged my holiday trip so as to meet him in Naples where he was an executive in a large American conglomerate.

The publicity was positive and plentiful. Victor did a very good job for Mensa then and for the duration of his enthusiasm. However he horrified the IGC by an error which proved to be damaging. Very much a self-starter entrepreneur he failed to realise that an IQ test published is an IQ test destroyed and, without a word to Mensa or the copyright owners, he 'gave permission' to a big magazine to publish an Italian translation of an IQ test we use. This so enraged the entire psychological profession in Italy (which at that time was minuscule) that, despite many attempts during business trips, it was many years before I persuaded the local doyen of the profession to forgive us and co-operate.

Dr Abbele of Milan was the psychologist concerned and when we did make friends at last he gave me a very fine contribution to Mensa thinking which I have repeated endlessly. 'It can only be', he said, 'the intelligent in each language and cultural group, who can comprehend each other across the semantic chasms that divide them.' It was more or less the same thought that Her Majesty Queen Elizabeth gave me later when I was introduced. Even the British Queen, you see, suffers from the same precognitive plagiarism that has always dogged me. People, especially Mensans, read my thoughts before I have them. It is a most disrespectful way to treat the Queen and even this humble Mensa President.

The second Italian beginning arose out of the faded rump of the first. It was centred on Como and fostered by Alan Henderson who was then living in Lugano. That effort faded away too and there was little heard of Mensa in Italy for a year or two until the appearance of the needed enthusiast in the form of the good Dr Mennoti Cossu from Rome whom I first met in a big Mensa Congress in Graz.

Mennoti Cossu is a man of enormous drive and enthusiasm

who makes things happen effectively despite being confined by an early illness to a wheelchair. His work, with the constant help of his devoted wife and of the team he has built up, is effective and he taps the vein of applications that is opened up by successful and favourable publicity. I myself was able to visit last year and we got TV and good magazine coverage.

I am certain that, at last, Italian Mensa is established as a permanent part of Mensa. It is part of the very difficult and so far rather insecure, breakout from Anglophonia (if you will permit my neologism for the English speaking world) where we have had our greatest appeal and strength so far.

Spain has had a similar patchy Mensa history with number of half-hearted starts which have been inhibited by the difficulties with the authorities there. Recently the omens have been suddenly better. Once we can establish Mensa firmly there I believe that folk in the southern half of the American continent will begin to want to join our world-spanning comprehending community.

Irish Mensa is still part of British Mensa but despite the border problems it embraces both parts of the island. There is no border in Irish Mensa. It is autonomous in everything except that it sensibly uses the facilities of the well-organised British office rather than undertake, at this early stage, the risky experiment of setting its own selection agency.

The relations between Mensa in Britain and in Ireland could hardly be better and some of the most enjoyable weekends for Britons have been in Belfast and Dublin alternately.

British Mensa's favourite Irishman, David Lalley the international and British archivist has played a great part in the development of Irish Mensa and of the good relations that exist. He is a good-looking young man who is one of the most ardent and least political of Mensa stalwarts. His collection of Mensa memorabilia (mementos) is unequalled and he displays them at all important meetings for new members to see.

Another Mensa enthusiast who has done much for the development of Irish Mensa recently has been their Chairman, David Schulman, a Dubliner who is now also the International Administrations Officer. Irish Mensa has grown fast since he began to be active and I believe we shall hear more of his contribution at the international level.

Africa has been a problem for Mensa with too many false starts and little solid progress until the mid-seventies. We have had a cell in what was then Rhodesia which was mistakenly recognised in the very early, over-enthusiastic days. Kenya made a fairly promising beginning after my business trips there but that faded too during the periods of political tension when attention was distracted.

During the dynamic period of Robert Lehr's presidency of French Mensa he made good contacts in Senegal and the Ivory Coast during business trips. We still have loyal groups of francophone local members in each capital. Nor are these expatriates. Both groups were prematurely recognised and have since had, sadly, to be derecognised as National Mensas because they have not been able to solve the very difficult recruitment problems in such countries and have remained too small.

The one striking success was in South Africa where Mensa has become strong and widespread but it is not yet fully recognised. My first approach in the sixties was discouraged by the government of the time with a stern note from the Ministry which informed me that South Africa had enough cultural associations and needed no more.

During the seventies I had to go there to introduce my electronic stress-grading machine for automatic quality control which was useful for their fast-grown cultivated conifers. During my trips I promoted Mensa as usual. I expected difficulties because Mensa cannot accept any other barrier to membership than the one we have all accepted. (Green members with yellow stripes will be welcomed warmly if they qualify.)

I was told before I got there that it would be impossible for members to meet in a mixed-race Mensa but I found, to my surprise, that the press published my statement of Mensa principles and no one seemed to object to Mensa's anti-racialist position.

There had been from the very earliest days a loyal handful of immigrant expatriate members but of course they were almost all of European origin. They helped with and welcomed the publicity from my visit. It galvanised the local group and they began to work towards national status as they recruited more members locally. I was able to reassure the International Committee that at least a few members were of Asian and African origin. In later trips I was able to meet these members myself in meetings in Cape Town and other places, so I can confidently say that South African Mensa does not practice apartheid. Further all my conversations with members of all racial backgrounds showed that in South Africa, among Mensans, there is no apparent support for apartheid. I do not claim however that Mensa has as many members in all the local race groups as I (and the local members) would like to see. Here is a problem in many places which will not be solved easily.

A bigger breakthrough came when Christine Chester emigrated and soon became the local chairman. She built up membership to some hundreds quite quickly and thus strong groups were formed in the main centres which took up the work and continue to thrive today.

Christine is a graduate linguist. She joined Mensa and was later, briefly, my extraordinarily competent personal business secretary. But later still, my friend and business associate, South African Solly Tucker, came to England, met her at a trade show I was in, and took her back as his own PA to Pretoria.

That is how we got a fresh surge of Mensa growth in South African Mensa. It now has a large and thriving branch which seems stable and viable. I know there are some who regret that we have members there but I stick to my view that we should recruit sapient humanity without any exceptions of our own making. Mensans have no collective views but I am sure the overwhelming majority of them condemn apartheid. Constitutionally we may not practise it ourselves by excluding those who can qualify, no matter where they are found.

There is a conclusion to this world Mensa tour. It demonstrates how, by a chapter of seeming accidents, we have spread abroad from our starting point in Oxford. Unplanned, opportunistic and sporadic is what it has been. For that, those who have done the work have often been criticised.

There have been vociferous demands, especially from hopeful election candidates, for systematic, budgeted, planned campaigns and the like. There have even been attempts to make such plans and carry them through. But, so far, it seems Mensa is simply not that kind of animal. Mensa has been like the wind which bloweth where it listeth and may not be commanded.

I am sure that the highly developed recruitment systems that we have in a few countries could be adapted and transported, predictably and reliably, across language and culture barriers, but it would require an amount of risk capital that we have not persuaded members to provide.

Until we provide it, or try other methods, we are very reasonably dependent on what may be called the serendipity factor which I and some others seem to have made to work after a style. We are in the business of helping members in new national regions where the entrepreneurial enthusiast makes his unheralded appearance as an expression of Mensa's will to be in that land. Then, opportunistic and erratic, we move in. When the local effort flags we do not grieve. We turn to aid the next enthusiast. There are always plenty.

I believe that with 67,000 members Mensa is still in its infancy and I firmly join with that other rather more important president, Mr Ronald Reagan, in saying about World Mensa, 'Y' ain't seen nuthin' yet'.

What will ensure the real breakout from Anglophonia that will come will, I believe, be the professionalisation of a franchising system. The recruitment function should be performed by small, reasonably profitable, professional organisations who would specialise in the recruitment function, being paid by results. They would be strictly supervised and would hand over to Mensa nothing but a stream of members.

In October 1971 it was announced in the *International Journal* that my Unity Slate had been returned unopposed as the International General Committee. I was elected as International Chairman and Bob Van Den Bosch, who was an officer in the Dutch Army, became the International General Secretary. Herman Blumenthal was Treasurer and there was a Dutch member, Adrian Visser, a British solicitor, Raymond Allen, the Swiss, Henderson, and an American, Dr Max Fogel who has been a great contributor to Mensa since the first in America.

In amendment to the American Mensa bylaws were passed at the June AGM.

During 1971 Mensa celebrated its Silver Jubilee with a reception which was held in Lincoln's Inn where many of the Mensa old timers met each other again. Soon afterwards Dr Ware arranged for the installation of the blue plaque of which I have spoken on the wall of the house in Oxford from which Berrill had set out with the copy for the printer in 1946.

Looking back now, 1971 can be seen as another of Mensa's new beginnings as well as the year of its Silver Anniversary. The political storms and public scandals had died down a little although there was still dissension on the American Committee. But good things began to happen. In France another of the short dynamic men who often seem to be Mensa promoters, Monsieur Robert Lehr, began to galvanise French Mensa and soon became its Chairman.

What Lehr showed conclusively is that the Mensa dream can be exported outside Anglophonia. For the few years while his effective enthusiasm lasted, Mensa France shot up in numbers to over a thousand. Expansion ceased abruptly when he retired as Chairman. I toured France with him that year on a publicity tour in which we did the usual round of interviews, radio and television appearances. My French is fairly fluent so both he and I spoke to Mensa groups in Paris, Nice, Cannes, Marseilles, Lyon, and other towns I have forgotten.

But I must mention Nice where I met an enthusiastic young Mensan psychologist, Jean-Paul Terrassier. He had an interest in pediatrics and able children. I told him about the gifted children's movement in the UK and USA.

I have written of my early contacts in the USA with the American pioneers of that movement. I had reported this in my first Mensa book and had been approached by a pediatric nursing sister, Margaret Branch, for material for a television story on the subject. I had loaned her all the books and literature I had collected from the USA and she went on to publicise the idea and to found the British National Association for Gifted Children of which I have always been a member.

I told Jean-Paul this story at a dinner party and asked about the chance of a French association on the same lines. He was positive and later did indeed set up the French 'Association National pour les Enfants Surdoués' (ANPES), which developed well and still survives. Jean-Paul has become famous internationally for his work with gifted children.

The 1971 American AG was at Houston and two hundred members turned up. Sander Rubin was re-elected to the Chair. He proved to be a good chairman and the Committee he chaired laid the organisational foundations of the expansion which followed his term.

There was an IGC Meeting in Paris with a lot of publicity and some rewarding meetings of minds.

I had been nominated for a post on the British Mensa Committee as well as for the post of International Chairman and I was somewhat embarrassingly elected at the top of the poll in Britain. I had not known that the Unity Slate would be unopposed and I was hedging my bets in my desire to get back into the action, building Mensa at a time when auguries were good.

There was other bad news and good news. The bad news was that on 10 October, the first President of Mensa, Professor Sir Cyril Burt, died. The good news was that his death at the age of eighty-five ensured that he should never know of the vicious world campaign of ideologically motivated character assassination which was performed on his reputation later.

Possibly I have become too emotional about this late friend of mine and of Mensa. His help and influence over many years had been a decisive factor in our success. Without his many interventions and active help I would never have persuaded psychologists in many lands to give the aid that was essential in Mensa's progress towards psychological respectability.

This seems to be the moment to mention another famous psychologist who was a Mensa friend. Professor Raymond Cattell, another very supportive psychologist introduced by Burt (whose pupil he had been). Many Mensa members were tested as Berrill had been and I myself had been on his Superior Adult's Test, of which Mensa must have used millions of copies.

I have had a thirty year correspondence friendship with this expatriate Briton who ran the Institute of Personality and Ability Testing at his University in Illinois. I only met him once when he addressed an American Annual Gathering in Chicago in 1974. He has been a constant and faithful supporter of Mensa through bad times and good.

British Mensa was at a low ebb in 1971 and there seemed to be fewer local groups. The decline had been slow but continuous although the trend was to change as the effects of the first Superbrain competition began to be seen.

George Atherton gave up as editor then though he was to resume later. A young member from Canada who had been coming to parties at my house took over. Tony Buzan was the best editor of the *International Journal* we had had until then. Suddenly it was lively, controversial, intense and full of good authors. Buzan was one of a little group around a London American member, the polymath journalist and prolific writer, the late Heinz Norden. Round him there formed a group of young members. Tony Buzan was one and another of that vital and later significant group was the inventive entrepreneur and Mensa activist, John McNulty.

Today Tony's broadcasts and books, published in many languages, have given him international fame. His especial line is the development of human mental potential.

1972 saw the end of the plateau on the American Mensa growth curve with the publication of the first Superbrain competition. It appeared in the TV Guide and membership shot up from 12,400 to 16,400 that year in a trend that was to continue until it began to level off again in 1980.

Mensa journals began to discuss the appointment of a new president to replace Sir Cyril and there was much argument and discussion in central circles. A few wanted me as a candidate but Marvin Grosswirth suggested that Professor Buckminster Fuller had made just the kind of international reputation built on applied intelligence that would be the right image.

I was back on the British Committee and was able to work up some successful publicity schemes in England as well as to do my work on the International Committee where the main problem was to repair the finances after the period of extravagance under the previous regime. The main international meeting that year was in Aachen. The International Committee and the British Committee had, without realising it at the time, the same basic problem. Both lacked a sound, stable and enterprising professional base such as Margot Seitelman had built up in the growing suite of offices in her apartment building in Brooklyn.

The SIGRIM-nominated panel had set up a little office run by a housewife in Brighton much as I had done in London and New York. The excellent and efficient lady was a good secretary but would not claim the sort of versatile self-starter entrepreneurial ability that we had found in Margot and later in Harold Gale.

British Mensa, in its urgent desire to 'be master in its own house' after Mensa's internationalisation, had shifted the office to Wolverhampton where the current chairman, John Lishman, lived. This did not work all that well compared with what came later.

The staff were constantly changing, poorly paid and supervised because there was no effective professional boss in charge. It was the old problem of leaving control to a changing series of elected officials popping in in their spare time. Though British Mensa began to get more applications the results in membership were disappointing.

As International Chairman that year I did another American Mensa tour with lots of publicity again. I think I was first at the Canadian Annual Gathering in Toronto and then at the American one in Denver. After those organised by Codella, none of my American and other tours abroad were at the expense of Mensa. Some were arranged when I had to make business trips, some were out of my personal holiday budget and some were partly funded by Mensa local groups who wanted to attract me to their town for the sake of the publicity. These trips cost me little because I was offered such generous hospitality (and warm friendship) by Mensa hosts and hostesses everywhere.

My tour that year included Louisville where there was a television show at the airport and the newspaper interview that produced my favourite headline about me: 'INTERVIEW WITH A MAN NOT BURDENED WITH HUMILITY'.

Some will have guessed that my outrageously unhumble posture is a gimmick, a little deliberate and posed. But I do have a real point. A decent degree of self-regard is not harmful and the fashion for an exaggerated outward show of humility has gone too far. Further, I am sure that the able people I meet in Mensa lose more by overdone humility than they would by overdone pride. I recommend a realistic but sanguine self-assessment which hides behind a teasing mock pride. I do not recommend humility: it is nothing to be proud of.

Only obvious and excessive over-achievers like Clive Sinclair and the present Pope can afford to be really humble. You have to be very good indeed and very sure of yourself to be that humble and still be respected and effective.

In 1972 British Mensa broke important new ground when it arranged for its members to use the Arts Theatre Club, which had been founded by a member. Members then had a place where they could meet and have small functions. I am a member of the Savage Club which is for those who work in the Arts, my qualification being as a writer. I used to have my Think-In meetings in the comfortable library there but we were not allowed to use the members' bar. The Arts Theatre Club was much better as all members were welcomed at all times. I transferred the Think-In events to the Arts Theatre Club when that connection was made.

There should be more of this kind of development. It seems still to be true that London is the only big city where any Mensan from anywhere can find Mensa company, restaurant, bar, other services and accommodation on club premises.

The club which accommodates Mensa today is that enormous turretted Victorian pile on the Embankment, the National Liberal Club. This is a monument to the past pre-eminence of the British Liberal party (which is now a rather shrunken but very hopeful rump). It keeps going by opening its splendid revolving doors to other groups like Mensa.

In 1973 American Mensa continued its new surge and achieved a peak membership of nearly 16,500. It was at this point that we got our first *Reader's Digest* exposure. It was achieved by Margot and her helpers at the New York office. We have had several of these now. We get a one page simple puzzle quiz in that journal with a little background about Mensa and an address. Each of these has produced a dramatic deluge of applications and a sharp increase in membership wherever Mensa has had the local organisational strength to cope. The *Reader's Digest* publishes in many countries so that this American achievement was very good news, but a challenging problem to the struggling little national Mensas. To American Mensa it was the best kind of stimulus because they were well equipped. By 1975 there were to be 20,000 members at the peak. (The peak under the annual billing system comes in March when subscriptions become due. This causes an apparent slump in paid-up membership in April which causes an apparent drop of approximately eight or nine thousand in membership as the office waits for the dues to trickle in. Britain uses year-round billing which spreads the work load and cuts out these dramatic seasonal losses. Another British advantage in this respect is the facility for payment by banker's order which is not usual in the USA.

In America in 1972 under the Chairman Sander Rubin there was a continuation of the harassment on the American Mensa officers with some members being extremely unhelpful and contentious. Rubin handled this with persistence and patience. But American Mensa was static.

1973 was the year that Marvin Grosswirth took the chair of the AMC. The kindly, universally liked and respected Marvin began to suffer from the same problems from which Sander Rubin had been suffering and from which the International Mensa had freed itself.

There were very contentious, long, miserable meetings of the committee in New York. Often working by proxy, the dedicated objectors and obstructors moved in to create difficulties. The disputes were incredibly complex and could only be understood through long, close study. I had no notion of what they were about although I had all the reams of reports and papers about them. Scalding intemperate accusations and long patient explanations and refutations were what they seemed like. Boring beyond belief they really were. Marvin (Job) Grosswirth with tact, patience, firmness, persistence and tough-minded resistance to threats and coercion, held the fort and kept things afloat.

Then the Litigious Men of Straw moved in with senseless but troublesome lawsuits called at remote locations against Marvin and his colleagues in American Mensa. An appeal fund was launched and funds for legal fees were donated by members to protect those who took all this nonsense because they loved and worked for Mensa.

This damaging nonsense went on for a long time and caused endless problems and waste of time but in the end every one of the suits was settled or withdrawn with a favourable outcome from the Mensa point of view. The problems caused as much revulsion among members as they had in England but, strangely, in another way they strengthened and consolidated Mensa's fragile unity in the end. Marvin was so patently decent, honest, long-suffering and patient that a ground swell of support welled up from the grass roots in local groups which finally led to better times and a resumption of the spectacular growth of American Mensa.

1973 was also the year of the next International Election and the Serebriakoff panel was returned with a good majority vote against another panel which was based on a Canadian group. The international panel contained a number of American members in deference to the increasing American membership. I was very busy in my business and also because of the growing burden of work as international chairman, but I had the odd experience of being the only person that I know of to lose my place on the British Mensa Committee due to one of those rules imposed by a floor motion at the AGM. According to this curious rule a committee member had to get *prior* permission by a motion to be excused attendance. I was a world traveller selling an innovation. I could not know six weeks before of the need for a trip, so I was summarily dismissed for absence without prior leave after missing some. I can claim from subsequent work when I was elected later that such rules can rob Mensa of useful workers for no good reason.

British Mensa was to suffer much from such impulsive floor motions passed in the excitement and passion of a crowded Annual General Meeting. This system was a tradition left from our informal beginnings and it throws a curious light on intelligent people in the mass. As I have said intelligence works in teams and a crowd of very bright people are capable of a collective decision which seems stupid to any thoughtful individual.

In Britain there were vigorous and good publicity campaigns which were ineffective because there was not the office organisation to cope with the flow of enquiries that came in. British Mensa began to get into a mess financially because of overspending and the excellent newsletter edited by Steve Odell had to shut down for a time. It reappeared, without Steve, in a sadly slim and shoddy form after a month or two. The British Committee adhered to the expensive practice of issuing a separate sheet to British members and not combining it with the *International Journal* which continued to be well printed and edited by Tony Buzan.

In America things were very good and 1974 saw a big increase in American membership with the March peak at 20,000. *The American Activities Bulletin* was improving markedly and was well printed and readable. It included the *International Journal* which came from the IGC.

That year, the aged Professor Buckminster Fuller became the second World President of Mensa.

In May British Mensa suffered a minor schism as Channel Islands Mensa broke away, having been dissatisfied with the magazine service.

Both Buckminster Fuller and Professor Raymond Cattell spoke at the American Annual Gathering at Chicago where a record crowd of 450 members turned up. Chicago was then a good spot for Mensa and a leading light was Charley Fallon who had been a tough and staunch Mensa defender in the days of difficulty, especially in Chicago. Another business trip was combined with a holiday so I managed yet another wide Mensa tour with the usual big publicity and very warm and hospitable American welcome everywhere. All this was organised at local level by the many friends I now had in America.

I remember Chicago well because it was a turning point. The outlying members in the local groups had at last begun to accept that which they found hard to believe at first. People of goodwill and decency, that is to say the overwhelming majority of Mensans, began to accept that there really are ill-disposed members or sincere self-deceiving ones, who harass elected Mensa workers without just cause. There is no smoke without fire but seeing smoke does not tell us who lit the fire. The boring old accusations of autocracy, suppressing 'legitimate criticism', and fixing elections which were hurled indiscriminately at any one who was vicious enough to win an election, were patently absurd when applied to the patient, friendly, compassionate chairman Marvin Grosswirth. So it was the accusers who came under fire. They were a tiny group of people who seemed to be acting from an inbuilt hatred of anything that could be set up as an 'authority' or indeed anyone who achieved any prominence. They get frustrated. They get nasty.

At Chicago there was a very healthy and overdue counterattack from the local secretaries and local journal editors from the very constituency the disruptors relied on to create uproar. Uproar there was but they themselves were its victims.

It was not easy in a society which is divided by its very protean principles, but a sense of order and unity in Mensa was growing stronger. It was a fine meeting with quite the atmosphere of intellectual interaction that I remembered from the early days. One of those who came to the fore in American Mensa at this time was Gabriel Werba, who had been elected as American Ombudsman. He was helpful to Mensa in the troubles I have been describing. He later served on the IGC under my chairmanship and later still was American Chairman.

There was a meeting of the IGC there with myself as Chairman and we tried to set up an international phone link with Mensa in Austria and France. It was a badly stage-managed failure. My fault.

I talked with Charley Fallon who was coming to the fore as the best known Chicago M. We wanted a survey to be funded by International to investigate the gifted children problem using Mensans as a convenient sample of those who once were gifted children. Their experiences might throw light on the best educational methods for the gifted. Charley proposed one of our Mensa academics for the job.

Professor Philip M. Powell was at that time a lecturer in psychology at Yale. His beginnings in life had not pointed to academe. He told me about a delinquent black youth from the seamier part of Chicago where he had been a gang leader. Someone had dared him into applying for Mensa, and such kids have to take up dares. Philip was accepted with a maximum score. Hooked on Mensa and learning things, he found he could not kick the habits. So the poor man finished up at the University of Yale. And worse, as a lecturer! He now has a fine family of bright kids and a good career.

In Britain Dr George Atherton became British Mensa Chairman at another smaller AGM at The Victory Ex-Services Club near Marble Arch.

In the office in Brooklyn that year Margot and her gradually growing team struggled manfully with a great surge of enquiries from another *Reader's Digest* quiz. American membership soared and the same quiz published later in Britain helped there too. But the organisation was poorer. The American membership peaked next year at nearly 22,000 but Britain lifted out of decline by only a little.

In 1975, glowing with the success of the renewed growth, American Mensa started something which proved to be a vital and important step forward and which was to break new ground for the rest. First and most importantly the committee meetings ceased to be in New York. Charley Fallon became the American Chairman and began to arrange a peripatetic series of meetings around America which did much to increase the contact of the Committee with the members and also to give members more opportunities to meet each other. It was the answer to the disruptive pamphleteers who were now writing about real people and not the far away figures you read about.

That year the Committee met in three locations: San Antonio, Chicago and Atlanta. The latter two were the Regional Gatherings or RGs, which were now to become an important activity in American Mensa and elsewhere. Without Charley's important initiative it would have proved to be much more difficult to preserve the unity both of American and International Mensa over the years. Growth and dispersal present problems and the shape of the solution was appearing. From then on I began to get many reports from returning visitors of these excellent events.

Clive Sinclair was especially impressed and the RGs renewed his close interest in Mensa.

Each Regional Gathering has its own special flavour and these reflect the delightful cultural diversity which is a special feature of Mensa in America. It is an aspect that is often missed by the casual foreign visitor who sees only the mono-cultural exterior which coyly hides the delightful, subtle, sweet, and protean local cultural savours beneath. Mensa seems to bring them out.

There are scores of them every year and Mensans vote increasingly with their cash and their feet in favour of them. The attendance varies between thirty and twelve hundred or so and they are usually held in a good convention-type hotel. There are all the locals and a faithful crowd of Mensans from further afield who seem to go to many or most of them. The Friday evening registration is usually an uproarious affair with people falling into each other's arms like long parted sisters and brothers. Mensans and especially American Ms either started or were early to follow the modern habit of increased physical contact on greeting. Soon hugging became a Mensa cult with a Hugger's Special Interest Group run by Jimmee Stein. There were even hugger's competitions at many RGs for a time. It may be laughable but it was something that had to happen. Intelligent people are still people. They have bodies and the usual emotions and the need for caresses. They are different, at an extreme of human variation on one parameter. Those at the extremes, any of them, may have a body-love and physical approval problem, an unsatisfied hunger. It is right and proper that Mensa members should have a permissiveness about bodily contact and reassurance between them. The condition is that it is not abused or considered compulsory. Sensitivity is needed. We offer, do not press our contact. There was in fact a reaction to overdone hugging later.

Too many of the brighter people, like early Christians, have hidden feelings of rejection and, to my own amazement one of the real advantages that members found in Mensa was in this unexpected area.

There is usually a great deal of variety in the RG programme. There are workshops and seminars on a great variety of topics, all in separate rooms and each drawing in a crowd of enthusiasts for whatever special interest is concerned; education; gifted children; local newsletters; computers; sociology; psychology; man –woman relationships; logic; philosophy; religion; the occult; fundamental physics; mathematics; hypnotism; higher education; lower education; anarchism; love and marriage; sexism; puzzles; chess and other board games; computer games. These are some of the subjects that may be dealt with in the many little meetings which last all through the weekend. Outdoors in the hotel grounds they will be throwing boomerangs, flying kites, swimming and always, everywhere, continuously and incessantly arguing, discussing and disputing anything and everything.

Meals? Only exceptionally are these really good. At the public meals we usually get the standard American conference banquet which is all right if you love bland, meek, submissive food served with pallid inoffensive coffee. English tongues are tolerant but tongues educated in Europe or the East, grow limp and wilt a bit.

There is always the secretary of the local gourmet's SIG who will lead those with the more adventurous tongues, who like wine with food, to the secret local delicacy or to the standard but excellent Italian, Chinese, Jewish, Spanish, Mexican or Japanese restaurant.

And yes, the physical side goes a bit further than hugging and some wicked members sleep around a bit after the numerous fairly alcoholic but friendly parties in private rooms. This is an unvarnished tale and I shamefully admit that a Regional Gathering is to a small extent, the place where the eggheads get laid.

So when the assembled Mensans·go off to the airport there are some very sad and almost tearful farewells after a Mensa gathering. We go away renewed, refreshed and intoxicated with thought and talk and waiting for the next time.

1976 saw the further steady growth of American Mensa with another record attendance of five hundred of the 24,500 members at the San Antonio AG. The peripatetic AMC meetings got into full swing with the AMC meetings at Santa Barbara, Detroit, Kansas City and Boston. The new team with Fallon as Chairman and Werba (who had gained reputation as Ombudsman), as first

Vice Chairman was now a responsible and constructive one. The specialists in long, whining, incomprehensible memoranda and meritless lawsuits seem to have disappeared in the electoral process. The expensive lawsuits dragged on for years. None succeeded.

American Committee meetings now took on a much more business-like and constructive air and the results were visible in growth, activity and atmosphere in American Mensa. It had learned its lesson and stopped being over-tolerant of its dedicated contention-lovers.

At the international level in 1976 another Serebriakoff panel of candidates won the election without too much problem. International Mensa was in fair heart but under increasing pressure from the American Mensa Committee to cut the international component of the subscriptions.

Cuts had been made and despite this the inherited deficit reduced and a surplus built up. My plan was to build up the reserves to finance a move to plant the successful American recruitment methods in other countries. But I had to engineer consent for it and that was not easy.

The first essential was to create a revenue producing a self-sustaining office like that which the redoubtable Margot had built up in America. It was going to be a risky venture and in retrospect we were too cautious, we delayed the adventure too long.

A young bank official, David Warren, was the International Treasurer and over a number of years he tough-mindedly and competently guided us in a cautious policy of economy and retrenchment to build up reserves. We took no risks and helped aspiring new Mensas only with small grant loans and any help that could be given by we amateurs in our spare time. A pool of international members was built up and we planned and budgeted with the hopes of establishing the essential professional base but dared not take the plunge in view of a quite natural feeling coming from the AMC. They claimed to represent all American members who provided eighty percent of the cash because of their numbers. Although the eight officers of the IGC were elected by the votes of all members, including Americans, it was the AMC that controlled the subscriptions of which the IGC took twelve, then ten, then eight percent. Some of the AMC thought they saw better uses for the money in America.

I became distracted by an idea that had been festering in my mind for years. Back in 1958 there had been a period during which I had what I saw as an insight concerning self-organising systems. This had obsessed me for a time after meetings with many pioneers in the cybernetics field that I found in Mensa and in the Philosophy of Science Society.

After brooding on my ideas and reading everything I could find on information theory, cybernetics, neurology, computers and theories of social organisation, I had managed to find an adventurous publisher to publish my book *Brain*, which was an attempt by an autodidact outsider to propose a theory of self-organising intercommunicating systems. I felt that all systems like human organisations and institutions, markets, cells, and brains had common tasks and methods and that there were ways of understanding them in a generalised form. Working on this difficult book, which I confess does not really communicate well enough, and then, when it was published that year, answering letters and giving university lectures on it, took up a lot of the reduced time I could spare from my now rather tough job.

British Mensa was a worry then as things were not going at all well since the internationalisation split. The British Committee was constantly changing, there were a series of short term chairmen who were none too inspiring, there was no one to take the essential central role of the vitally needed 'motivator who keeps his eye on the ball'. And the Committee was divided and distracted by the same dissidence problems which the International, American and Australian Mensas had suffered and resolved or outlasted.

There were endless damaging quarrels, arguments, lawsuits and childish pamphleteering. The reduced newsletter was full of accusations and refutations. Much of the lengthy, incomprehensible nonsense which fascinates the participants and bores everyone else was circulated.

Exploiting the Superbrain idea in March British Mensa got many new members but many others resigned and lapsed in apathy or disgust. Very large numbers of these rejoined in the better days that were to come. Things were at a very low ebb. There were fiscal problems, and a member tried to get a special Annual General Meeting called (apparently thinking this extra expense and a big meeting would help somehow). The Committee resisted. There was also an argument about loans and expenses claims. All were trivial in comparison with the final heavy legal costs.

All this led to another interminable, incomprehensible, complex dispute which rolled on for years and finally cost British Mensa members very large sums in legal fees, resisting lawsuits by litigious men of straw who had little to lose and represented themselves in court.

British Mensa was deep in debt and the first task of the newly elected International Committee was to bail it out with a loan to prevent default. As International Chairman I insisted on conditions.

Here was the chance to get the professional office we needed both for British and International Mensa. This was the plan and the condition. We closed down the little home IGC office in Brighton and, merging it with the British one in Wolverhampton, we built up to the required minimum effective office scale. The economies meant that we could afford a professional boss for the whole operation, to be called the Executive Director. To avoid disputes about priorities there was to be a little company called Mensa Administration Ltd with a board appointed by the IGC on one side and the BMC on the other and with an independent chairman. The International General Secretary at the time was Ian Palmer, a pioneer of data base programs for computers. He set up a small committee which found a schoolmaster who was willing to take on this unpromising job and that is how Harold Gale was appointed as Executive Director both of British and International Mensa.

He was engaged in April 1976 with a brief to make economies, get British Mensa back on the rails and repay the international loan. He was to start serious recruiting in non-Mensa countries and service the British and international committees. It was an uphill job at first as he tried to establish his authority and deal with the muddled fiscal and legal problems in the UK.

In 1977 American membership peaked at 24,000 and American Mensa continued to run smoothly apart from the fading aftermath of the lawsuits.

This was 'Get Burt' year for the press of the western world. Our late president came under fire in an organised international campaign of journalistic post mortem character assassination.

I published a counter-attack on Burt-bashers and weighed into them in the book I was writing for an American publisher called *Test Your Child's IQ*, which was published in many languages subsequently. My collaborator, who composed and validated the tests, was a Chicago Mensan, Dr Stephen Langer. There was an IGC meeting with more than usual overseas representation in Paris and an International Mensa Congress in Bristol.

The 1977 British AGM was a black disgrace to Mensa. It was, and it shames me deeply to admit it, almost, but mercifully not quite, as bad as a bad question time in the British House of Commons. The numbers in British Mensa were down and a version of Gresham's Law applied. At this kind of meeting a claque of the noisy and obstreperous members drove out the majority of well behaved ones. It was the same bad time for British Mensa as those in Australia, America and International.

In a long, noisy, confused and disorderly meeting there was the spectacle, in a society of intelligent people, of both the Chairman and the Secretary being unable to establish order and resigning on the spot. High intelligence is no defence against mass stupidity.

In morphostatic systems (self-sustaining ones that preserve form through time), and Mensa was proving to be one, trend lines are contra-indicative because such systems are homeostatic. British Mensa had gone down enough. When Harold Gale started there were just 1,350 members left out of the more than 4,000 I had handed on to British Mensa in 1962.

But from then on British Mensa began to get well and grow. In 1984, eight years later, British Mensa had just ten times the membership Harold started with at that low point. How that happened is an interesting story with a moral.

In the 1977 American election there was another sound political move in American Mensa: regionalisation. The central committee was augmented by a number of Regional Vice Chairmen. There were now fifteen instead of nine members and much more input as to what was going on all around American Mensa. I believe this strengthened and unified and is a pattern that could well be copied elsewhere. I feel it will prove to be a better way of doing it than that recently adopted in French Mensa where the regionalisation has been more thoroughgoing. Both experiments are of great importance and we shall learn much from the way they work out respectively. My own worry comes from the fear that if the catchment area of a Mensa selection agency is too small, it cannot be self-sustaining and produce surpluses. Decentralisation is good up to a point but we should try all patterns and avoid rigidity in our effort to preserve our fundamental form.

In American Mensa the test income from the *Reader's Digest* quiz had given the financial strength to afford good professional publicity advice such as that we had had from Codella and this began to show in excellent exposure with a consequent lift in applications, test fees and thus more money for publicity in a self-reinforcing chain reaction. The talented publicist behind all this was Alice Fixx, wife of James Fixx, a Mensan who helped Mensa with an excellent puzzle book which popularised Mensa. Alice had been doing, unobtrusively, a very professional job with and for Margot and Mensa. I suspect that she had no small part in her husband's world fame.

AMC meetings in 1978 were at Chicago, New Orleans, Minneapolis and Portland with the AG at Cleveland. In March that year there were reports of major Mensa international meetings in Geneva, Santa Barbara, the Catskills, Dundalk, Paris, London, and most important Philip Poole's well organised and splendid International Congress on the Channel Islands where we had the States, that is virtually the King and Queen of the islands, present at the sumptuous formal dinner.

French Mensa benefitted a lot from a publicity meeting in Nice for the French Gifted Children's Movement which was now begining to flourish under the leadership of Jean Charles Terrassier. I was invited as one lecturer. The press attention was intense and I got hundreds of French clippings later. The journals took the cautious, quizzing, critical line, with the ritual lip service to anti-elitism.

Yet I could see a real but underground constituency in France for the ideas that inspire both Mensa and the French Gifted Children's Movement ANPES.

Unashamed recognition of mental differences and heretical discussions about finding, educating and using human talent from all social and racial origins for the general benefit is largely taboo among modern intellectuals, even in France, because of the fashionable egalitarian and anti-elitist ethos.

There is no mystery about today's clerical treason. It arises simply from the fear of Marxism. Eyes are closed to real genetic and cultural differences because they are secretly seen as influencing class differences. About these Marx made frightening predictions.

I do not believe in the risk of class war because class analysis is too crude. Class structure is more changeable, complex and permeable than Karl's simplistic binary theory would have it. The wars we now have, even those that can be depicted as class wars, are really intercultural battles. I see no interclass ones.

When, as in Nice that year, bold or foolish heretics resist our century's damaging anti-sapience, anti-mind, anti-life, anti-excellence trend, break the taboo, and sound off, the attention and interest is vital and fascinated. Taboo talk enthralls. This is why, after nearly 40 years Mensa is always fresh news, again and again.

1978 saw another miserable year in British Mensa with another uninspiring and quarrelsome AGM in Birmingham.

But, under the surface, things were better as Gale began to reorganise in Wolverhampton. The *British Activities Bulletin* kept getting worse under a series of ever changing editors and the members, especially the new ones that were now beginning to join, began to complain. The last straw for me was December that year when the cover was a hippy figure with a joint dragging from his lip, snapping his grubby fingers and saying 'See you at the AG man'. Possibly even worse was a series where an enormous Mensa logo mercifully and completely obscured the close print on the front page. This Bulletin was supposed to be the attractive lure to

retain the new members. That is the bad news. Something would
have to be done.

This is the good news. 850 members attended the American
AG in Cleveland, Ohio. With professional publicity and an
expanding staff in Brooklyn membership continued to soar.
American regionalisation with local democracy was a success.

In fact 1979 was the beginning of a trend-setting epoch, though
again it could not be seen at the time. It started with the gradual
accentuation of the transatlantic rift of which there had always
been some sign.

British Mensa and all non-American Mensas had not matched
the strong American progress and eighty percent of our 42,000
Mensans were then American. The American committee had
been enlarged and strengthened and unified under Charley
Fallon. That electorate had rejected the fractious and contentious
ones and the AMC was now confident and optimistic.

The IGC under my chairmanship was also working smoothly
but its task of pioneering in new countries was more difficult and
its success was less spectacular. Certainly the new administration
in Wolverhampton and the appointment of the very hard-working
and devoted psychologist Abby Salny as psychological adviser
had made it possible to start steady recruitment in non-Mensa
countries but this was moderate. The international skein of
isolated members, the seed corn of later national Mensas was
rising by some hundreds each year. But that looked small beer by
American progress.

Elected by all members, the International General Committee
usually met in London. It had the central responsibility for
Mensa, the whole.

In the American Committee this was seen as gross imbalance.
One of the seventeen national constituencies (some of them tiny)
which made up the whole, America, was four times the size of the
rest put together. Under the international constitution no one had
foreseen such a thing.

There was a vote for each of the internationally elected panel of
eight officers but also each national Mensa, however small, had
one vote (the same bad principle as the United Nations Assembly). Eight votes represented all members (including Americans)

directly, sixteen votes represented non-American members. Only one vote represented the eighty percent of American members via their own committee.

It did not work out too badly because in fact the many little Mensas only rarely voted. But anomalous it had become. Everyone agreed there would have to be a new constitution.

Because of this imbalance, looking to our main constituency (and paymaster), America, we had a practice not to pass a motion where the American representative's proxy (usually Tony Littman) was against it. We also had a budget committee under the American Treasurer's control.

But some of my good American friends could not distinguish well between British Mensa (which was in a mess) and International Mensa (which was not).

To AMC eyes the International Committee met in Europe, mostly in England the founding country. They were seen as all the same inefficient bunch. It looked, maybe with eighteenth century eyes, like English colonialism all over again. The phrases 'The tail is wagging the dog', and 'taxation without representation', and threats of a 'Boston Tea Party' appeared more and more on the scolding but always friendly letters I got from my American Committee contacts. The American Committee wanted more say in International Mensa. The fact that their members had voted for the international officers did not satisfy them. The AMC treasurer had to sign the cheques.

I wanted nothing less than the mildly threatened American breakaway, but domination by one national Mensa would be bad too. I knew it would be a long uphill job to do what had to be done. To get a world-wide Mensa we had to create a balance by growing vigorously elsewhere.

But I had been too opportunistic with my numerous American publicity tours, getting members where it was easiest. I had done much to create the problem. Now I had to solve it if Mensa was to remain as one, which was and is my passionate desire.

I decided to stand again as candidate for International Chairman if I could in concert with Charley Fallon, the outgoing American Chairman, and a more American team so that we could get influential and effective Americans interested in the international problem. I wanted a united team of which the Americans could really feel part.

Charley said he found the idea of a Serebriakoff/Fallon Slate in the 1979 election favourable but asked for time to decide. According to our thinking, after the election and a hand-over period, I was to be 'kicked upstairs' to a non-executive honorific role and help with the publicity tours I was so experienced in after my retirement. He was to tell me by the end of 1978 which was a bit tight for comfort. My own electoral following in America was very strong by now and he had to get a strong slate to run against me if he decided to.

Charley's decision was to go it alone. He left me waiting till past the agreed decision date. This was politically astute as it left me less time to adjust to the change of tack. Only when I phoned him in January 1979 did I learn that he intended to run an opposing slate. It was a crucial decision and much flowed from it.

Charley got together a formidable slate of popular people. Himself as Chairman, Gabriel Werba almost certainly the incoming American Chairman, the much loved Harper Fowley, a very successful and effective West Coast Mensa stalwart, Len Rickard, Karl Ross, the hard-working Bulletin Editor, the English accountant and experienced Mensa activist, Tony Littman, John Meredith, a British banker, and Professor Philip Powell.

Short of time, I also got together a slate, contended the election, and won again by a comfortable margin during 1979. My slate had four Americans including a past AMC Treasurer, Art Gardner, Philip Powell (also), Jan Williams and James Sprague, three Britons: Dr Atherton, Dr Madsen Pirie, and myself. The eighth member was Karl Schnoelzer.

This International election result was not received with acclamations of wild joy by the American Committee which came under the leadership of the new Chairman, Gabe Werba, that June. We started a new period of contention in Mensa but this time it was a civil and orderly contest between decent people.

I had decided to retire from my industrial job and, even during that last year of nine to five in which I was handing over to my successor, I had more spare time and tackled what I saw as the Mensa transatlantic problem in this way. Something dramatic had to be done in Europe and the starting place could only be the UK.

I looked around for help and turned to an old friend. I have spoken of Clive Sinclair when he was the thin, carrot-haired youth of nineteen I first met at some Mensa do and sat with in a car all night, deep in fascinated talk. He impressed me enormously then. Today he is one of the growing band of distinguished and famous people who became so *as members*.

We had to wait for this to happen because those already famous have a disincentive to risk failure to qualify by applying to join Mensa. They do not know of, or knowing, do not see why they should trust, the confidentiality of our selection agency. (It is, truly, very strict. I as President may not find out the name of an unsuccessful applicant.)

A few bold spirits among the famous – Leslie Charteris, Isaac Asimov, Don Pederson, the President of the Ford Motor Company, Jimmy Savile – have been sure enough, bold enough or trusting enough to risk the dread Mensa test. But not many.

One of these risk takers is the very famous TV cook/humorist and British MP, Clement Freud. He published a lovely knocking article with the headline, 'CLEMENT FREUD, MENSA (FAILED)'.

But Clive (now Professor Sir Clive), Sinclair was one of our home-grown heroes and a beloved personal friend. He seems to have had an article about his achievements in every magazine on earth so I shall not recount them more than to remind you that he started by designing and selling match box radios without capital from his lodgings and went on to design and market the first really commercial pocket calculator in the world which really did fit into the pocket. He made his first million pounds from a capital base of nothing. The stream of electronic and other innovations from the team he built up, much of it from Mensa contacts he says, reminds me of our joint hero, Eddington. And now between the ZX80 and 81, the Spectrum, and the QL personal computers, his companies have sold far more computers than any other company on earth.

Mensa has to thank the many warm American Regional Gatherings for Clive's renewed interest in and enormous contribution to Mensa. Obviously he had been put off by the bad

years I have described in British Mensa but he told me with
delight how good he had found it, wandering round America on
many business trips, to find convenient friendly convivial groups
of interesting like-minded people in Mensa everywhere. That
rare, golden commodity, good talk, was to be found easily around
the American Mensa scene. Praise of American Mensa hospitality is universal.

Knowing how intense was his preoccupation with the expression and realisation of his innovative genius I had never pressed
him for help. But now, I was getting (though not feeling) older. I
was desperate to preserve my vision of a truly international league
of multicultural comprehenders that which seemed to threaten it.

An old man in a hurry, encouraged by Clive's good report from
America, I asked Clive to be further over-extended as the 'busy
man' to whom one gives the new, difficult, trouble-shooting job.

His rapidly growing prestige was certainly going to help Mensa
with its bad British image. After the dedicated industrious mud-
fighting by the fractious few, Mensa was publicly seen as Brain-
proud Quarrelsome Under-achievers Limited.

So the busiest of men in the country and its most obvious
over-achiever let himself be persuaded to join a campaign to
revive and reinvigorate British Mensa. We were going to improve
its image and make it what Berrill said he had failed to make it, a
pleasure to belong to. How? By gaining from and improving on
the best American experience. And John McNulty, another of our
home grown inventors and a long time friend of mine and Clive's,
was in there, too.

And there was another. Dr Madsen Pirie was a Mensan who
turned up at a Think-In which was then being held at The
National Liberal Club. He won my heart by actually understanding and liking my almost incomprehensible book *Brain* (as Clive
did), and I was vastly impressed by his erudition, his brilliant use
of language, and extraordinary ability to think on his feet at
an exceptionally profound level. He was the President of the
Adam Smith Institute which was then a tiny new political Think
Tank.

I picked a winner because he has achieved national fame in a
few years by a succession of brilliant publicity campaigns which

have had a strikingly visible effect on British politics. Madsen is another Mensan who has built a team which makes things happen. Margaret Thatcher, the British Prime Minister, found it necessary publicly to deny that the Adam Smith Institute was making Government policy. That Madsen's ideas get close attention in high quarters has not been denied.

In that year, 1979, Madsen impulsively accepted my nomination as an international candidate and was catapulted into Mensa politics overnight as International General Secretary when we won the Election. Both Clive and I stood for office on the British Mensa Committee and were both elected in November 1979. It was for me like a place bet in case I lost the International Election. Embarrassingly I won both.

The *British Mensa Newsletter* was now being edited by Michael Clift, who had certainly improved it but soon came under fire from the many unconstructive critics around Mensa at the time. The Bulletin was still full of quarrelsome, meaningless disputes. Clift published the slanging and his own counter-slanging. It could hardly help being better than before; edifying it was not.

A member I knew who was an executive for the *Reader's Digest*, Ian Redpath, phoned me to bitch about the magazine and I persuaded him to offer to be Editor. He did and the newsletter was once more readable.

The American AG was a rather splendid affair at Kansas City and since I was invited to give a speech I went.

The British AG in Liverpool marked a return to sanity because of the same sort of grass roots revolt that had happened in America. The claque of disruptives were outvoted by postal votes or by the fact that trusted members were there with masses of proxy votes. I had twenty or so unsolicited ones and one member had collected sixty. In any case the membership was increasing and there were lots of new members who could not be relied upon by the disrupters.

Under the constitution in British Mensa Ltd, which had been changed by referendum during the Chairmanship of John Lishman, any member could put a motion to the AG for general vote and there were thirty or so ill-thought out, unbudgeted, motions to be debated by a large meeting. There was no way they could be

properly debated. British Mensa was in the same silly fix that
some political parties get into. British Mensa had the problem of
the Annual Conference Motions.

The idea that a meeting with hundreds present and thousands
of postal voters can work on the same lines as a small committee is
plain silly. But there is great resistance among those who enjoy the
annual cathartic uproar to any change in this scheme of things.
After a very unjust and unfair debate the editor was rejected by a
motion and Ian Redpath replaced him. Most of the other silly
motions were defeated. But one, that the editor should be an
electoral post, was passed.

In the new committee I took the post of Developments Officer
and so got back into a position to help with the growth and
recruitment problem. I had done it before. Maybe I could do it
again. Clive was now an active participant in a committee which
remained under the Chairmanship of Michael Collier Bradley.

Clive's first thought was to create in England something as
good as the American Regional Gathering. He was living in a
lovely stone house in Cambridge at the time and his business was
there. Working with John McNulty and myself, he proposed an
annual week-long Gathering at one of the colleges with a holiday
flavour but a strong intellectual content. This was the beginning
of the now firmly established international Mensa feature 'Mensa
At Cambridge' which is now almost a national institution in
Britain as well as an international one in Mensa, judging by the
growing popularity and press attention.

We are now in 1980. The international election result was
declared and there began to be trouble on that front.

I remember being warned by American friends that Gabe
Werba, the new American Chairman, was a 'hard-nosed'
businessman whose professional job was shaking ailing companies back into efficiency and profit. This is what he was going to
do with International Committee. If ways were not changed
American Mensa would refuse to go on subsidising this dog-
wagging tail in Europe, cast it off and go it alone.

This was the sense of the rumours. They were exaggerated I
am sure, possibly deliberately.

The next two years saw big changes: very rapid growth in

British Mensa; paralysis and politics in International Mensa; relative stagnation after the sharp growth in American Mensa; civilly conducted conflict and arguments around World Mensa. And then at the end peace, a new accord, a referendum and a new constitution which put the elected American Committee virtually in voting control of the international body for the time.

Early in 1980 the new American Chairman, Gabe Werba, came to England to negotiate with the newly elected IGC and there were a number of sticky meetings in which Gabe pressed the case that the new American Committee was making. The American Mensa Committee was under pressure for more funds for local activities and there was a need to show better results from the international expenditure. Further, there were objections to the fact that nearly all IGC meetings were held in London which meant that the many national Mensa representatives could only be represented by proxy. It was unfair, Gabe said, that the expenses of the national Mensa representatives had to be paid by the national Mensas, all delegates should attend and all should be funded out of international funds.

This demand was welcome to the smaller national Mensas and that ensured a majority for that decision on the committee. In fact from that time forward Gabe had gained the political initiative because the internationally elected officers (the Serebriakoff panel) were outvoted by the seventeen national representatives. Not all voted with Gabe but he soon won enough of them over after a good deal of telephone lobbying to have a majority.

Gabe Werba's further demands were that the change in the International Constitution, which the committee had been considering for some years, should now be pushed through quickly and it should be such as to give the American committee the voting strength relative to American membership and financial contribution. With eighty percent of members in America that would mean control of the international body by the American committee. Gabe also said that international development should be conducted to a budgeted plan with clear targets.

He was forthright and demanding but the atmosphere was not unfriendly. He represented himself as a dedicated internationalist in Mensa. But he said he was under pressure from his committee and grass roots members, some of whom were indifferent to the international aspect and concerned to cut the financial cost of the IGC.

As a result of another *Reader's Digest* quiz in 1979 American Membership peaked at 43,000 in 1980, a net gain of over ten thousand members in the year, a record that still holds. There were confident forecasts of continued growth in America. The American attitude on the IGC seemed reasonable to the smaller national representatives.

At a London meeting in January more of these national representatives turned up than usual and, after a private lunch together, Gabe and I prepared a statement which was to be agreed by the committee which he could take back to satisfy his committee.

We accepted that there should be a referendum for a new international constitution and asked Gabe to chair the committee to prepare the draft which was to be discussed at a meeting in Athens in November. We agreed to plan a budget on the lines he asked and generally accepted that the IGC had to take more account of the views of the American Committee.

Gabe did some canvassing and lobbying with the national representatives of the small national Mensas both then and later by telephone to press his point of view. He was active and persuasive and he soon gained the marginal control of the committee which was now divided into factions.

One faction was impressed with American growth and progress and welcomed Gabe's leadership, the other faction was worried about the idea of the international body being controlled virtually by a single committee which had been elected as the committee of one of the national Mensas, even though it was the largest.

Seven of the eight international officers, four Americans, three British and an Austrian, were behind me as Chairman and leader of the internationalist faction. The British, French, Austrian and Channel Islands representatives also voted with the internationalist faction and the rest tended to vote with Werba on the few questions of dispute. At first the contention was not great and we agreed on most things. The tension caused by the schism was constructive; it increased motivation and effort on both sides.

It was a year of international meetings, London, Charlotte (North Carolina), Paris and Athens, following the Werba plan that the international committee should become peripatetic so as to increase contact and gain in publicity.

The friction and dissent warmed up a little as the year went on and the lobbying and canvassing on both sides continued. I was worried because a very carefully prepared and budgeted continental development plan, prepared to meet Werba's ideas, was turned down flat by a vote so that all expenditure on the main job of the committee, developing new Mensas, ceased while the international travel expenses threatened to eat up the reserves that had been built up for this development effort. But politics is the art of the possible and we set up another more modest budget only to have that turned down later at Cambridge. 'We' were Clive Sinclair, Dr Madsen Pirie, the Fallon Slate International Treasurer candidate, a banker called John Meredith, Philip Poole and some others.

The first Mensa At Cambridge conference at Trinity College in 1980 was a huge success from every point of view except finance, but it had been underwritten by Clive Sinclair and we learned how to do it thanks to his generosity. It was to the theme 'The Eighties' and got glowing reports from the international crowd of Mensans who came, and a lot of press attention and TV time.

The underlying idea of this five day series of lectures in a comfortable and beautiful college was that those who are at the cutting edge in science and philosophy should come together with an international sample of multidisciplinary comprehenders so that in a few days of comfortable, unhurried interaction in holiday atmosphere the Mensans could try to grasp what is happening. Then, in a humble way, they could try to act as an interface between the often out-of-touch mental pioneers at the interface with the unknown, and the general public who may not have the time, leisure, or in some cases the comprehension, to grasp what is changing the world in which they live.

Mensa At Cambridge was again a very good week from every possible point of view. This was a new kind of success which renewed my faith in what we were trying to do. Here was the fundamental concept of a ubiquitous, truly international multi-disciplinary agora come to life. The sour note at the end was a fraught and miserable IGC meeting. In a gloomy windowless room at the back of a Cambridge hotel there was a meeting of Mensans which was not one of minds.

The two factions were more evenly balanced but the Werba faction scraped up enough votes to win on contentious decisions. A vote for his side came from a decision to recognise and accept a proxy vote for a national Mensa in Africa which had about twenty members.

The British AGM that year was at Aston University. As was becoming usual there a long printed agenda with the tedious list of motions from a little group of members giving unbudgeted detailed instructions to the committee. The boring routine of wading through these and rejecting the silly ones caused considerable impatience in the new members but attempts from the floor to short cut proceedings only made them worse. The meeting dragged on contentiously with more procedural motions than discussion and much head-shaking about such meetings of supposedly intelligent people.

After the meeting Clive Sinclair was elected to the Chair of British Mensa. I had been elected as Editor of the *British Mensa Newsletter*. Clive and I felt that we had to do something to improve that if we were to hold the now rapidly growing membership. It had improved a lot under Ian Redpath but, since it was the only contact most members had with the society, it had to be better and even more professional.

Attendance at meetings was not good because the local group structure had not expanded to cater for the surge of new members coming in as a result of the development drive. After a very successful year I retained the office of Developments Officer. I saw British growth as the only answer available to us, to correct the imbalance that threatened us.

I put much more time into Mensa now that I was retired. Being inhibited from doing much at the international level by the refusal of a second more modest budget at Cambridge I had to throw my weight where I could.

Clive and I wanted to find a way to do something we had never been able to do before. We were good at getting enquiries from free publicity but this was erratic and the staff had to work in surges. We needed a flow of enquiries to fill the gaps. Large-scale advertising had often been considered but had never been thought economic. Later that year we were to try a new adventure. But first back to the international scene.

In November the IGC met in brilliant autumnal Athens and the atmosphere began to improve. The new team seemed to begin to understand each other. A large and representative international group of Mensans met on a hotel roof in the land where democracy was born and in the shadow of the benignly approving white columns of the Acropolis we came to accord. We went carefully through the proposed new International Constitution which Gabe Werba's American sub-committee had produced and we reached agreement. There were things that I did not like but my faction thought that this was the best we could get. We had to take account of the weight of American membership and the very strong determination of this American Committee. The money we used came from all members but it was their treasurer who was signing the cheques for most of it.

There was a strike and some trouble in the streets in Athens at the time so we had to break up in a hurry to get away. Unfortunately we had not dotted all the i's and crossed all the t's on the new draft. Werba was to tidy up some details and we were to pass the whole thing and put it up to a referendum when the final draft was approved. I left Athens with a good feeling, I wanted to see that my thirty-odd years work on Mensa did not come to nothing and so I was interested in arranging succession. I was desperately anxious that the enormous imbalance in membership should be corrected so that we should not become just an offshoot of a largely American organisation.

I was afraid that any emasculation of the IGC would hamper the policy of developing parallel growth in other countries and especially non-anglophone ones. But I thought we could live with the Athens proposals even though they put control largely in the hands of the American Chairman.

1981 started in Britain as another good Mensa year with even faster growth, an enlarged and typeset newsletter and other improvements.

In America too, things went very well with a flattened but continued growth curve peaking at 47,000 members. The March drop in membership had become a bigger problem with so many new members; it was around nine thousand that year.

There were many more meetings and Regional Gatherings in America as the excellent local group structure absorbed the influx of new members into the network. The system of local elections and succession which governs the local chapters there is better at providing for the incoming member than the British Mensa system which has not yet elaborated democratic local structure.

But on the international scene things did not go well. The Athens accord broke down harshly at the next IGC meeting at Baltimore. It was a perfect example of my saying that what ever great minds do, high intelligence thinks unlike. We had two meetings of sincere and dedicated Mensa workers and stalwarts on successive days. All parties were pro Mensa and there were no musketeers or any real self-interest.

The American Committee met under the chairmanship of Gabriel Werba and the International Committee met under my chairmanship and, on an important matter affecting the whole future of Mensa they were poles apart! Such was the Baltimore Disaccord which led to a new bad time for Mensa. We dispersed in serious disagreement. There was disunity as we stood to leave the Mensa table.

Peace in Mensa was to return but not before some undignified scufflings, hard words, numerous proposals for a plethora of referenda and talk of another Boston Tea Party. Not in Boston Massachusetts this time, but in Boston, Lincolnshire, England. Secession in reverse was, for a time, in the air.

The problem was that it had taken some time to tidy up the last details of the agreed Athens Draft International Constitution and the draft had only gone out a few days before the meeting. Some international representatives saw their copy only when they got to Baltimore. There were even new amendments which the American Committee had insisted upon the previous day. There was no great opposition to the draft by the IGC members but they were deeply offended by the high pressure atmosphere in the American meeting (which they attended as observers). There were some hard words and, unwisely, a threat. 'This must be passed tomorrow at the IGC meeting or it will be withdrawn and replaced by something you will like less.'

The American Committee thought that my faction was simply stalling. They insisted that the draft must be passed then and there because they wanted the referendum to happen at the same time as their own election next June. This would save money. It would also maximise American participation.

Some of the things that were said at the AMC meeting were so anti-international that I had American members apologising on behalf of their committee members. Charley Fallon stood out as a moderate and a friendly voice in an unfriendly meeting.

So the IGC met next day and was not going to be rushed into a hasty decision on an important matter just so as to help the American Committee to get its votes out. The support for Gabe had faded completely and there was a large majority against an immediate decision in the IGC vote. Gabe Werba was very upset at his failure to carry the IGC and talked of resignation. He did not turn up at the next meeting and sent Henry Schofield Noble in his place. Henry was seen as a hard-liner then.

That we were not stalling is proved by the fact that the Athens proposals were passed nem con after some insignificant editorial amendments a little later that year at the next meeting in Oslo. Even Henry Schofield Noble did not vote against these.

By that time however the American Committee had fulfilled its threat, repudiated the internationally agreed draft and put up another one which was much less acceptable to my faction on the IGC. Among other things the referendum was to dismiss myself and the other elected international officers in mid-term and put what was virtually a controlling block of votes on the new 'International Board of Directors' into the hands of the American Mensa Chairman (so long as the imbalance of membership lasts). Pending the next election the international officers who had been elected by all members were to be replaced by officers appointed by the new board.

When copies of what had unfortunately been represented as a

'punitive' new American draft appeared in Europe there was a 'we can all play that game' feeling and one by one various national Mensas began to put up their own drafts of the International Constitution for referendum as they could do under the existing constitution. They would be withdrawn if the new American one was withdrawn when all would go back to the Athens draft.

After the Oslo meeting we waited to see what would happen at the American AGM at Louisville in June. The news was bad. Relatively few of the 1,200 members present attended the AGM at which only one voice spoke for the internationally agreed Athens/Oslo draft. It was repudiated and a re-elected Werba put the new American draft to the AGM. It was passed to go forward for referendum.

This news caused more National Mensas to put up drafts until there were six altogether. There was much dispute as to how six long complex motions could be put to referendum. If, in the normal way, it were done one at a time in order it would take years and cost a mint. There was no precedent or method for multiple choice. If they all went out at once how could one get a majority of the voters with six to choose from? It was a big mess. And the argument around Mensa became vexed and fraught.

But Irish Mensa was beginning to prosper along with British Mensa and the new leading spirit was David Schulman. In May they held the first of what has become a series of first class international meetings. This was on the occasion of the Irish AG. We all listened eagerly to the American visitors who told us how the grass roots American members were reacting as the quarrel warmed up.

The parties in the constitutional dispute had put their case to the members by various means. The British, the International and the American Journals featured articles, discussions, arguments and some none too pleasant personalities on the subject. It was dramatised as a dispute largely between myself and Gabe Werba and someone in America set off a letter-writing campaign. I began to get dozens of letters from America by every post pressing me to accept the American point of view and put the American draft to referendum by itself and out of turn. Others wanted all drafts to go out immediately. I replied to them all, setting out the thing as I saw it, and also began to circulate letters to American local groups.

Feelings were high in Europe and I was seriously afraid of a break-up of Mensa with some of the Europeans breaking away from a Mensa dominated by one national Mensa. It was feared that this would happen if the proposal from the American AGM was passed. The British, Channel Islands, Austrian, and French committees were seriously thinking of a breakaway movement and I had to use my influence against this again and again. At one British committee meeting the decision had almost been made. I was to be late and Clive persuaded the meeting to hear my ideas before the final decision. I managed to hold the fort for unity by a small margin.

The second six day 'Mensa At Cambridge' was another success. It was followed by Ferdinand Heger's similar and splendid weekend meeting at Graz in Austria. The lecturers there were Clive Sinclair, Madsen Pirie and Northcote Parkinson. I met the new activist in Italy, Signor Mennotti Cossu, with good tidings from Rome. These two meetings were in a new class and gave us courage in adversity.

The international situation now looked so bad that a break-up of Mensa seemed unavoidable and it was at this point that I got a call from Hyman Brock, the chairman of Canadian Mensa. Hyman had been a vociferous supporter of the internationalist faction at Baltimore but, like me, he was beginning to fear disunity more than anything else. He proposed that Clive and I should get to an RG of reconciliation with Werba, Noble, Fallon and Gardner, to be held in Miami in October, and this seemed like a good idea to me. But blood was now up and my faction in Europe were against compromise. I was warned that we should be misled and that we should make no concessions.

October in Miami is hot and sunny and there was a very pleasant weekend of swimming and good talk before the big meeting. It did not take too long. Everybody was fed up with a muddled and harmful squabble and there seemed to be no good uncontested solution. We had to make peace. We had to get our knees under the Mensa symbol and talk until we agreed. And Mensa won.

Clive and I argued for some amendments in the features we liked least in the draft. We wanted more American faces on the board rather than a one man block vote with the American chairman deciding everything. That conceded, I was ready to accept my summary dismissal by referendum, taking it as a compliment that this was assumed to be the only way of getting rid of me. Holding on to unity was my priority because it is not easy to get it back once you lose it.

So we signed the Miami pact. It was a personal agreement which had no official standing. All parties were to accept the new draft and all were to use all their influence to get the whole batch of differing drafts withdrawn so that the new, agreed Miami draft could be put to referendum early in 1982. There was no guarantee that all the national committees could be persuaded to withdraw what had in many cases been decided at an AGM but we were pledged to try our very best.

I was in sore trouble when I got back to England, as the negotiator usually is with those who were not there. 'Sell out!', was the cry. Some have not even yet forgiven me for what was seen as a betrayal but I have not the remotest doubt that what Clive and I agreed was the best for the future of Mensa.

And we did it. The Miami signatories managed to convince their supporters to withdraw all drafts so that the Miami draft should be put uncontested. I published an article in December in which I put the case for the agreed draft as the only way to keep Mensa in one piece. 'We can split up anytime, let us give this a try first.' This was the burden of my case.

The outcome was surprising but we were not surprised. Both sides kept their word on the pact and the signatories turned out to be as influential as they had hoped. All the contending drafts were withdrawn and the Miami draft was put to a referendum passed by a very substantial majority. In 1982, after twenty-eight years with a three-year gap of Mensa leadership, I was kicked out in mid-term. The majority of American membership would now exercise control through their committee rather than directly. The control by an array of small National Mensa representatives was peacefully over.

On reflection I can see that, after their own lights, both factions had a case. We could have made the necessary changes more peacefully but, considering that we were scattered around the globe and the parties could not know each other really well, we could have done a lot worse.

As in many such disputes the *casus belli* seems to me to be more symbolic than real. Two years later we can see that little has really changed. Constitutions and changing them are really distractions from the real problems. Once composed they are hardly ever looked at and so cannot really have much effect on what actually happens.

What happens depends on an astonishingly small group of activists and constitutions neither help nor hinder in finding them. What had happened was that American Mensa activists had begun to insist on the recognition of their success, size and contribution. They were over-impressed by my own influence and felt that a change in the rules was the only way to diminish the influence of a leader who needed to be replaced. I was seen as the classic 'ageing supervisor problem'. Of course no ageing supervisor can be convinced that he is a problem and I am no exception. However, that I was not clinging to office is proved by the fact that I went consenting and that much earlier I had suggested it myself to Fallon. Whether I was right in my guess that I was still young enough in spirit to have more to contribute to my life's work must be judged in the light of what happened then.

All that year I had been working on plans to 'go professional' with the British Mensa newsletter and planning a big advertising campaign for recruitment which the generous Clive Sinclair was prepared to underwrite to the extent that the cost per applicant should be economic. It cost him a lot of money but the experiment taught us a vitally important new technique which has been an overwhelming success. It has led to a five-fold boost in British membership in as many years and has changed the whole Mensa scene radically.

Further, fighting for a better newsletter to hold the great new surge of incoming members I found what seemed to be a good firm of publishers who would try, within our existing budget, to take the newsletter up-market to a properly printed glossy journal.

Clive had to threaten resignation to get this move accepted at a British Committee meeting in Devon. The committee was divided by the new surge of growth and vigour that had started when Clive Sinclair and I came in two years before. The earlier committee members were disturbed by the changes and the up-market moves that had begun. As the chief instigator and motivator of these I was soon, as is any activator, under fire with constant niggling criticisms of the newsletter under my editorship, despite the fact that members generally approved of the improvements.

The idea of 'glossy paper' became the symbol and this was strongly resisted as somehow 'elitist'. I even had campaign-type letters from those who claimed that it would hurt their eyes. Underlying these objections was a suspicion of any change. There was also discomfort at the transformation of the small comfortable Mensa of the under-achievers. There is a strand of this in every Mensa because successful bright people are often too busy in other fields to give voluntary service to Mensa. So far we have not, frankly, been seen by many achievers as a sufficiently worthy cause. But this changed as we spread wider and became more respectable.

Later in 1982 at a meeting in Toronto, the first of the new style International Committee, I was asked by my successor as International Chairman, the successful Canadian businessman Hyman Brock, whether I agreed with the proposed motion to recognise Dr Ware with the self-chosen title *fons et origo* and whether I would accept the honorary non-executive post of International President of Mensa.

Never averse to a bargain I said yes to both questions and at the formal meeting I was installed as President and Dr Ware was officially recognised as the fount and source of Mensa on the basis of his claim to have suggested the idea to our Founder Roland Berrill.

Dr Isaac Asimov, who had been dismissed also by the referendum, was reinstalled as Vice President. Professor Buckminster Fuller (also dismissed) was installed with the title President Emeritus.

The same IGC meeting planned for the next meeting to be in

Auckland, New Zealand, in pursuance of the dispersed meetings policy.

In Britain my own plans to improve the newsletter in Britain came to fruition when the December edition 'went glossy' with a much enlarged newsletter renamed *MENSA*, with photo-typeset printing on the eye-scorching glossy paper.

The Toronto IBD meeting had been preceded by the American AG at Trenton, New Jersey, at which there were 750 present. There was a reduced rise in American membership of two thousand to 49,000. The British membership continued to grow more rapidly as the improved publicity methods Harold Gale and I were developing began to work.

The British AG was at the famous Metropole Hotel at Brighton and it marked a very distinct change in image and atmosphere which reminded me of the change at the Chicago meeting when the disruptives had been put in their place by the grass roots members. There was a big crowd of new members at Brighton who took a sturdy negative view of the AGM exhibitionists and dealt in short order with the usual batch of member motions. The fun for the tiny group, who enjoyed the cathartic yearly feast of discord resulting from lots and lots of motions, had been curtailed by the rule passed previously that there had to be ten signatories to an AGM motion. A couple of them scornfully resigned after the meeting and everyone had to adjust to the shock and disappointment of their parting.

Clive Sinclair retained the British Chair despite a challenge and the Gathering, well-organised by Lorraine Boyce, was regarded as an excellent one by all except those whose yearly bout of points of order had been spoiled.

The important news in 1983 lay in the continued resurgence of British Mensa, cessation of growth in America, relative stagnation on the international front, the re-election unopposed for a further two-year term of the international officers appointed by the IBD in Toronto.

The big IGC and IBD meeting in New Zealand was very expensive and this caused some criticism. But publicity was in the Antipodes and the Far East was good because it threw emphasis on Mensa in places remote from our usual sphere. There was another big success with very great publicity for Mensa At Cambridge and an important meeting in Nice of the IBD and IGC.

American Mensa membership just held its ground at 49,000 at the March peak. But Britain had taken over the lead in the most friendly penetration competition.

The new feature in British recruitment was the scheme which resulted from the Sinclair funded experiments with large advertisements. The breakthrough was an absurdly simple idea which I suggested and Harold Gale energetically and successfully worked out and applied.

Large adverts in high circulation journals began to carry a mini IQ test. Those who can solve this are invited to apply. I had learned from the very great response to my own 'kickself' puzzles in the newsletter, that people who have solved a puzzle want to tell somebody.

The most interesting article would attract four letters, a simple 'you will kick yourself when you hear the answer' puzzle and, with the prize of one of my books, would bring in two hundred letters to claim it. The *Reader's Digest* quizzes worked the same way. The simple lesson I had failed to see was that we could buy the *Reader's Digest* effect and did not have to wait to be given it. The marginal extra motivation to potential Mensa applicants made all the difference. It pulled us through a threshold to self-financing large adverts. We could now control the flow of applications and fill in the gaps to order.

British Mensa growth took an even sharper upwards surge. In 1983 we passed the 9,000 and the 10,000 mark and I bet John Meredith ten pounds that we should pass the thirteen thousand mark before the AGM in 1984. Some weeks ago in November 1984 I paid him his ten pounds. I had missed by seventeen members.

On 1 July 1983 Professor Buckminster Fuller, who had been the second President of Mensa and was President Emeritus, died.

Not without serious teething troubles the newsletter, restyled *MENSA*, continued in 1983. Now in December 1984 it has now settled down with a new widely approved, enlarged new format and my recent economies made it possible to afford to have a three colour cover and a professional editor without an increase in the cost per member. We have something that begins to justify the subscriptions of the majority of members for whom we have not yet evolved sufficiently attractive meetings.

My career in Mensa has been like my career in business, successful but stormy. This is because I have the faults of my virtues. I am essentially a self-starter entrepreneur, an ideas man who is plagued by far more new ideas than he can ever implement. Long experienced in dealing with the frustrations of those who sell novelty, I tend to get on and try things. I do not spend as much time engineering consent and agreement as I should. Many beneficial ideas and projects must either go off before they are ready or not at all.

I have also noted that many schemes which have the much vaunted 'careful preparation and detailed planning' take more time, cost more and are less successful than many quickly modified, learn-as-you-go schemes which have a precarious start. The power and freshness of an idea and the enthusiasm it attracts are always diluted by the attempt to be more sure than is needed before the start. The compromises that come with a 'please-everyone' negotiated agreement often ruin the deal.

The problem in 1982 started from my belief that Mensa would in the end greatly benefit internationally from the use of micro-computers to perform the final supervised test. A slow, difficult, demotivating stage would be removed from the induction process and people everywhere could be passed through exactly the same procedure simply and easily in their own home.

So, thinking to prepare the ground and start people thinking by an unofficial personal initiative, in 1982 I got a micro-computer and learned how to program it.

With help from my family and the permission of my friend, the author Ray Cattell, I wrote a program that would put a candidate through the Cattell IIIA test, supervise it in a standard way and mark the test with due age allowance. This out-of-date test is no longer suitable as a Mensa acceptance (or any other) test because it has been compromised by the fact that Mensa used it for thirty years as a preliminary unsupervised test and sent out millions of copies, not all of which have been returned.

As a start towards the controversial goal of a computer test I arranged to market this as a micro-computer tape. As with my several books on Mensa themes I feel that the authors of such things benefit Mensa by writing them and are entitled to normal royalties as an author. I see no reason why Mensa should claim royalties from the programs written by its unpaid honorary President. I had made no secret of my plan and told those I thought should know. I think perhaps that they had hardly listened or did not believe the unlikely story that, at my age, I was going to be able to write saleable software. So it was only when I had invested much money and time and informed everyone in writing that the tape was on the way that a completely unexpected outcry started against me.

I had a whole year of acrimonious correspondence and was accused of exploiting my position as President for personal gain and ruining the (already ruined) test. Critical letters were sent to psychological associations and Ray Cattell was pestered with Mensa objections.

The matter was referred to the Ombudsman, Eric Hills, and people dropped everything else to send scalding letters around. Eric Hills had many depositions which were very critical and Dr Ware was very critical. Eric Hills listened patiently to all the attacks and then in a long careful report exonerated me and recommended that the matter be forgotten. But there were some members of the new IBD who felt that this judgement was not acceptable and the matter was 'retried' at the meeting in Nice.

The IBD meeting there was a bit fraught. My friends Clive, Madsen, John McNulty and some others were indignant at this personal attack and even I, though used to such stuff, felt annoyed that even after I had been kicked upstairs I still was a target for such things. But matters were resolved peaceably with the understanding that the publication should cease after the first batch.

The sad thing is that this time, for once, the idea I was promoting – computerised testing for Mensa – was set back rather than advanced by my experimental personal initiative. I look to the day when the idea can be revived. One thing we have learned is that the fear that the answers could be easily obtained by the computer-wise and that Mensa would be discredited somehow have not been realised. My way of hiding the answers seems to have thwarted anyone who has bothered among the 4,000 or so purchasers. Experience tells me that if anyone had found the answers we should have heard of it in the computer press. (One expert did get to one of the decoy sets of answers that were set as traps.) When, as we must, we get to the stage of a micro-computer Mensa test, the answers need not be on the tape or disk.

The Auckland meeting in 1983 was a success and was the biggest meeting ever held in the southern hemisphere. I was gratified by a motion acclaiming what I had done for the British newsletter. This enraged and exasperated the diminishing band of my dogged detractors on the British Committee. (As President I could not stand for the British Committee so I was not a member.)

So we come to 1984. A very sad event was the death after a long and painful illness of Marvin Grosswirth.

American Mensa broke the 50,000 barrier at last as it peaked in March but finished the year with 47,404 members. British Mensa finished the year with 13,139. World membership reached 68,058 by the end of the year.

At the end of this history my aim to correct the membership imbalance is a long way from realised, but the imbalance is slightly less. Over eighty percent of members were from the USA when I was returned as Chairman in 1979. Since then American Mensa has grown fifty percent but the new American total is now sixty-nine percent of all members.

All members, I am sure, especially those from Britain and America, welcome the day when the proportion of Mensa members to the general population is as good in the rest of the world as it is in Britain and America today. In Britain there are 234 members per million of the population against 20,000 per million who are qualified to join. In America there are 209 members per million. I shall draw a veil over Philip Poole's ridiculous performance on the Channel Islands with over a thousand members per million. That is indecent.

Here is a State of Mensa report on the membership of Mensa

around the world as I finish this account a few days before Christmas in 1984.

International Mensa

MEMBERSHIP AND MEMBERSHIP PENETRATION

COUNTRY	DATE OF RETURN	POPULATION IN MILLIONS	CURRENT MEMBERS	MEMBERS PER MILLION
Australia	9/84	14.42	712	49.37
Austria	10/84	7.65	466	66.91
Belgium	9/84	9.89	176	17.79
Britain	12/84	56.20	13,139	233.79
Canada	6/84	25.00	2,088	83.52
Channel Isl.	6/84	0.13	153	1,177.00
Finland	6/84	4.76	380	79.83
France	10/84	53.80	425	7.89
Japan	9/84	116.12	228	1.96
Netherlands	6/84	14.03	389	27.72
New Zealand	8/84	3.15	502	159.36
Norway/Swed.	3/84	12.34	159	12.88
Switzerland	6/84	6.55	114	17.40
USA	10/84	226.50	47,404	209.28
			66,335	

*　　　*　　　*

Germany	12/84	62.30	168	2.69
Greece	12/84	9.18	23	2.50
Hong Kong	12/84	4.60	31	6.52
Italy	12/84	56.20	252	4.48
Malaysia	12/84	13.67	241	17.62
Singapore	12/84	2.31	48	20.77
South Africa	12/84	27.80	289	10.39
Spain	12/84	37.80	78	2.06
Unattached			603	
WORLD TOTAL			68,068	

Date of issue: 14th December, 1984

The American AG this year was in Washington. It is said to have been a very good meeting.

The British AG was again a very well-attended success with an excellent atmosphere except for a messy AGM with the usual small group raising confusing noisy points of disorder and shouting down the Chairman, Clive Sinclair. Apart from this there was just that feeling of a meeting of minds that Jaques Schupbach described in connection with the first few Annual Gatherings which started thirty-seven years before.

There was an excellent international meeting with the IGC and the IBD coming together in Kerkrade, Holland, for a real meeting of minds which made some very sensible decisions.

I was encouraged by both the atmosphere and the press coverage which seemed to me to be positive. The meeting had the same feeling of excitement and the press and TV coverage that the seminal meetings in London had had in 1960 and 1961 which had led to the first big surge in membership. But this was in Europe where we have never had very great success but where always, despite everything, survived.

The Board decided to set up an international office in London and to employ a professional to undertake the job of projecting Mensa firmly and decisively abroad. We have found a promising linguist entrepreneur; we have the money, the will, the knowhow and the resources. Take no bets against us.

I am very hopeful that by the time I revise this on my ninetieth birthday we shall be counting members by the million – in fifty languages.

The last words on this short Mensa history by Mensa's third President are the same as the last recorded words of Mensa's first President: *Floreat Mensa.*

4

Can mental ability be measured?

Mensa arises from the idea that mental ability can be scientifically measured. That anything as complex can be measured is a thought which needs defence.

Science has transformed the modern world, whether for better or for worse, and, in the long run, remains an open question, but no one denies that scientific methods have brought great short-term benefits to offset the disadvantages and risks that we are all so keen on frightening ourselves about. We have to balance longevity, health, comfort and wealth for some, against the possible ecological and war damage.

The first great achievements in science were in realms where precise measurement was possible. The hard, or exact, sciences were the pioneers. Astronomy, physics, mechanics and chemistry were fields in which progress and practical dividends for humanity were most quickly and easily gathered.

Precise measurements led to the expectation of precise predictions and the successive testing and falsification of these led to better hypotheses. The greater the precision the more likely that errors in theory would be exposed, so that there was a rapid advance in both theory and practice, each interacting supportively to the other. Many of the most important general discoveries have arisen from the observation of tiny discrepancies in data. With better instruments and more accuracy, a point was reached even in the exact sciences where the observations were confused with the background noise, the chance effects which were unrelated to the hypothesis. A theory of errors was needed.

It was work in this region where data and noise intersect that led to the development of that very powerful weapon in the armoury of the applied mathematician and scientist, statistics. This is the mathematical technique for dealing with uncertainty. This was an extraordinary idea to the scientists of the time. Some asked, 'How can we be systematic about random error, about chance?' There was an impasse. Rigorous science was held up at the border represented by the limits of accuracy. Oddly, it was the green baize gambling tables of France that produced the unexpected spin-off which renewed scientific progress. Aristocratic gamblers hired mathematicians to make observations there. That began the systematic study of chance and probability. They studied what other scientists thought to be a contradiction in terms, the laws of chance. The unlikely gamble came off in a way which hardly helped gamblers but did a lot for science. The resulting discoveries have proved to be the most important tool of science ever since.

Statistics and probability theory are the measuring instruments for error, indeterminism and uncertainty. Where we cannot measure with sufficient accuracy, or where the relation between phenomena is variable but still significant, predictive, there is no need to give up the idea of an adequate theoretical structure. Statistical techniques enable us to develop 'better-than-guesswork' predictive theories where measurement cannot be precise or predictions exact.

It proved possible to be rigorous even about uncertainty itself. Probability, significance and reliability can be measured rigorously. The vital importance of this was only fully recognised when, early in the century, the hardest, most exact, most rigorous science, fundamental physics, found itself in need of the same tools to deal with problems at the level of the microcosm. Progress in that field was held up until Planck, Dirac, Heisenberg and Schroedinger showed that uncertainty reigns even at the heart of things. Statistical methods are necessary even there.

Once methods were developed to deal with the errors in exact measurement and observation, it became possible to extend the methods of science to fields where observations could not be certain. There were the 'soft' sciences such as meteorology and the life science, biology, with its branches, medicine, psychology, and sociology. In these fields rigorous scientific methods had been held to be inapplicable. But once the hard sciences had been forced to accept them, statistics and probability became the probes of psychology, biology and medicine so that predictive theory and explanatory concepts at last became possible.

In the new science, psychology, the statistical tool was seized upon and even developed. The concept of a correlation coefficient arose in the very field which concerns us, the measurement of mental differences (from Galton, Spearman and Burt); it is now in general use in the hardest of sciences and technologies.

One of the approaches to psychology was Individual Psychology, the study of mental differences. The early workers, trying to understand the differences in personality and ability which were being revealed by the development of mass education, turned to the new mathematical techniques with avidity. But the true beginning was a little earlier.

A year before I was born in 1912 a man died who was in every way remarkable. Several of his ideas have made an indelible mark on the culture of our times. One, which he would have considered trivial, is used by every law enforcement agency in the world. As the pioneer of anthropometry he was the first to discover the uniqueness of finger prints and suggest their use for identification. Sir Francis Galton, it is widely conceded, was a genius and perhaps the first systematic student of human genius. And he was the first man to apply statistical methods to the examination of human differences. Read this letter to his sister: 'My dear Adele, I am four years old and can read any English book. I can say all the Latin substantives, adjectives and active verbs, besides fifty two lines of Latin poetry. I can cast up any sum in addition and multiply by 2, 3, 4, 5, 6, 7, 8 (9, 10, 11). I read French a little and I know the clock. Francis Galton, 15 February 1827.'

Those who cannot accept the large differences in innate ability which show up in children and babies have to explain what could be so different in the feeding and treatment of that tiny child that would account for the early ability shown in that letter.

Among the little boy's close relatives were Erasmus Darwin, Samuel Galton, who originated the three colour theory, the towering figure of Charles Darwin and Suzanne Wedgwood, eldest daughter of Josiah Wedgwood, a Fellow of the Royal Society. Young Francis was educated in Boulogne and at the King Edward School, Birmingham. He complained about 'a period of stagnation; I learned nothing and chafed at the limitations. I craved for an abundance of good reading, solid science, and well taught mathematics.'

Later, at the General Hospital, Birmingham, he became a physician, but found his way to King's College where he preferred laboratory work. He studied mathematics and began to travel. In 1869 he published his highly influential book, *Hereditary Genius*. As the first man to think about human ability and talent in a scientific way he was the real founder both of individual psychology and of the study of eugenics. Galton was the first to perceive the difference between general and special abilities. This took thinkers in the field past an important mental block which impeded understanding before his day.

Previous writers about genius, ability, and talent had wondered to what extent they were hereditary. Galton started the first objective studies to establish the facts. Fechner in Germany was the first to apply statistical methods in the field of general psychology but Galton was the first in the field of individual psychology, as he put it, 'To treat the subject in a statistical manner and arrive at exact numerical results.' He was the first to suggest that human ability might have a normal or gaussian distribution like bodily weight and height. He started down an entirely new track by trying to define both genius and mental defect in exact, and therefore generally comparable, terms.

Galton examined the pedigrees of nearly a thousand very able people: judges, generals, statesmen, scientists, poets, painters and divines. Then he looked among the relatives of this sample. He discovered 89 equally eminent fathers, 114 eminent brothers, and 129 eminent sons.

Galton concludes, 'if for simplicity, we suppose that the number of male children born to each of the population, whether a genius or not, is on an average four, then the chances that the son of a genius will himself be a genius will be 129 times as great as that of a parent chosen at random' (Galton took no account of such a possibility as a female genius).

To accept the view that there was no hereditary influence here is to believe that the middle class environment of the concerned families was wonderfully better than that in families in the advancing working class at the time.

Galton was very conscious of these environmental advantages and in his books and papers deals with them at length. He remained convinced however, that it was impossible to explain the facts he had uncovered on a purely environmental hypothesis. 'The moral and intellectual wealth of a nation', he wrote, 'consists largely in the multifarious variety and the gifts of the men who compose it'.

Having investigated the individual differences which could be explained by 'nurture', he then went on to discuss those attributable to 'nature', thus setting the neat apposition of the two concepts in a way which no commentator since has been able to ignore.

He had very clear ideas on eugenics, a subject which has become discredited since Hitler's racialist crimes. However, Galton's ideas could not have been more different. He felt that the ideal would be an intermixture of races which would provide the raw material of human variety for selective advantage to work upon. So in an imperialist age, he seems to have been the first proponent of the multiracial society. 'The more diverse the nation and the greater its range of variation', he proclaimed, in the face of the perfectly normal chauvinism and racialism of the times, 'the better the chance that genetic excellence will emerge'.

'Such a nation', he went on, 'once it has realised the importance of encouraging and educating its ablest members, will become a dominant race.' Here is a view to astonish and perplex the multiracialists among today's intellectuals.

In 1884, Galton established in London that enterprise which led to the mental testing movement in many countries. The birthplace of that movement was without doubt, Galton's 'Anthropometric Laboratory', which was opened during the International Health Exhibition in London in 1884.

To use Galton's words: 'The leading idea was that the measurement should "sample" a man with reasonable completeness; factors or traits should be measured absolutely where possible, otherwise relatively among his class-fellows by ranks and percentile grades'. In his second book, *Natural Inheritance*, Galton put forward a remarkable anticipation of the experimental results established by Gregor Mendel, of which no one in England knew anything then. Galton spoke of the 'multiplicity of quasi-independent elements which combine to produce the graded distribution of genetic differences'.

Galton's anthropometric enquiries led him to develop the method of correlation, undoubtedly one of the most important advances in the science of statistics. According to Professor Sir Cyril Burt's account, he even anticipated the statistical technique called 'factor analysis' for dealing with that set of problems where there is a need for multiple cross correlations. Burt observes, 'When Galton took it up, individual psychology was just a speculative topic for the fancies of the poet, the novelist, the biographer, the quack and the charlatan on the seaside pier. By the time he left it and handed it on to others, it had been transformed into a reputable branch of natural science.'

Early in the next century and some time after Galton's death a number of workers in several countries began working on the problems which had attracted his attention. Binet, Stern, Burt, Terman and Spearman are only a few of these pioneers in psychometrics, the application of rigorous measurement in the new field of individual psychology.

What Galton had done was to investigate families which consistently produced great talent in generation after generation. He reached the inevitable conclusion that there is a strong hereditary influence affecting them. Galton's underlying concern, the recognition of the importance of outstanding talent in a highly developed, interrelated world was well expressed by one of those who followed him. Professor Lewis M. Terman spoke thus: 'It should go without saying that a nation's resources of intellectual talent are among the most precious that it will ever have.' Psychometry, intelligence and personality testing is a branch of Galton's anthropometry.

What were the human differences that were most important in the social circumstances of Galton's time? It was natural that

Galton and the scientists who followed up his lead should look for these first.

One of the human differences that was proving to be much more important than ever before in the new industrial age at the time was, as I have said, intelligence. The intelligence of a small number of inventors, industrial and agricultural innovators (informed and guided by the brilliant insights of the new breed of objective and intelligent scientists), was being combined in a new way. It was being amplified, in the new type of industrial institutions which were arising. Man's life in industrial countries was guided much more by the best brains than ever had been before.

So it was natural that the workers in the new science of anthropometry should follow Galton in taking very great interest in this quality which was now having a much greater effect on the world. What was this important difference, that which meant that some people were much more able than others to solve problems, invent things and push forward the new ways which were to enrich everyone in the end? What is intelligence?

We are talking about an age when, for the first time, mass education was beginning. Vast numbers of children had to be catered for in the new schools that were being hurriedly organised to meet the need for new skills, literacy, numeracy. There were a thousand problems. How could a teacher cope with these great classes of children from all sorts of backgrounds and of widely different abilities?

It was, in fact, problems with the slower children in the new schools that first attracted enough official concern to trigger scientific investigation. A young professor, Alfred Binet, was called in by the authorities in Paris. The new schools were in trouble because no one quite knew what to do about the retarded and mentally deficient children who had been drawn in by the sudden crude trawl-net of compulsory education. Few had dreamed of sending these poor children to school before. Suddenly the unfortunate duller children became not just a parents' problem but the State's problem.

Binet was asked, in the first place, to find some simple way at least of diagnosing the problem, sorting out the problem children in case it should turn out that they could be helped. Could they be given specialist attention away from the discouraging and distracting pressures from other children? Would that help? Following Galton's own methods, he tells us, Binet worked out methods of constructing a simple battery of tests so that children could be compared, not as before, just with their classmates but with the whole cohort of their age group in the population. Alfred Binet put forward the few simple ideas which proved to be the foundation of intelligence testing.

Visiting schools in Paris and testing children of all ages on a range of tests, he gradually elaborated the idea of a graded series of mental tasks, arranged in order of difficulty. He found he was able to fix on a level of achievement on simple, easily administered tests, which represented the average boy or girl of each level of ability. This enabled him to propose the concept 'mental age'.

A child whose performance is at the level of the average child of ten is said to have a 'mental age' of ten regardless of actual age. Binet then divided the mental age by the child's real age, which he called the 'chronological age' to get the fraction MA/CA. He took this as an indicator of the general level of mental ability of the child, disregarding age. A bright ten year old who could equal the performance of the average child of twelve would be ascribed a 'mental ratio' of 1.2. The reverse configuration would give a mental ratio of 0.8.

Professor Lewis M. Terman modified this to produce the now familiar 'intelligence quotient' concept. He simply multiplied the ratio by 100 and took the integer value so as to work in simple whole numbers. Thus:

$$IQ = INT \ \frac{\text{Mental Age} \times 100}{\text{Chronological Age}}$$

Binet's aim was to find a way of expressing the underlying mental ability of the child, regardless of age.

Binet made a very important but very usual assumption. He assumed that mental ratio tended to remain constant, that those who exhibit high intelligence as adults are almost always found to have shown intelligence at an early age. This implies that there is some underlying quality there from the start or which appeared very early. In fact, consciously or otherwise, he assumes a genetic contribution to differences in intelligence as in every other trait.

It was not a very risky assumption. As a psychologist he ascribed a semi-permanent characteristic to the child, one which had not constantly to be revised with age. This was why his idea was so successful; this was what was needed if remedial action was to be taken for retarded children or if the most was to be made of the talents of able ones. From a constantly revised measure across a range of tests resulting in an ephemeral profile, he advanced to a useful general diagnosis which could guide action. Since the intelligent quotient is designed to remain constant through changes of age it enables those responsible to help the child in the light of reasonable expectations of what it should try and what would waste both child and teachers' time. It was a lucky guess because, by and large, IQ scores do remain remarkably constant. If this had not proved to be so his scheme would have been forgotten long ago.

So much is made of the occasional exception that it is hard to remember that, overwhelmingly, the expectations resulting from the Binet assumptions are fulfilled in practice. Examples of very bright children who turn out to be dim adults and vice-versa are very rare indeed. When they are found it seems likely that there are circumstances which leave the Binet assumption unassailed.

It will be obvious that by this method the average IQ score should be 100. The range of scores is from those who are untestable (score below 50) to those who (on some tests), score 210 or more. To talk of genius scores on an IQ test is absurd. There is no way to standardise a test to a level of one in millions.

Much of the subsequent work in the field has been seeking limitations and criticisms. It has revealed limitations to the strict validity of the simple generalisations upon which the method is based but its general truth is not in doubt except where doubt is an act of a political faith. A very great deal has been made of these limitations by those whose bigotry is threatened by them. But despite many urgent detractors the tests remain a very useful tool for the clinical psychologist, the educationalist and the industrialist.

They are as good as, and a lot fairer than, any other method of predicting academic promise or problems. Those who want to abolish IQ tests because they discriminate against minority cultures, are asking us to throw away a life raft because it is not a boat. The IQ test may still retain some cultural bias if it has been standardised on a host population but it is far less biased than any other type of examination, assessment, judgement or method of selection. Throw it away and you are back in the murky world of individual human judgements when it comes to the essential task of fitting people to roles in a very complex society. It cannot be done by lottery. The bright child from a minority culture has a better chance with an objective standardised test than with the attitudes and judgements he or she usually encounters. Even those who favour the practice of positive discrimination are dishonouring and handicapping the recipients of this insulting favouritism. The effect of their well-meant discrimination will inevitably be counter-productive as people over-allow for the bias.

The really important underlying fact, which is being pushed aside because only exceptions are newsworthy, is this. Children whose mental ages are notably higher than their actual age do, in the overwhelming majority of cases, retain that advantage as they grow older, they *do* show every evidence of high intelligence as adults and the widely believed story that precocity 'burns itself out' is a myth. This came out strongly in the work of Binet, Cattell, Spearman, Thurstone, Burt, Terman, and all the workers in the field ever since.

Yes, we are dealing with tendencies, not with inflexible laws and the quoting of an occasional exception is not a valid falsification. Yes, there is a small class of 'late developers' whose ability is not visible so early. Yes, another small class fail to live up to their early promise. These cases comfort those who have difficulty in accepting the fact that ability is not distributed 'fairly' but they are arguing from rare exceptions, not from general experience. And policies based on exceptions are more likely to be wrong than those based on the generality.

Another important discovery made by these pioneers of mental testing is that intelligence ceases to develop at around puberty. Their researches on a large sample showed that the mental age ceases to advance after the age of fourteen. It later came out that the slow down did not occur until eighteen or so with very intelligent children.

Like most human variables (ways of being different), measured intelligence has a gaussian, or normal, distribution. This is a way of saying that the further you are from the average the less people like you there are.

The Bell Curve diagram illustrates this. If you were to take a large, random sample of people, test their intelligence and make them stand in a great hall behind numbers ranged along a wall from about 80 to 160 according to their Intelligence Quotient, then the shape of the crowd (after this absurd procedure) would be that of a bell. The top of the bell would be at the average, IQ 100, the lips on either side would be the tiny minority of those on each side of the mean, those of exceptionally high and exceptionally low IQ.

Unfortunately the statistical characteristics of all tests are not the same. (The standard deviation differs.) A score on one test is

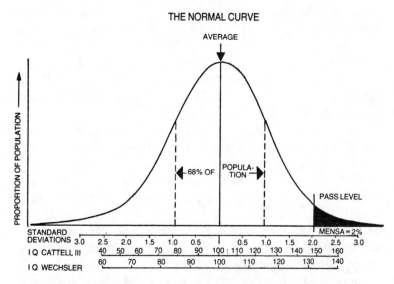

The bell curve diagram shows how intelligence test scores are distributed in the population.
The 'I Q' score which is equivalent to a given number of standard deviations is seen to be different for different types of test.

not equivalent to that on another. However, we have another, better way of expressing a level of intelligence. The percentile rating is calculated from the standard deviation of the test used so it is comparable across different tests. We can find the proportion of the population that would get any given score. Any one who comes out on the fiftieth percentile in an IQ test is of average intelligence. (Fifty percent of the standardisation population are likely to score less.) If you score on the ninety-eighth percentile, you have scored better than ninety-eight percent of people, you are in the top two percent, and you are eligible to join Mensa if you care to. This seems a better way to express the differences and it is in fact the one Sir Francis Galton pioneered.

One cautionary note: beware of bogus precision. The measurement of intelligence is a long way from being an exact art. The percentile system gives a feeling that the gradations are very fine. We cannot sensibly say that a percentile rating of sixty-two is better than one of sixty-one. It would be like a proud mother boasting that her Freddy was a millimetre taller than your Joe. But it would be astonishing if someone who scored on the eightieth percentile was not markedly brighter than someone who scored on the sixtieth.

I have given a brief description of the work of the pioneers of mental testing and the state of the art at that time. There have been few essential changes and most of today's tests are based on that early work. A vast mass of confirmatory information has been accumulated and the statistical techniques have been much improved. An enormous amount of time and work goes into the standardisation and validation of a modern test but there has been little fundamental change since those days.

At this period at the beginning of the century, when new ideas of social justice and equality were developing, there was much concern, especially among these pioneers of mental testing, about the existing educational system. Universal free education had indeed been established in many countries, but the upper reaches of the education system were still the perquisite of the middle and upper social classes. They had the money to send their children to the 'independent' schools. There were places at the public schools and at the middle class grammar schools for those poorer children who could pass an academic examination and earn a scholarship but the chance of this for children from the poorer backgrounds was not good.

The educational reformers were seeking some means of selection which could peer below the educational disadvantage of the bright, less privileged child and they naturally turned with enthusiasm to the intelligence test when it appeared. The tests were devised to avoid or at worst diminish bias and bring out underlying hidden ability. They were standardised on a large and representative sample of the population and not, like school examinations upon a selected sample from the educated classes. By the 1930s tests had been devised for adults and they were in widespread use in the armed services for recruits, by universities for candidates and for industrial and commercial appointments.

As I have said there were several trends in the nineteenth century which prepared for the development of Galton's ideas. Galton's own work on statistical mathematics and its application in anthropometry and psychometry, were followed by the systematic development of experimental psychology, which started as a branch of philosophy (and still is in France).

The industrial revolution was making most people in Britain more prosperous but there was a revulsion against many of the painful disruptions and harmful side effects of the traumatic changes. From a land of farms, Britain was becoming one of large new factories. Disturbing changes cause discontent, and there was a powerful movement towards industrial reform.

Science applied to work had changed people's lives, some saw a need for scientific management as well as science based work. Such things as vocational selection tests were developed to solve the resulting problems. Educational reform and scientific child study all underlined the need to devise intelligence and attainment tests which were not influenced by environmental factors and which did not emphasise disadvantage.

Everything was changing with the advance of industrialism and the mass urban society. The old ways of sorting people out and fitting them into the world of work were breaking down while a thousand exacting new roles were being created which had to be suitably filled. And society had not developed techniques of selection for these new occupations.

Science, applied via industrialism, had transformed, largely but not universally beneficially, the life of most people. Could it now solve some of the problems created by that transformation? Could it take on the problem of putting people optimally into work roles? It was established that, at least in schoolchildren, mental ability was measurable and normally distributed. Early predictions about mental ability and defect were the best indication available of future achievement.

Useful social predictions about what people could achieve and how they could function had proved to be possible but were these reliable on a long-term basis? The opponents of intelligence testing, and the art had opponents from the start, said that the assessments were of doubtful predictive value in the long run. 'What', said the critics, 'can be predicted for the bright child when it becomes an adult? Will the early promise be fulfilled?' This question could not be answered at the time because there was not yet a population of adults who had been tested as children. Today, exactly one hundred years after Galton's tentative beginnings we can answer very firmly. The answer is an unequivocal 'yes'. The early promise is, speaking statistically of course, fulfilled in very good measure.

This chapter will have given the reader something of the background to the art of intelligence measurement and an idea of the motivation of those who worked in the field. But no reader today will be unaware of some very negative political attitudes towards mental tests which are current today. In contradiction to charges of bias and class origin which are made I have shown that, so far from being created as a means of discrimination and exploitation as some modern critics claim, the intelligence test was devised to correct and replace a class system of selection in which the educated middle and upper class child had an unfair advantage.

I was brought up in a London slum in the twenties. I have seen how it was for myself. My experience in Mensa confirms that seventy thousand Mensans, selected for high IQ, come from all social classes and backgrounds. Knowing them in many lands gives no support to the view that intelligence tests select only those from privileged parents. That suggestion is a socially dangerous untruth. It has no warrant.

The criticisms that IQ tests face are welcome to those who believe in them. It is right in the provisional world of science, that everything should be repeatedly challenged. Nothing should be allowed to harden into dogma. Intelligence testing has not been without this needed stimulus. It has had much challenge. But some of the challenge is unhelpful because it is itself based on dogma.

It is preferable that the challenges to scientific ideas should themselves be scientific and objective, not dogmatic and personal. Mental testing is an art and a nascent science that has always irritated a political nerve in the world culture. The Victorian middle and upper class academics did not love a method which threatened the established social order by undermining traditional methods of academic selection.

As a result of Burt's ideas and mental testing the system became fairer to underprivileged children in the forties and fifties in Britain, and middle class parents found that their children had to compete in ability for the grammar school place which they could no longer buy for them. Many such parents joined the egalitiarian socialists in an outcry against selection by any method, however fair and disinterested. There was a fatal alliance of the political extremes but the onslaught on objective tests from the left was of a quite different nature. Many puzzled intellectuals had turned away from the confusion of an age of disruptive, if largely beneficial, change. The accepted religious dogmas had failed them and they turned to the security and the simple and beautiful certainties of Marxist dogma as a substitute. To them, the attempt to replace unscientific, traditional ways of allocating roles in society by a new system based on scientific methods smacked of an attempt to revive the aristocratic principle with a modern rationale. They had read their Rousseau too well and believed that equal rights were the same thing as equal people.

The Leninist view is that the cadres and elites required to transform 'a corrupt society' must arise from self-selected working class-conscious band of brothers. They must form a party to take over all power and responsibility. They would not dare to have truck with any system of 'bourgeois' scientific selection. They wanted to correct one class bias by another.

So the fiercest attack upon the idea of mental testing arises out of left wing dogma. But it is not contained in that dogma. It was Vladimir Ilyitch himself who said, 'From each according to his ability, to each according to his needs'. And his writings contain passages in which it is clear he knows of the need for intelligent leadership.

So in the west, not in Russia, the scientists who have tried to order our thoughts on differences in mental ability and mental excellence are labelled racialists, fascists, elitists and scientific frauds by socialists and Marxists.

One of the strongest Marxist traditions is that of personal attack upon opponents of the prevailing fashion in dogma. This tradition is followed faithfully by the Western Marxists who join the clamour about mental testing.

SO WHAT IS INTELLIGENCE?

The meaning of the term is well understood generally. It is questioned and probed only by those whose political ideas are upset by the idea of human differences.

The thinkers whose ideas helped the formation of the open free society today put forward three powerful and attractive ideas: democracy, liberty and equality. These were to regulate men's dealings with the new, more powerful State. The people shall choose the government which shall govern by law. We shall be free to do as we wish within the law and we shall be equal before the law. There are some throughgoing zealots who interpret the word 'equality' literally. They want equality of outcome rather than equality of opportunity. Where liberty and human differences exist there cannot possibly be equality of outcome. There is not anywhere in this world.

The egalitarian zealots prefer not to face the idea of abolishing liberty as a way of ensuring equal outcome so they are forced to disbelieve in human differences and assert that the visibly diffe-

rent outcomes must always result from different treatment, different opportunities. They are quite happy to take people as being
born indistinguishably alike so as to condemn all economic
differences as discrimination and exploitation.

People with ideas like this have come to many positions of
influence in society in the western world and especially in the
educational field. They have set themselves to play down all
human differences as unimportant. Especially they downgrade or
refuse to accept differences in intelligence because they cause
differences of outcome. The inheritance of intelligence is an
especially painful thought because it smacks of the rejected ideas
of inherited rank and privilege. These are the very things the new
ethos was against.

One brand of extremist is so desperate about the contradiction
to his thinking created by the differences in intelligence that he
claims that the concept is an unreal one, a reification, like
phlogiston. Intelligence is a word without objective meaning
invented to justify privilege!

It is from these quarters that the challenging question about
how to define intelligence comes most often. The most sensible
answer to the question, 'How do you define intelligence?' is
simply, 'You don't'.

There are many ideas and concepts which we understand
without need or ability to define them. I cannot define an elephant
or a flea. If I truthfully say that Joan is cleverer than Fred and you
understand me, there has been useful communication though
neither can define 'clever'. You will have more accurate expectations.

The attempt to conjure a well established concept out of
existence by the challenge to define it is simply a political posture.
No one really believes that 'clever' and 'stupid' are meaningless
terms. However the real challenge to understand that most
mysterious manifestation in the universe, intelligence, must be
met.

The science of mental measurement, psychometry, is the very
first attempt to apply the rigorous quantitative method which had
been so successful in other sciences to the human mind. 'The
proper study of mankind', said Alexander Pope, 'is man'. 'Poss-

ibly', we might reasonably reply, 'but it is also the most difficult'. Whatever the difficulties it seems to be a study we are wise to make because mankind has started down an adventurous track which has created new problems.

The track is the amplification of human intelligence by means of scientific industrialism. This has created a vast complex interrelated world civilisation. Relative to the span of man's history it is entirely new. It cannot be sustained in traditional ways. There is no going back. There are now too many of us on the earth for that.

The norm for Man on earth over millions of years has been small primitive territorial societies. These have depended heavily on the human propensity to classify and judge neighbours. In successful clans and tribes men and women have had to know what can be expected of each other.

Without some predictive knowledge of behaviour not even the smallest human social group can survive the challenges of a hostile environment. Mankind has always classified tribesmen as being strong-willed, lazy, brave, nervous, clever, stupid and so on. And the classifications have acquired labels, words which made it possible for tribesmen to communicate such expectations. In a tribe that lives by close co-operation in the hunt and war, the usefulness of such ways of verbalising expectations of behaviour is obvious. Clever, canny, thoughtful tribesmen have always been recognised and valued, with or without definitions.

Today's expanding society is only a few hundred years old. Our bodies and minds were not evolved for anything like it. Today we have to be in reacting contact with many more people and groups than the tribesmen we are designed to be. We have to learn to cope in large impersonal institutions such as schools, firms, local authorities, governments. There is a new need. The face-to-face group behaviour judgements are no longer good enough.

We have to try to systematise and order our behaviour classifications in a more rigorous and scientific and therefore more just way. We have to meet the new and unpredictable behavioural needs of an entirely new type of society. It will no longer do to make and pass on judgements of reputations; the circles are too large, the varieties of behaviour too many and too complex.

To develop the scientific ways of handling this old human skill we have to turn to one of the hardest of the admittedly soft social sciences, psychometry.

Psychometry, like all the other sciences, has to develop from the art that preceded it.

Those of us who, in traditional, small, face-to-face groups can best judge the character and ability of the others in our group will make better guesses at their behaviour and do best for themselves and for their group. Groups which are better at conceptualising each other's behaviour and describing and communicating ideas about it will function and survive better than those that fail in these things. This is the way at the pre-scientific stage, at the stage of the art of character judgement.

That is still all right in families and societies at the clan level. But the developed world has gone irretrievably beyond that stage. We have large mass societies of incredible complexity and the methods that serve simpler societies are no longer appropriate. This seems to me to be the reality behind the development of psychometry.

How do we develop the science from the art? How do we decide about the character we ascribe to our neighbours? Consciously or otherwise we compare their behaviour with that of others over a period. Now whether the conclusions we draw about the characteristics or traits we see in people are real distinguishable aspects of the physical world, or whether they are mental models set up to act as behaviour predictors, does not matter. There may be no such thing as 'bravery' as an observable, objective reality in the brain of the subject but there is agreement in any group about what is brave behaviour and who is brave. And the concept is socially useful, predictive. It communicates something which has its own reality, a reality which is essential to the survival of a hunter, gatherer group.

What the primitive human group member looks at are human differences, predictable human differences, which help a group to survive because the members know what to expect of each other.

One of these differences between people, which was of importance in all societies, but is much more important now, is difference in intelligence.

People are different from each other in size, strength, bravery and laziness. They also differ in their ability to collect information, conceptualise it, summarise it, classify it, codify it, process it, communicate it, and use it to plan and execute actions which will benefit their group, their family or themselves.

The science of psychometrics is simply the attempt to order, systematise and standardise whatever it is that goes on in the human mind when judgement of individuals, of characteristics, of reputation, is being formed. We do not have to define bravery, honesty, intelligence or manual skill in order to assess our fellows in these respects and benefit from our assessment.

Wide reading in this field reveals that the dismissive attacks on intelligence tests are advanced usually by those with leftist political views.

There are few that support them uncritically but those who accept their limited validity quote statistics, facts, problems and doubts. Their writings are mild and reasonable. They do not indulge in polemics. They take account of other views. They want improvements, more research, and think tests do a useful job.

The arguments associated with leftist political convictions are different. They are polemical, they include personal attacks. The writers use moral arguments. They write about subjective ideas, 'justice', 'exploitation' and 'discrimination' in connection with attempts to understand human differences. They are deeply concerned with the motivation of the researchers. They advance no evidence from their own field researches. The arguments advanced are selective, detailed, negative criticisms of psychometric researches and researchers.

Let me give just one example from Professor Leon J. Kamin. 'The IQ test in America, and the way we think about it, has been fostered by men committed to a particular social view. That view includes the believe that those on the bottom are genetically inferior victims of their own immutable defects. The consequence has been that the IQ test has served as an instrument of oppression against the poor – dressed in the trappings of science, rather than politics.'

In his book *The Science and Politics of IQ* he quotes examples of extreme views to support his case that IQ testing is a form of racism, which are selectively culled from a period at the beginning of the century when racial and political chauvinism were quite normal in the western world. Some people of racialist views *did* quote mental tests in their arguments, but it not safe to condemn a technique on the grounds that someone with views to which we object has quoted from it. We do not reject Christ because Hitler quoted from the Bible. Kamin ignores the evidence that most pioneers of testing had a motivation like his own. Accepting that societies have to allocate roles somehow, the test advocates an oojective scientific method rather than one based on class and privilege.

Kamin gained world publicity because the media love nothing better than discovering the 'feet of clay' of a respected authority. Kamin's book was a sustained and unscrupulous, posthumous assassination of the character of Professor Sir Cyril Burt, who had been the doyen of psychometric psychology.

I declare my prejudice and interest. Sir Cyril's kind, wise, patient counsel was invaluable to me in the difficult early days of Mensa's international development.

Kamin's main attack was on some transparently faulty work on twin studies. An ageing man's carelessness was presented as deliberate fraud and there was an enormous press scandal around the world in which Burt was castigated unmercifully as a scientific cheat and swindler.

But was Burt motivated by a desire to oppress the poor as Kamin suggested all such workers were? To anyone who knew him it is absurd to have to defend him from such a charge.

In his report to The London County Council of 1915/1916 Burt said that many educationalists were astonished by the difference in the proportion selected for scholarships (free places at grammar schools) in various districts by the old type academic tests.

At that time there was a big change going on in British education. The traditional system was one in which working class children went to free schools while the middle classes paid for places at schools for studious children called grammar schools.

The first change was that bright working class children were getting places at these grammar schools. Poor able children were selected by an academic scholarship examination.

Sir Cyril noticed that in 1913 prosperous districts had seventy scholarships per ten thousand compared with two in poor districts. Sir Cyril proposed intelligence tests to correct the unfair conditions which handicapped children who came from poor and sometimes semi-literate homes. He saw the intelligence test as a means to reduce the disadvantages: 'So far from the new test questions favouring the educated middle class type of parent, as our critics allege, the demonstrable effect was to reduce the disproportionate number of scholarships going to the privileged few. Thus in the sample borough in which our most intensive surveys were carried out, the number of scholarship winners coming from working class homes rose from 1.8 percent to 3.5 percent.'

Eventually, due to pressure from those in Britain of the same view as Kamin, the system of objective selection advocated by Burt was dropped in the interests, we were told, of justice.

The result was the reverse of what was intended. Professor Stephen Wiseman points out that when the tests were dropped in Hertfordshire in 1952 the number of grammar school places allocated to the children of manual workers fell from 14.9 percent to 11.5 percent. The percentage allocated to the children of professional and managerial parents rose from 39.6 to 63.6 percent. Wiseman was clear about it. 'The conclusion I draw', he wrote, 'is that although modern intelligence tests are far from culture-free, they are significantly less affected by adverse factors in the home and school environment, than are tests of attainment. Whenever we are concerned to perform educational selection, the use of such tests will reduce the dependence of our results on occupational class, on socio-economic level, on differences in the quality of teaching and schools and all other adventitious environmental factors'.

From this kind of evidence we begin to see the motivation of the middle class British parent who found that the fairer, more objective system of selection by IQ Tests brought a lot of working class competition for places in the schools suitable for studious children. Prosperous parents found they could no longer buy a place for the less academic or less studious child who had been displaced by the bright working class child. The political climate prevented a return to the older system. So the disappointed parents turned against any kind of specialist education for able studious children. They joined the vociferous left in the demand for comprehensive schools. There was to be no selection of any kind. Mixed ability schools, even mixed ability classes where all the children advance in lockstep at the pace of the slowest. This is what became the fashion. A single generation of British educationalists set about undoing the work of their forebears over centuries. They brought about the destruction of one of the world's best secondary education systems, the one that had brought Britain to a very respected place in the world of science and scholarship.

Over the next twenty years hundreds of first class grammar schools which had built up precious traditions of scholarship and excellence over hundreds of years were dismantled or destroyed in what amounted to a concerted campaign of cultural vandalism. A vast, cumbersome network of costly, inefficient, and often disorderly new factories called comprehensive schools was set up to replace them. Under the Burt scheme the class bias, which had certainly been a feature of these schools earlier, had disappeared because selection was on ability only but the enthusiastic destruction went forward just the same.

Very soon, as Wiseman showed, the inequality which was thought to have been thrown out of the door came back, as it always does, through the window. Today some comprehensive schools are more equal than others. In prosperous districts some have partially inherited the good traditions of the grammar schools and are fairly good. Others in areas of inner city decay are indescribably bad; they turn out the illiterate, innumerate young people that are finding life in our technological society so difficult. The highly intelligent child from the working class districts who would have got a scholarship under the benevolent Burt's scheme has now got to wait for the 'irreversible transformation of society in favour of working people' upon which the procrustean anti-elitist ideologues have set their hopes.

My point has been to show that the intelligence test is an instrument of social justice as well as a tool to make the invidious job of role selection which has to be performed more justly.

Those who from the same motives as the test advocates – concern for fairness, justice and equal opportunity – have taken the opposite path, pretending to ignore human differences. They have always and will always produce an effect which is the opposite of their intention.

Much worse, in an age when we shall need all our talent to solve our problems, they are neglecting and wasting that most precious human resource, conceptual intelligence. Their well-motivated but desperately mistaken actions have not only decreased equality; they have impoverished all.

It is interesting to speculate on the course that history would have taken if early socialists had been truer to their scientific pretensions and had recognised the importance of well trained brains to the planned society we sought in the twenties and thirties.

In a confused age of traumatic social change, most intellectuals were attracted by the idea of a centrally planned society which would bring 'reason' to bear on human political and industrial affairs instead of leaving them to the 'cruel, blind forces of the market'. Central democratic control, the nationalisation of all industry and commerce: these were to solve all the messy problems of the new, more prosperous but unfamiliar and confused society which was so painfully being born.

Eager Five Year Planners and Nationalisers talked the voters round. Large-scale planning by bureaucrats, for politicians became the fashion in the capitalist world as well as in the Soviet one. But they failed to make the most important plan of all: 'The Plan for Planners'. The socialist governments which suddenly found themselves in control of complex, highly interrelated industrial systems, both in the East and the West, expected that the right, high-flying, organisational talent would quickly be identified and attracted to serve. They forgot that entrepreneurial skill is self-selecting in the sense that it emerges best, unbidden, under competition.

And they selected and empowered a succession of civil service administrators, worn-out politicians and trade union leaders for the Big Job. Those they chose had not been trained to be self-starter entrepreneurs. They had been trained to limit and restrain them. So with exactly the wrong attitudes and habits, they were set to make and administer the largest scale, most complex, intercorrelated plans ever known in the world.

In the UK they supervised the destruction of large parts of previously dominant British industry. The nationalised industries became the political footballs of successive governments and were run so as to please vested interests such as trade unions and to make life easy for the Government by avoiding the tough decisions that are needed to keep industry efficient.

Things are a little better now but most nationalised industries, for most of their time, have led a parasitic existence with their begging bowls out to the taxpayer. They have become producers' monopolies, with management and workers able to take the soft option that is not available to those who pay for it.

It might have been a different world if the eager socialists had sought and found the high-flyer managers and administrators that could have given the planning experiment a better try. We tried to replace unfair class-based selection methods by those with the opposite bias.

If scientific and thus objective and fair methods of selection of ability and talent had not been condemned by egalitarian bigots, centralist policies would have had a better chance. But it was just the old 'jobs for the boys' with different boys. There are signs that some communist countries, belatedly, have learned this lesson and done rather better at locating, training and using talent within a centralist system, than the West has done at that difficult job. The West, of course, under the self-selection system it favours, has done much better overall.

So much for the politically motivated arguments against mental testing. They are not the only ones.

The more scientific doubts about the art are more reasonable; they are couched in a more temperate tone, reveal no ideological predispositions and are therefore to be taken more seriously. Most of them seem to be directed, not against the art itself, but against some of the more exaggerated claims for it that have been made by its enthusiasts or implied by its opponents. They can best be answered by a restatement of what is claimed for the art nowadays after nearly a century of development.

The claim is made that children and adults can be usefully classified on an approximate scale of conceptual mental ability by means of a simple test administered by a trained person. The claim is made subject to certain primary assumptions.

It is assumed that the subject is willing and is motivated by a desire to score as well as possible. It is not possible to test an unwilling person.

The test results are valid only if the conditions under which it is standardised are observed when the test is taken. It is the duty of the test supervisor, usually a professional psychologist, to make sure that every subject has the same time and works under the same conditions as applied to the original groups or individuals during the development of the test.

A further condition of the claims is that the subjects under test shall be very familiar with and within the range of variation of the language/culture group upon which the original test sample was based. It is, of course, a further condition that the subject shall be of sound mind and in reasonably good health at the time of test. They should also be within the age range of the test group. Minor things like having a cold, menstruation, and headaches have been shown not to be of great importance in test-retest validations.

Given all that, and bearing in mind that there are in many countries very large groups which are relatively monocultural from the point of view of education and language, the following claims and nothing more can be made and sustained for intelligence tests.

These are claims that, under the conditions, can be made. No more.

Carefully prepared tests, standardised on the relevant population can, after statistical validation, classify people with that population into predictive mental ability groups within a considerable degree of fairness and validity. The classifications derived seem to relate to some permanent and persistent aspect of the subject's personality and are more predictive and reliable than the unaided judgement or any other similar method of classification so far developed.

The classifications arising from the tests are useful to psychiatrists and psychologists for diagnosis and thus of great benefit to the patient. When used with knowledge, training and care, they are of great help to educationalists (those among them who wish to know), in helping students to make wise choices for education and career. They can help the teacher to avoid, and guide parents to avoid, either of the cardinal educational errors. They avoid encouraging unrealistic aims on the one hand and underchallenge and waste of talent on the other. Perhaps more important, mental testing has a place in singling out those who will be happy in and benefit from higher education or any other type of sophisticated education or training.

It is one of the claims for mental tests that, used with training, knowledge and skill, they can assist employers, managers, and authorities in the vital and difficult task of good and efficient and just allocation of occupational roles.

Although many mental testers think that there is a component in mental differences that is genetic in origin it is not a necessary part of these claims. If it were finally proved that all differences in manifest intelligence are due to the environment (a great compliment to child care by the middle classes), it would make no difference to the usefulness and predictive validity of the tests.

These and only these are the claims. They will be rejected by the politicised objectors and some of them will be rejected by some psychologists. To answer them we can only point to the amazing durability and world-wide spread of the art for nearly a century despite an unending barrage of objection. Intelligence tests are completely discredited several times a year in all the popular newspapers and even in the scientific journals of different disciplines, but the rumours of their demise always turn out to have been exaggerated.

If it is true, as it is the recent fashion to believe, that differences between people in the power to see relationships, understand concepts, and solve problems are entirely due to the way they were brought up then I dare say that the middle and upper classes whose children can be shown to do better at these tasks will manage to live with the implied compliment. Working class people whose children do not do well at school might resent the slur on their methods of child care and upbringing implied.

Mensa, as a world-wide body of people selected by a simple intelligence test, can throw some light. If some of the extreme critics of the tests are right, then what we have been selecting over the last four decades has been a random sample of people. By the time this is published there will be seventy thousand of us. Now I have met more Mensans in more places than anyone else and so my report may be of relevance. I can only ask you to accept my judgement that they are not random at all but an extremely bright and interesting bunch.

Earlier in the chapter I skated round the definition question, saying that we did not need to define a concept that was universally understood. 'We have raised a dust', said Bishop Berkeley and now we complain that we cannot see!

When a science emerges from the art which preceded it there is the problem of the words to be used. Older words with vaguer meanings are sometimes selected and the meaning is made more precise for the purpose of the science.

Galton and Binet made statistical observations which established a usefulness of a concept that had only been sensed intuitively before. They needed a word for it. What they began to see was that which Spearman was later to show very clearly, that among the many ways for humans to be different there was one which had no clear name that was free of other connotations. 'Level of ability at a wide range of cognitive tasks' would be a way of describing it.

What they observed unequivocally is that children who are good at any task involving the comprehension of conceptual or symbolic systems, such as words, patterns or numbers, tended to be good at any other such task. Those that are bad at one tend to be bad at all. I *did* say tend.

There was a variable quality, 'general ability', at this kind of task and problem. Ability at a range of such tasks was not randomly distributed but has a biassed distribution. Children with high 'g' scores do well all round. Binet chose the French word 'habileté' (skill, cleverness) for the quality but in England Galton and Burt chose the word 'intelligence', which until then usually meant 'information', as it still does in the sense of military intelligence. They might have chosen 'versatility'.

What was emerging and what has now been established beyond controversion is that, generally speaking, conceptual, cognitive ability is 'unfairly' distributed. 'To them that hath shall be given' applies.

Professor Thurstone thought he had established that the different cognitive abilities are independent of each other and his work got wide publicity, but he had to concede that he was in error. (He had worked with a sample of students who were all bright. This reduced the range of variation and invalidated the conclusion.) His retraction got much less publicity and I have seen recent accounts of the claim which do not mention the retraction.

Every attempt to use factor analysis to get rid of 'g', the general factor of intelligence, by 'rotating it away' has failed and Spearman's 'g' remains. Spearman's scheme was that, apart from the 'g' factor which affects our ability at everything we do, there are a number of special ability factors ('s' factors) which affect our ability at particular tasks and account for the unevenness underlying the broad general truth of the above.

Now I feel that the growing understanding of information theory and data processing gives us a base for a better understanding of this mysterious quality intelligence. I think we can make new distinctions and clarify thinking, so let me propose a newer frame of reference for the purpose.

It is quite usual to apply the word intelligence to other animals and even to birds when their behaviour shows evidence of optimisation, learning by experience. We use the word when behaviour seems to be influenced by a combination of observation and memory or where it shows anticipation or the animal is obedient to words and other signals. While this kind of intelligence corresponds to one sense of the word it is not this sense we mean when we use the technical word 'intelligence' as measured in people, the IQ type intelligence. The intelligence shown by animals corresponds to what psychologists called psychomotor intelligence in people the ability to learn bodily skills (other than speech). This is the ability to optimise behaviour directed to some goal.

When we try to make computer hardware and software perform the simplest animal tasks of perception, classification and adaptive response, we soon learn what an enormous amount of data processing is involved.

A man (or any mammal) has over one hundred million nerves simultaneously signalling to his brain and when he acts on this information he has to send out instructions to about a million nerves. So walking along the road while seeing, recognising and avoiding obstacles is a data handling task that is wildly beyond the possibility of any computer today. In sheer terms of the number of channels and the amount of data to be processed such 'simple' tasks are beyond our comprehension so far.

Now to the intelligence we rate so highly, the conceptual intelligence that deals in symbols, solves larger problems and begins to comprehend the universe. We can communicate 'thoughts', the output of this kind of intelligence, by means of words, a string of symbols passed one at a time at an extremely low rate of transfer. In terms of information theory the data exchange in speech and reading is insignificant by the standards of a computer and zero by the very much higher standards of the data handling in each of our brains when used for psychomotor tasks. So how do we come to rank this 'thinking–speaking' intelligence which stumbles along at a word or two a second as in any way 'higher' than psychomotor intelligence?

Riding a bicycle, playing tennis, and the physical act of writing out mathematical propositions are all data handling problems which are more complex by many orders than the manipulation of written and verbal symbols called mathematics. This is shown by the growing tendency for the computer to take over more of the mathematician's tasks.

The answer is plain. The primitive, slow, monolinear symbol manipulation systems called thinking, ratiocination, speaking and listening are ranked much higher because their effects on us and our society are much greater. The animal brain can command its one body to act. A human brain can command or persuade a team or a tribe or an army to act.

We are social animals. The actions of groups are more important to humans and their survival than the actions of individuals. We value conceptual intelligence because it passes detailed information within communities, tribes, firms, nations, co-operating groups of people. Conceptual intelligence is special intelligence. It is part of and belongs to the collectivity of which it is a part. It cannot be expressed or have effect outside it. We each perceive our little bit of it and think we see the totality, but our bit is simply part of the working of the social 'brain' that runs the group or institution.

Conceptual intelligence would be of little use to a non-social animal. It is unlikely that it would even develop in man in the absence of social contact. It certainly would not be observable or measurable. The behaviour of Helen Keller (who was deaf and blind from birth), before and after she was taught, shows the emergence of conceptual intelligence. Before teaching she had only psychomotor intelligence.

Let us take an imaginative visit to the emergence of this conceptual mentality in mankind. How did it arise? For some millions of years there have been wandering bands of hunter-gatherer hominids and we have an idea how they lived by observing primitive tribes and some of the surviving simian species today. They lived in mutually repelling, territorial, co-operating bands which are kept together and led by a dominant leader. It is a fairly successful long surviving life-style to be found in many places.

One could see the tribe as what I have described as a morphostat (any self-organising system which behaves as if it had the purpose of preserving its form through time with as little change as possible). Like an individual living creature the tribe seems to act so as to optimise its chances of preserving its existing form through time. The only kind of change a morphostat tends to accept is a progressive one, one which is an improvement. That is a change which *increases* its power to preserve its form with as little change as possible through time.

This surviving entity, the tribe, is a living thing itself, a morphostat. Its elements, people, were born and died, but the tribe survived and retained its form. Like all other active morphostats, the tribe needed an organisation structure, some sort of 'brain' to co-ordinate behaviour and a signalling system by which the centre and the elements (people) communicate, instruct and inform, each other. Apes have this in the form of the dominant male who acts as communications centre. They also have quite a language of cries and gestures and expressions for intercommunication. But all of these signals communicate a single emotional tone; none communicates a concept. But they served well enough. Mankind has cries and gestures too. But man has something else. Speech. Man got past the *cry* expressing emotion to the *word* expressing the thing and the *sentence* expressing a combination of things, an event.

Early forms of man seem to have lived in these co-operating groups by hunting intelligently in packs and by searching for and collecting food. For both these activities communication is very helpful. There was another activity. Fighting. Tribes had to deter others from invading their territorial back yard. Here even more performance can be improved by better communication.

We can learn about primitive life by looking at sport. Many sports seem to bring us a surrogate taste of the tribal life for which we were bred and for which we have a hidden yearning to return at least in play. When I played rugby in England I enjoyed a brief glimpse of the lifestyle of the preverbal hominids, we shouted and pointed during the game but once it started we were like any other hominid tribe. British Army rugby is no feast of conceptual communication. But American football has an element of the postverbal hominid, of nascent man, during the game. The difference is the plan. The little huddle before each play is a brief verbal exchange in symbol form, in words, and by its means much more elaborate, unpredictable, co-operative behaviour is possible.

I imagine that the system of cries and gestures in some hominids developed into speech much like this. Under evolutionary competitive pressure the communication improved and the noises made carried more meaning until the word meaning 'the thing' instead of the cry meaning 'how I feel' arose. And the word led to the most important human development of all, the sentence. When words could be combined then, at a stroke, a new kind of mental activity had arisen, for this is an activity which works at an entirely different level. This is what made complex social interactions possible. Intelligence in the tribe had risen from a tactical to a strategic level. Much more complex, adaptive and surprising plans could be made for war and the hunt. Places where food could be gathered could be communicated by words so it was not needed to take the slow journey to show.

And very much more importantly there was a means of social heredity. Knowledge and skills could be passed on through the generations in a tribe instead of lost with the dying man's brain. Successful social practices could be passed on so that a new, more rapid kind of evolution could start, the evolution of tribal patterns. Those tribes passing on successful and viable patterns of behaviour with this new verbal tool survived and spread; those that stumbled on to poorer patterns died out. Those that had no social heredity method had no speech and also died out.

The development of speech must have caused a very sudden leap in the evolution of the brain because of the interaction between brain development and speech development. Once there was conceptual speech then a conceptually skilled brain became a great advantage to the tribe. Speech made the developments of artefacts possible because there was now a medium for the communication and preservation of arts and skills in the tribe despite the death of the skilled individual. There was a new social heredity to back up the old genetic one. The tribe, the social unit, had the essentials of progress and evolution: a source of mutations and a basic social heredity for selection to operate upon. The earlier form of such social heredity may have been religion which carried socially valuable behaviour practices between generations. And different, competitive ethical and moral systems (behaviour modifiers) were subjected to trial-and-error elimination or replication on the substrate of a competing world of tribes. Our moral codes are survivors.

So, according to this way of seeing things, thinking is a social act. It is part of the mental activity of the various groups in which and upon which you act. Conceptual intelligence is your networking ability.

Each cell of your body has a nucleus, an informational organisation centre. Its language is messenger RNA. Your whole body has an informational and organisation centre, your brain; its language is nerve impulses. You live in and completely depend on surviving social entities of various kinds and, this is more confusing, each of them has its central organisation system or networking system in which information is being exchanged. The language in this case is symbolic: words, written or spoken. But the function of this network of information is the same as in the lower level cases, the preservation of the institutional form (and its members with it).

The confusion is that, unlike the tribesman who is part of a single social unit, you can function in a plurality of institutions taking a different role in each. The individual social unit is *not* individual. It can break up and reform like another, different morphostat, a swarm of bees.

But your thinking in words, your conceptual thinking is just a part of a group's social activity with a purely social function. And I suggest that when we say that someone is intelligent we mean he is good at that part of his mental activity which is communicable, which has a social function. I may spend a year writing this book and may fool myself that something has happened. In fact nothing has happened until you complete our joint social act by reading it. The fact that you can read it and understand it shows that you must have a receptor thinking organ that is fully prepared for the message. Thus you are part of the activity and it is without effect on the universe unless you or some other prepared receiver participates.

The social (conceptual, IQ-type) intelligence is much simpler in terms of data handling but much more important because it works at a higher, that is, more strategic and less tactical level. It can have an enormous amplification factor in its effect upon the world. It can move armies and mountains, change the face of the earth, for better or for worse. This is why it is right to try to measure it and understand it and wickedly wrong to sweep it under an ideological carpet as a politically inconvenient notion.

Let me try to put the idea of intelligence into an even wider context.

It was Descartes who first put forward the idea I mentioned above when he asserted that animals could not think because they have no language. I think he was right at least in the normal sense of conceptual thinking. It was also Descartes who said, 'I think therefore I am'. His own existence is the only incontrovertible fact. But note that he said it. Who was he talking to? He established grounds for solipsism and proved he did not believe in it by the same statement.

Due to the interaction of many intelligences within a growing international communications network, knowledge and understanding are advancing at a frightening pace. So I propose to look at this world-changing quality, intelligence, from an even broader perspective.

Some experts who are working at the interface between us and the unknown are beginning to promise us or threaten us with the possibility that there may soon be another sort of conceptual intelligence on Earth to compete with or combine with man's intelligence. This will not be an alien intelligence in space ships but, they say, a human creation, Artificial Intelligence.

Some other experts seem to have the faith and courage to say that such a thing is by its nature impossible but those that know most about computers and the brain seem to lack so much blind faith. I incline to the more cautious view that it would be unwise to rule out the possibility of thinking machines.

Given that, the implications of this possible advance in technology are so immense that it might be worth your time to look at an overview.

We in Mensa may have to think, for instance, about what we shall do about an applicant in the form of hardware, what test we shall need, and whether we accept android voting rights or just discriminate.

I ask three questions about Intelligence and I use the tricky word now in a sense akin to 'mind' or 'sapience': What? Whence? Whither?

WHAT?

I have already said that the communicable, strategic level

intelligence starts with man but in the extended sense we see it manifest in the higher animals and, if we go downwards on the *scala naturae* towards the primitive forms, we cannot see any sharp dividing line where it first appears.

May I accept the teleological nature of intelligence. There is or seems to have to be some purpose before it can be manifest. The essential feature is the act of using information to optimise the probability of some *desired* outcome. If that is accepted then we can go as far as we like down the evolutionary scale and we shall not find any place in biology where there is not the use of information to make optimising decisions between options. The feeding and excretion of the simplest prokaryote cell is a form of choosing, accepting and rejecting, optimising.

And what is that chooses? We think of it as a material thing, but what we are looking at is a thing like a fountain, not a thing like a stone. It is not a thing at all but a form. The genome and the cytoplasm of a bacterium are a flux of change. The material substrate of the persistent form is ever-changing, the atoms and molecules are constantly being exchanged and the genome is under constant repair. What remains, the bacterium, is not material, though it exists only on a material substrate; it is form, pattern. The laws of form-like entities can be different from those of physical ones because the forms are not material at all.

And living form behaves teleologically, as if it had the purpose of preserving that form through time. By repair, maintenance and replication it seems as if it wants to go on existing. The word intelligence comes from the Latin *intellegere*, to choose. It chooses. It optimises. It has in some tiny measure something like we have to use when we use information from the universe and transduce it into actions as we try to avoid that irreversible change in our form that death brings. It has primitive intelligence.

WHENCE?

Any starting point for intelligence other than the beginning of life brings an arbitrary line, a falsification. All living things are not in fact what they seem, solid objects; they are surviving forms; they are immaterial; they are like information itself which is again form and only form. I can replicate or transduce a string of signals on to many different substrates but it retains its essential nature and effect, its form. Words mean the same as sounds, marked paper, or something happening in my brain. I can put a computer program on tape or disk or carry it in RAM, and it is unaffected. I can make a billion copies and each will have exactly the same effect on a proper receiver. Life and information alike are immaterial forms carried as far as we know, always on a material substrate.

Now I suggest that information and that other thing like it called 'life' are a higher order reality which exists in the universe and, while entirely subject to its laws, or what seem like laws, its patterns of probability. Life and Mind can create their own set of overriding laws which are independent of but consistent with the physical laws. We do not need the concept spirit. These are not mystical statements.

Of course if the universe were, as some think, really governed by strictly determinist laws, what I describe would be impossible. But, since Heisenberg, we know that we cannot either affirm or deny strict determinism. We can account for all we see without it and our direct perception that we have choices and options should encourage us to accept an indeterminate universe as the default hypothesis. What seem like inflexible laws are really enormously high probabilities at the level we live, in the mesocosm (which is between the microcosm and the macrocosm). Nothing anyone can say in words can make me disbelieve what I directly perceive: that I have choices and that my life depends on the choices I make. Amplified microcosmic interdeterminism can, as Eccles showed, explain mesocosmic options.

WHITHER?

So I can begin to describe the pattern of life and intelligence at various levels and see which way the trend line points.

(1) At the lowest level we have what Schroedinger called that aperiodic crystal, the genome, the self-repairing double helix, billions of pairs long, which is like a computer program, a long string of information which can be read by its CPUs, the ribosomes in the cell, to make and replicate its proteins. It

seems to have an internal variation mechanism which chooses and offers slightly mutated forms of its pattern, its form, for choice by the physical world. World chooses the viable. The cell replicates, preserves its form through time, accepting only changes that make it better able to do so. The eukaryote cell has an organisation centre, a brain, and a constant traffic of networking chemical signals carried by messenger RNA.

(2) The next step arises from the symbiotic combination of cells to make more elaborate, more viable living forms, metazoa, animals. These evolve a different form of central processor, organisation centre, a brain and a network of nerves to carry information around the system.

(3) Some animals combine in social networks to live symbiotically. These social combinations are also morphostats, form-preserving, non-material beings, they too develop internal networks, signalling systems, to aid them in survival. The information here is carried in symbolic form, the bee's dance, the antennae language of the ants, cries, gestures in animals and speech in man. And in man who depends on his sociality, each has developed a part of his personal communications centre, brain, which is also part of the group or tribe centre, the speech areas where the social activity of conceptual thinking goes on.

(4) As I say in a later chapter, there is now a combination at an even higher level which is bringing together human groups and institutions into a world-scale, intercommunicating entity which I call the 'world culture'. What we call the 'market' is a brain, a part of the 'world culture'.

(6) So, following the trend, we may expect, that a very long way into the future, the Intelligence then manifest on Earth will contact other Intelligences, other forms of 'mind' and form a new synthesis. Perhaps Earth brain will then have biological form, perhaps it will be an artefact living upon a non-biological substrate produced by the bio-form. Perhaps it will be a symbiotic combination of the two. Perhaps Earth Intelligence, or as it may then be Solar System Intelligence will contact, contest and finally combine with other Intelligence, other forms of 'mind' out there in the galaxy or beyond.

Coming back to Mensa is a steep descent. But perhaps for a time it may play some small part in this rather large scheme of things.

— 5 —

Nature or nurture?

I have pointed out that it is irrelevant to the usefulness of mental tests whether or not what is measured arises from nature or nurture, or both. It is equally irrelevant from the point of view of Mensa. It might be comforting for those who do well on tests to accept the compliment to themselves and their family implied by the environmentalist view. There is more merit in what we achieve through effort than in what we get without it as would be the case if mental ability were settled at birth. Either way it makes no difference. The tests are helpful and predictive either way. Mensa has a stimulating and attractive atmosphere either way. Tests have no effect on human breeding so the genetics of mental excellence does not matter.

However, the question in the title of this chapter is a vexed and contentious one upon which people and the media are curious to hear my view. I must first emphasise again that Mensa has no collective view on this or any other subject. In fact, members have a wider range of views on this subject, as on all others than will be found in unselected groups of similar size. That, at least, is my experience. But there may be a majority view.

The questions are put simply, too simply. Are the wide differences in general mental ability seen among people due to genetic heredity or social inheritance? Are they due to differences of upbringing and lifestyle, which are passed on by family upbringing, or are they predetermined by the genome (the set of genes inherited from the parents).

I am a layman, but I am a very interested layman who has, for obvious reasons, read most things on the subject for thirty-five years. All I can do for my reader is give a general impression. What is the effect of a mass of contentious and contradictory views on the subject upon the mind of an unbiassed autodidact who had no possible professional or political axe to grind?

My strongest general impression is that the whole subject generates a disproportionate degree of polemic and emotional invective. The area of the debate has become a desperate intellectual battle ground, and all the proponents are enjoying a great and glorious battle of insults in which common sense and truth are equally forgotten.

It will be as instructive to determine the reason why the contenders are so heated as to investigate the question itself. I shall try to throw some light upon both questions.

My first task is to point out the false antithesis in the way the question itself is posed. The hidden assumption is that the differences in mental ability we observe can only have one of the two causes. The possibility that the differences may have dual causation seems, suspiciously, to have been left out of account by one side in the dispute, as we shall see. I say suspiciously because the view that either heredity or environment can possibly be completely without effect on mental performance is so glaringly silly. It can be decisively disposed of in two sentences. They take the form of thought experiments:

1) Separate two similar twins at birth, bring one up normally and have the other brought up by deaf mutes in a bare cell.

2) Rear a new-born baby and a new-born chimpanzee together giving them identical treatment.

Those and only those who expect either of the two pairs to be completely alike in mental powers at the end of the test step forward. Congratulations! You have excelled in the human quality, credulity. You have excelled either as a genetic bigot or as an environmentalist one.

It is so glaringly obvious that both what you are born like and what happens to you must have some effect on mental performance that we are going to be a little hard on those who seem to claim that it is otherwise. I have to report that the extreme degree of bigotry is to be found on only one side of the dispute. The most extreme hereditarians claim no more than that eighty percent of the variance is genetic but that is the limit. The hereditarians argue a lot about how much of the variability is caused by heredity and how much by the environment. Some argue pessimistically that it will never be possible to make any estimates of the differing contributions of the two factors. The hereditarians seem to cover the whole range of political views. They disagree among themselves, argue in a mild and moderate fashion, avoid personalities, invective and emotion and give the impression that they are seeking to find the truth in harassing and difficult circumstances.

The environmentalists are very different. They pin their colours to the absolutist mast. They do not want to hear of any genetic influence at all. They would have us act on the assumption that at least within the human species the genome, which is acknowledged to shape the whole form in humans and animals, is completely without effect on one aspect only, that of cognitive activity. From the point of view of how brainy we are we could all have been cloned from one fertilised egg. In all other respects heredity determines the individual constitution which separates us from the rest of humanity and makes us unique. As regards the most important ability we have, the ability to think and reason, everyone starts the game with exactly the same hand. All is fair and square as it should be.

In case the reader doubts that anyone could really believe such stuff I shall have to turn once again to Professor Kamin who, unashamedly, on the first page of the book I mentioned in the last chapter wrote the following sentence. He says that it is one of the major theses of his influential book: 'There exists no data which should lead a prudent man to accept the hypothesis that IQ test scores are in any degree heritable.' What can one think of the prudence of any man who is prepared to deny the existence of anything at all? Proving negative and detailed inspections of all the data in the universe is a tall order. Even if we accept that he meant to say 'of which I am aware', we find the conclusion extreme and very trying on our overworked credulity.

I am suspicious about two things. Firstly I am suspicious that this controversy generates so much heat and secondly I am suspicious because those in this debate who take the environmentalist view seem, all of them, to be of a particular leftist political persuasion. The effect is so marked and the arguments they put are so similar and so vehement and consistent that I am unable to avoid the conclusion that they have unconsciously been doing what they think everyone else is doing, allowing their political views to colour their views on this subject.

The environmentalists are at least frank in that they disclose their socialist or Marxist bias. They seem to accept it as axiomatic that it is wrong and unfair that people should be born with differing mental potential and so, from a sense of justice and human compassion, they manage to believe that there are no such differences or that any there are can only be due to the unjust inequalities of an oppressive, corrupt society. They are indignant because they see tests as an instrument of oppression. They have convinced themselves that social decisions are still based on mental tests which result in disadvantages for the poor. For this serious charge they bring no recent evidence. The evidence that supports this assertion is a careful selection of out-dated quotations from racialist writings early in the century when such views were widespread. The fact that no modern instances are quoted makes me suspect that none can be found. I have seen none.

What I have found is evidence for an opposite conclusion. It is, I believe, the able children who are being handicapped by an increasingly procrustean egalitarian trend in education which often prevents their access to education and training suited to their ability.

There was, for instance, in America, an enormous programme called *Head Start*. Children of low academic achievement were given a very elaborate enrichment programme in carefully arranged surroundings. This was supposed to make a great and beneficial change in their environment which would bring them up to the level of other children. We heard enthusiastic predictions about the programme when it started. After a year or two, things went very quiet. There was no publicity when the expensive experiment was terminated. It turned out to be a complete failure. None of the good results so confidently predicted for it were fulfilled. It was quietly dropped. Programmes like this for high-flyer children are much needed and almost certain to succeed, but there is little enthusiasm and cash for them.

The views of environmentalist bigots about the *deprivation* to which *the poor* and the *handicapped* are subject are further contradicted by this. Public expenditure on retarded children in all the countries of the Western World is very much greater than that on gifted children. There is a great and successful charity effort to ameliorate the lot of those unfortunate children who are mentally handicapped but the funds attracted to support and foster the talent of less privileged gifted children are minimal. And these are the golden ones who hold the key to the future. These are 'the seed corn of humanity' who will make the future. As never before we *do* care for the poor. But for those who, with the right education, can work to abolish the poverty, we do not care. The heated, repeated accusations that intelligence testing harms the poor is truth free.

What of those who take the other side in this dispute, those that believe that we should not dismiss the possibility that genetic heredity may play some part in causing the differences which are so manifest to anyone who looks with open eyes?

Let me summarise the evidence from the other side, from those researchers who have, against the trend of the times, and often facing personal abuse and unpopularity, supported the hypothesis of dual influence, the idea that both heredity and environment have an effect on differences in intelligence.

Much of the counter-argument to *dual effect* views seems to obfuscate rather than clarify, emphasising difficulties and doubts about evidence produced rather than producing falsifying evidence. I must therefore spend some time explaining the ground that is being defended so that it can be seen that most attacks are upon empty positions which are not.

It might be thought rather curious that there is a school of defenders for the *dual effect* view since this was the normal common-sense view which was never questioned until late in this century. That children take after their parents in cleverness as well as everything else has been traditionally taken as obvious. This was not thought to be an environmental effect. No one has expected the resemblance to apply equally to, for instance, adopted children.

The proponents of *dual effect* have, rather courageously, come forward because they feel that someone must counter the views of those who contradict this ancient human belief. They seem to be motivated only by the fear that social policy based on a false view will be mistaken and damaging. They fear 'the Procrustean and intolerant treatment of human individuality in the name of equality', as one of them put it.

So to clear the ground first. This is a summary of the dual effect position.

It is very difficult without experimental control to estimate the respective influence of heredity and environment on mental performance, and it can only be done effectively on fairly homogeneous populations, genetically and socially. However, in an advanced society, where centrally planned social policy reaches to and influences every person, there is a need to make sensible first approximation guesses about it. Otherwise resources will be misspent and ill-directed.

If environment alone is responsible for intelligence differences, social workers could on reasonable humanitarian grounds take retarded children away from parents to cure their handicap. This would be mistaken, cruel and inhuman if the effect might be genetic. Environmentalists should recommend closing those institutions for retarded children which fail to bring their charges up to the average performance.

Families that produced high-flying children ought to be subsidised and encouraged to become foster parents in the interest of improving the nation's mental resources. These policies sound pretty daft but they do follow from the single causation environmentalist hypothesis.

The following approach is a simplification, perhaps even an over-simplification, so as to get a working hypothesis which will serve to guide policy until deeper investigations on the workings of the human brain enable us to get to the roots of the problem.

All research reveals a single obstinate factor, general intelligence, which refuses to be eliminated. It is accepted, in the normal fashion of science, provisionally.

General intelligence varies markedly between people, from the helpless idiot through the retardate, the normal, the bright to the rare genius whose score will not fit on any scale.

Properly devised standardised and validated tests can make orderly and predictive patterns of general intelligence distribution and make predictive assessments of it for individuals.

There is much evidence that throws light on the origin of variations in intelligence. It comes from studies with uniovular and fraternal twins, with siblings and unrelated children, all reared together and apart, and also with relatives of various degrees. The evidence is unequivocal and it is strong.

The evidence is, all of it, consistent with the view that much of the variability in the sort of intelligence that can roughly be measured on tests, could be accounted for most simply by positing a multifactorial genetic trait (or bundle of associated traits) which varies in the normal way between people.

The correlations between the test scores of relatives, the way they vary according to the degree of relationship, the distribution of the scores about the mean, all make a good fit with what would be expected if the effect of environment on score differences, in a fairly homogeneous population of the same broad culture is about a third of the effect of genetic heredity. More simply, the data fits a theory where our genes have about three times as much influence on the differences in test scores as our upbringing.

All the other studies that have been made to support these unexciting conclusions seem to confirm rather than falsify this guess. Children of different heredity brought up in exactly the same environment from birth have a normal range of difference instead of the greatly reduced one that would be expected under a purely environmental hypothesis. Studies of the mean scores of random samples of those from the range of occupations fit in exactly with the common-sense general view of the rank order expected. Studies of the academic and career achievements of parents and children fit very closely to the genetic model and much less closely to the environmental one. The genetic explanation on a multifactorial hypothesis predicts a regression towards the mean. The average score of the children of a parent group that is much above or below average tends to revert towards it to the extent of about half the variation per generation. This accords with Galton's law named in honour of its discoverer, our Sir

Francis. The observed regression fits well with Galton's Law but not with an environmental hypothesis.

The problem of disentangling the two influences is complicated by the fact that, as would be expected, genetic advantages are amplified. In the free and prosperous societies where this kind of research is done the more intelligent persons tend, regardless of their social origin, to create advantageous environmental conditions for their offspring. This makes it more difficult to sort out the influences but there are techniques for handling the problem and the results tend to falsify the one-cause environmentalist explanation of mental differences.

One word of warning, the accounts in the popular press in this field are not to be trusted. The environmentalists have had a signal success in muddying the waters in this field. Being politically motivated they are experts at propaganda, while those who oppose their extremist one-cause views are trying to get an audience for an unpopular view. Half the population is below average and most are close to average so there is a majority who listen to those who say that great mental talent is evidence of class privilege, not of an innate difference. There is a natural envy which has to be faced by those of high intelligence. It is that envy that the egalitarian would-be transformers of society hope to draw on as the engine of change.

The unfortunate Sir Cyril Burt's carelessness and senile dishonesties as a scientists have given these Procrustean Educational Levellers the perfect propaganda tool with which to throw doubt, not only on Burt's own work which is reasonable, but by a sort of sleight of hand, on many other researches which have similar results. They have managed to propagate the view that instead of proving nothing at all, bad research proves the opposite of what the researcher claimed. So, since the 'exposure' of Burt I have found many reporters confident that the genes have no effect on intelligence. All the other studies, and there are very many of them, supporting Burt's general conclusions are ignored or taken to be as flawed as his were. And they were not.

My conclusion on this question is that if I have to choose between the dual cause hypothesis and the single environmental cause hypothesis I must choose without hesitation the traditional view and reject the new, untested one. This has gained wide acceptance not by showing evidence of its truth but by arguing how unfair it would be if it were not true and claiming to refute one man's faulty evidence for an alternative view.

We can ask the question, and it is a reasonable one, which of the two hypotheses should be the default hypothesis, the one to be accepted by society until the matter is resolved by general consent, as most scientific questions are in the end. We cannot always defer all decisions until this happens. We have to go on living and deciding social policy. We might be able to make that decision by thinking about the kind of errors that would result from getting it wrong in either case.

I have already pointed to some of the unusual things we should be doing if we accept the revolutionary new view that genetic inheritance plays no part. We should be blaming decent parents, teachers and social workers if the children in their charge were of low intelligence. We should be constantly changing the environment of retarded children. Any working class groups who are prosperous would be blamed if their children were not up to the standards of middle class people of the same economic level. We should be giving undeserved praise and support to the parents, many from the prosperous classes, who produce very bright children. Those who speak for this view suggest that the only remedy required is to give more spending power to all poor people. But in spite of great increases in the standard of living of the poorest people in all the advanced countries they fail to show any great improvement (judging by the continued complaints of the environmentalists). I feel that the sort of working class family in which I was brought up – one in which we were suffering from what would now be called severe deprivation – was a much better climate for the development of intelligence than many much more prosperous homes today.

The environmentalists never suggest the kind of policy I, satirically, proposed earlier. Yet these silly ideas are perfectly consistent with the views they profess to have. It is not difficult to see why they do not.

I do not accept that they really believe in the nonsense they preach. If we knew the decisions for the education of their children that they have made we might find inconsistencies between declared beliefs and the beliefs which seem to lie behind decisions. This should not astonish anyone. Encapsulated, irrational belief-systems which influence decisions about words but never those about deeds are as common as can be. No one, not even the brightest of us, is immune.

What is so worrying is the bad effect that such popularist preaching is likely to have on educational policy at a time when, because of the informational revolution which is going on it is vital to base administrative decisions on sound, probable and pragmatic grounds. Nothing can stop the rise of a competitive form of intelligence, artificial intelligence, which will be a challenge – I hope a helpful and beneficial one – to human intelligence. To handicap the discovery, motivation, education and training of the best human intelligence at such a time is badly mistaken.

I conclude by saying that there is no data available to the interested and industrious seeker, which would lead a sane and sensible person whose mind is not imprisoned in an irrational dogma, to act on the assumption that all differences in intelligence within the human race are post-natal in origin. There is, on the other hand, plentiful though not conclusive evidence that it would be wise and sensible to act on the traditional view and default hypothesis that many or most of the wide differences in manifest intelligence in fairly homogeneous cultural groups are genetic.

──── 6 ────

What are gifted people like?

The last chapter tells how the measurement of differences of intelligence came about. We may now ask the questions, 'What are highly intelligent people like? Do they differ in other ways than mental ability?'

The art of mental testing was based on research which began with children and was used with adults by extrapolation. There is an underlying assumption, supported by experiment but not fully proved by the pioneers (because it could only be proved after a long time had elapsed), that the differences they were measuring were a permanent feature of the subjects, that the intelligence ranking tended to remain the same as the children grew older. The question was 'Would the early promise be fulfilled?'

There were plenty of urgent voices from those who felt that this ranking of children for mental ability was somehow divisive and unfair. They liked the idea of a natural compensation by which those who were good at one thing would be bad at others. The stereotype of the very bright child was a weedy, unsporting, bespectacled, bookish swot. It was only fair. But was it a true picture?

The intellectual egalitarians also loved that piece of folklore that declares that very high intelligence in young children is 'precociousness' which always 'burns itself out'. Now that a hundred years has passed since Galton's first speculative approaches. What have we found out? Is there a 'fair shares' compensation principle behind the distribution of abilities? Is the 'burn out' theory correct? Are bright children deficient in other ways?

Because of a monumental research of great thoroughness and very long duration and scope the answers are now known. But the conclusions of the research were distasteful to the popular egalitarian fashion in opinion and they clashed with political views which have become very influential in the field of education in the middle of this century. So the research has dropped out of sight, swept under a political and ideological carpet.

But before I give a summary of the results I have to start with a disclaimer.

When you measure differences in human traits such as intelligence you have, whether you know it or not, made the assumption that the traits are (at least to a large extent), independent variables. That is implicit in the research method. It follows then, almost by definition, that there are no other characteristics that correlate with intelligence. Other than in general conceptual ability, very intelligent people should be random. This would dispose immediately of the 'compensation', or 'physically deficient' hypotheses if followed through.

However, the research I mentioned established that the underlying assumption that intelligence was an independent variable was only partially true. While intelligent people are spread right across the range in measurement on all other traits, the distribution is not random. It has biases. The traits turn out not to be fully independent variables: there are intercorrelations significantly above zero.

Intelligent people and Mensa members do spread across the range of human variation on every parameter. I suspect that they have a wider spread of variation than the average, more at the extremes. There are saints and sinners, geniuses and under-achieving dullards, heroes and cowards, mean people and generous ones, energetic and lazy ones, strong and weak ones in the ranks of the bright but they are not there in the same proportion as they are in the population in general.

Mensa itself has people of all occupational and social classes, of all ethnic, cultural and religious origins in its ranks. We have had neurotics, psychotics, criminals, suicides, lunatics, extremists of all kinds and at least one rapist among the hundreds of thousands that have become members through the years. But they are very few relative to our numbers. We have also a very, very large number of fine, decent people who have made and are making a very positive social contribution.

Let us turn to the neglected research I mentioned. Professor Lewis M. Terman was mentioned earlier as he who adapted Binet's 'Mental Ratio' to the new form 'Intelligence Quotient'. His life work was the monumental study that I mentioned above. It was started in 1921 and covered four decades. It must surely be the biggest longest term and most thorough research in the whole field of the social sciences.

What Terman and his associates did was to select a sample of 1500 Californian children of high intelligence, about the Mensa level, using the standard IQ tests. At the same time he contacted another group of 1500 children, the control group, who were a good match for the first group except that they were random for intelligence test scores. Both groups were followed for over forty years with frequent enquiries to the subjects, their parents, peers, teachers, and any other kind of contact. It was this research that produced the unequivocal answer to the question I posed above.

Here are the answers. There is absolutely no doubt at all about them.

1) Overwhelmingly, on average, the early promise of children with high IQ scores is fulfilled in later life.
2) Far from there being evidence for the 'compensation' hypothesis there is a reverse tendency for the high IQ scorers to be above average in physical and other ways.
3) There is nothing in the evidence to support the idea that precocious children lose the advantage in the long run. Nor is it true that they gain by being held back in case they should 'burn out'.

It emerged from the first that the gifted group, the Whizz Kids as they were called by the eager media at the time, were, on average, at each age taller, heavier, healthier, more athletic, as well as being much more advanced scholastically than the match-ed control group. That was not 'unfair' enough. They were rated by teachers, peers and other contacts as having greater perseverance, self-confidence and a greater sense of humour than the matched controls.

It is no surprise that such results were not popular. The very popular and influential idea of Heaven was that disadvantages in one world would be corrected in another. Compensation is a very attractive idea to those who come off second-best in a competitive world. The demonstration that mental superiority was not corrected by a 'heavenly handicapper' came as a great shock to a stunned world.

The egalitarian critics moved in in droves to discredit such unfair ideas. Buckets of cold water and finicking criticisms were poured on Terman's work. His sample was biassed. His observers were prejudiced. It was all a 'self-fulfilling prophecy'. And the work got overlaid and forgotten until the fashion changed again.

Professor Terman's 1947 report[1] (Terman and Oden) gives 'a composite portrait' of the gifted child. This portrait is made from the average ratings of the gifted group. The range of variation is great in every respect, but a general image emerges. The parents of the Whizz Kids were judged superior both in culture and in innate qualities. The Whizz Kids were slightly superior physically, and were educationally advanced over the average for their age group but at least 14 per cent. They were much more able to master the subject-matter of written material, and in this respect were advanced by 44 per cent.

Most of them, however, were engaged on tasks two or three grades below their potential level of achievement. There was no correlation set between achievement and the length of school attendance. Schooling seems to have less effect on gifted children than on average children. The gifted group showed a preference for difficult subjects. Their interests were many-sided and spontaneous.

They learned to read quickly and they read more of what their teachers judged to be better books. They educated themselves. They were keen on collecting and were more knowledgeable about play and games.

[1] L. M. Terman and M. H. Oden, *The Gifted Group at Mid-Life* (California, 1959) (also Oxford University Press).

Their play preferences were advanced by two or three years beyond the average for their age. Ninety per cent of the gifted group were above average in intellectual interests. Eighty-four per cent were above average in social interests. All children were given a battery of seven character tests and the gifted group showed a higher score than average children on all of these. The gifted children were less inclined to boast or to overstate their knowledge. Other tests showed them to be more trustworthy under the temptation to cheat. Teachers rated their preferences of character and their social attitudes as more wholesome and they were rated as having much greater emotional stability. The superiority of the gifted group was greatest in abstract subjects, least in penmanship, spelling, and routine arithmetic. It was best in subjects involving 'thought' (concept manipulation).

This was the general picture. But there was a wide range of variability and variety of patterns. Every type of personality defect, social maladjustment, behavioural problem, and physical frailty could be found among the gifted. The only difference is that these deviations are, in varying degrees, less frequent than in the general population. The children were selected at ten and eleven years of age, yet their subsequent educational and occupational success was accurately predicted. In follow-up studies they went into better jobs, earned a higher income, and had superior achievements in the arts, in science, and in all practical human endeavours, than the average individual. Eighty-six per cent of the group finished up in the top two socio-economic classes. In the Second World War the gifted group in the Services showed a stronger tendency to rise into the officer class and gain promotion.

The Whizz Kids exercised more forethought, were rated as better leaders, and they were considered to be more modest. It may be asked how these qualities can be judged; and the answer is that a large number of careful checks were made among their parents, their teachers, their relatives, and their fellow pupils and in all cases the mean ratings proved to be superior to those of the unselected group.

While the range of variations was wide, the children were, on an average, markedly superior to the general population in ability and in personality, and general social performance as adults. Even their death rate, and their delinquency, divorce, maladjustment, and insanity rates were much lower than the average. Over 80 per cent of the men finished in the highest professional groups, and even during the depression of the 1930s, when up to 20 per cent of males in the normal population were unemployed, only 1 per cent of this gifted group were without jobs. This small group had produced between them, even in their early twenties, 90 books, 1,500 published articles and more than 100 patents. Twenty had already been listed in *American Men of Science* and seven in *Who's Who in America*. Forty-five per cent had become professionals and 26 per cent business men. They had achieved better status, were in better jobs, and were earning far more money than the average even of college graduates in California, to say nothing of the average Californian.

But though Terman clearly showed that the group which was selected by an intelligence test in early childhood turned out to be very much more successful on the average than an unselected control group, there was still a smaller minority of failures among the gifted group. While the early test proved a reliable predictor of the *mean* future achievements of the group, there was still a very considerable spread and many children failed to realise their early promise. What was the explanation of this?

Terman tried to find out. He confined his investigations to the boys and in 1940 set three independent judges to work on the young men (now twenty-five years old) and assess them for general success in life to that point. He then divided them into three groups: the top and bottom 20 per cent, and the middle group of average achievement.

The average income of the top fifth was two and a half times that of the bottom fifth, but during the elementary school years no difference had been visible and their achievements at school had been about equal. The two groups drew apart as they attended high school. The difference was not explained by the tendency of the lower group to engage in other pursuits because the top group had twice as many extra-curricular activities as the bottom group. As they were retested on intelligence tests the IQ scores drew apart, but this effect was only slight.

What were the differences? The home background of the two groups differed markedly. The successful group came from a background which was more academic; three times as many of their fathers had graduated. Twice as many of the successful group had fathers who were in the professional classes, that is to say they had a tradition of education. There were three times as many Jews in the successful group.

What perhaps is more interesting is that there *had* been an early sign of the future divergence of these groups whose IQ score was equal. On early personality ratings (eighteen years earlier) parents and teachers had made remarks which made it possible subsequently to separate the groups in a distinctive way. There was no significant difference in physical health nor in nervousness or emotional stability. But the evidence of social maladjustment in the unsuccessful group increased with time. The successful group displayed more evidence of leadership qualities. Not unexpectedly the unsuccessful group had a lower marriage rate and more divorces. On the other hand, when the intelligence of the wives of the two groups was measured it was found that the successful group had married wives of superior intelligence on the average. A much greater percentage of the wives of the successful group belonged to professional classes. The wives and parents of the successful group rated them far higher on perseverance, self-confidence, and integration. They also rated them as being less subject to inferiority feelings, but this effect was less marked.

Strangely enough, people who knew them made little difference between them on happiness, good nature, egotism, sensitiveness, moodiness, or impulsiveness. But the successful group were considered by those who knew them well to be superior in appearance, attractiveness, alertness, poise, attentiveness, curiosity, originality, speech, and friendliness. The greatest contrast was in the ratings on 'drive to achieve' and in all-round social adjustment.

The evidence here may not be conclusive, but it points clearly in one direction. High intelligence is not the sole determinant of success in life but it is a most important ingredient. It increases the chances of success in a very significant way, but is not enough to overcome all possible disadvantages and deficiencies. Early home background plays a very influential role, and an academic or an achievement-oriented tradition in the early home background is a very significant determinant of success. The frequency of Jews in the successful group pays a tribute to the Jewish traditions of upbringing.

The results of these inquiries seem to me to be of very considerable significance because they suggest the best and quickest way in which we can improve the contribution of gifted people to the general welfare. We cannot do much in regard to the genetic component, the underlying potential – this is the 'given' of the educational situation. We can, however, do much to improve the environment, the motivation, and the upbringing of the gifted children.

It is this type of thinking which has led to the establishment of the growing Gifted Children Movement. This subject is dealt with in a later chapter.

The Faults of Intelligent People

Terman and others have shown that those who have been selected for intelligence have been found, in general, to have other virtues. Intelligence predisposes people to have certain desirable characteristics. I believe that it also predisposes them towards certain faults. Most of these seem to be to be due to faulty adjustment of the able person to those around him. There are social pressures upon those who have the power to excel from which most of humanity are immune. At home parents often take an ambivalent attitude towards the precocity which has been shown to be the usual sign of intelligence in children. Especially in homes where intellectual values have not been accepted, the 'clever' child is often discouraged, and in subtle ways punished for his cleverness. At school he tends to become 'teacher's pet', but the pedagogue's delight in a bright mind is more than counterbalanced by the social rejection of his schoolmates.

As young people trying to make their way, the intelligent are handicapped by the suspicion of supervisors who may be their intellectual inferiors. It is often only when maturity has been reached that the intelligent person is accepted at his proper value and the contrary pressures upon him relaxed. Many intelligent persons, at least in the social context of the Western world, are subjected to paradoxical pressures. They are in a 'double-bind' situation, one in which they cannot win. There are pressures upon them to excel in scholarship and in other ways, pressures which come from a social order based on ubiquitous competitiveness. At the same time the intelligent person is under an opposite pressure from his peer groups, his mates, his fellow pupils: they envy and punish his successes. In my view most of the faults of the intelligent arise from a faulty adjustment to this situation. According to his character, the intelligent man reacts in one of three principal ways. They may be classified generally as

1) Rejection.
2) Dissimulation.
3) Escape.

The reaction of rejection includes rebellion, iconoclasm, disengagement. The subject adopts a pose of revolt against the people and groups and codes with which he is surrounded and he turns his energies to destructive criticism.

The dissimulator takes on a protective colouring of mediocrity and normality, repudiating the excellence which brings the social rejection. He takes refuge in excessive modesty and humility and betrays humanity by depriving it of his gifts. A majority of Mensa members confess to some degree, at least, of dissimulation. They confess, for instance, that it is their practice to adjust their conversation to the level of the company in which they find themselves, so as not to embarrass by showing a degree of erudition beyond what is acceptable.

The third group, the escapers, try to find a compromise between the incompatibles of being excellent and not excelling, but by permitting themselves to excel only in some success-proof field. These are the cranks, the devotees of flying saucers, mystic religions, unacceptable philosophies, odd hobbies – those who dissipate the treasures of their intellect in private and ineffective channels. They are the esotericist coteries, the cliques, and the intellectual extremists. There are also the Jesuits of the intellect, the complexifiers who love intricate obscurity and who hide the deliberate barrenness of their thought behind obscuring jargons and verbal games.

I believe many intelligent people have an unconscious will-to-failure which is the expression of the 'don't be too clever' values which have been built into them as a result of the social pressures of the groups in which they grew up.

These are the faults which may be excused because they are the faults of reaction to a society which does not accept them. There are other faults which are the especial trap of the intelligent.

> If all the good people were clever
> And all clever people were good
> The world would be nicer than ever
> We thought that it possibly could
> But somehow, 'tis seldom or never
> The two hit it off as they should;
> The good are so harsh to the clever,
> The clever so rude to the good!
>
> Elizabeth Wordsworth

The intelligent do not always suffer fools gladly. They are sometimes impatient, sometimes conceited, and inhuman towards those who do not have their gifts.

They are also subject to a kind of indecisiveness which comes from trying to see too many sides of a question. They fail to see that, although thinking and planning is the best prelude to action, the pre-action processes are never complete; and when a decision is made it is always on the basis of insufficient evidence or preparation. To go on with pre-action activities after action has started is to ensure failure.

These remarks about the faults of the intelligent are not supported by any research work. They are my impressions from many years of association with numerous gifted persons.

The Demand for Gifted People

We have seen that it is possible to select people both for intelligence and for other facets or traits of character. We have also seen that these qualities are normally distributed (or nearly so) in the population and that the numbers of able and less able people in each generation are likely to remain approximately constant. We might now ask ourselves whether the need for people of the various levels of ability and of the various types of character will equally remain constant.

There is considerable evidence in the more advanced countries that this is not so. There is an increasing need for peoples of the higher levels of capacity and a decreasing need for those of lower levels.

In his book *The Industrial Revolution* T. S. Ashton comments on the importance of mental ability during the Industrial Revolution. Among the causes he cites for that period of rapid industrial advance during the nineteenth century are:

1) High vertical social mobility.

2) Cheap money and a free economy.

3) The sweeping away of legal impediments on free enterprise.

4) The interplay between industry and the newer empirical sciences.

Men of great ability began to interest themselves in the mundane concerns of industry; and the result was the Industrial Revolution leading to the opening of a cornucopia of plenty, the enrichment and lengthening of millions of human lives. As Ashton puts it:

'Physicists and chemists such as Franklin, Black, Priestley, Galton and Davy were in intimate contact with the leading figures in British industry; there was much coming and going between laboratory and the workshops, and men like James Watt, Josiah Wedgwood, William Reynolds and James Keir, were at home in the one as in the other. The names of engineers, ironmasters, industrial chemists and the instrument makers from the list of the Fellows of the Royal Society, show how close were the relations between science and practice at this time.

'Inventors, contrivers, industrialists and entrepreneurs – it is not easy to distinguish one from the other at a period of rapid change – came from every social class and from all parts of the country.'

William Hutton, in 1780, said: 'Every man has his fortune in his own hands.' This was not quite true, but anyone who looks closely at English society in the mid – and late – eighteenth century will understand how it was possible for it to be said, for at this time vertical social mobility had reached a degree higher than of an earlier or perhaps any succeeding period. Ability was free to move into the key positions in the social network where it could achieve most for mankind. Ashton also said: 'Invention is more likely to arise in a community that sets store by things of the mind than in one that seeks only material ends.'

There is clearly an evolution in the field of occupation and employment, and this trend is accelerating. There is thus an increasing need for gifted people and a decreasing need for those of average and lower than average ability, and the rate of change is likely to go on increasing.

The Supply of Gifted People

It would be pleasant to believe that the supply of talent is unlimited, that mankind is infinitely educable, and that every soldier has a field marshal's baton in his knapsack. It might not be wise, however, to conduct our affairs on this happy assumption. Since the demand for human ability of a higher order is increasing, we might now ask whether the supply of talent is adequate, whether this too is increasing.

There are estimates today which indicate that in advanced countries there are already more workers engaged in handling information than there are doing physical work. Even those still doing physical work find the data processing side of their work is increasing.

This is a marked and increasing trend. The implications for the future of the world are great. Unemployment is seen as a major problem in the West and the fact that the standard of mental ability required in work roles may, without intention or plan, have advanced so much in the course of industrial progress that there is an increasing number of good citizens who, through no fault of their own, are in the lower tail of the normal ability distribution curve of employability. What happens to those who have joined the increasing fraction that are now unemployable rather than just unemployed? This is an unanswered question.

On the other hand those of higher mental ability are likely to be in more demand as time goes on. Is there a limit to this supply? Here is a daunting future social problem that needs the attention of the best minds. The solution of this problem will be much hampered by the unpopularity of any thinking at all in this sphere. My thought here is a hot potato that no one wants to touch. But the touch-shy experts who prefer not to know will be no friends to those who are likely to be painfully affected. The problem will not go away if we shut our eyes.

I suggest than an important area for future research lies in the field of the identification and fostering of human ability, estimating the demand for and the supply of those most important of all resources, the Mental Resources of Humanity. We need a computerised Mensa Talent Bank to start with. This might lead on to an international Talent Bank; a Register of the Mental Resources of Humanity.

7

About gifted children

If there is anything in the technique of intelligence testing, if giftedness includes such a factor as mental ability which appears early in life, then it follows that adult Mensa members are ex-gifted children. Mensa has a large sample of them. Members know about the problem.

Mensa's third aim is that of fostering intelligence for the benefit of humanity and that means attention to the young gifted.

One glaringly obvious gifted child was the child prodigy who grew up to become Professor Norbert Weiner. Weiner was the first to systematise the mathematics of control systems and one of his discoveries was that cybernetic systems have to have means to overcome the problem he called hunting: over-correcting successive deviations on either side of an optimal target or norm. Weiner established that hunting was an aspect of all continuing stable systems such as animals and including Man. And hunting even affects organisations and institutions.

Man as an animal has a wonderful mastery of the problem of hunting in his muscular behaviour and, since Weiner, engineers have been able to overcome the problem in our machines. But as Weiner pointed out we have not been able to overcome hunting as a fault in our society. Fashions and trends often over-correct past deviations from the desirable norm, sometimes wildly.

One such over-corrective trend is visible to the thoughtful today in our world culture. There has been a trend away from inherited power, wealth and privilege as that which governs educational choice. In some ways there is still a long way to go in this desirable direction. In other ways the trend has swung too far.

The effort to extend educational opportunity to all has for the best motives been extended and has become, as I see it, a threat to the very fundamentals of education. Today we see a demand for equality itself rather than for equality of opportunity.

From a desire to do the best for, and get the best from, all pupils, which must mean extending range and raising ceilings, we have moved to a demand for equality of outcome, achieved only by lowering ceilings.

Teachers have been taught to see the differences in educational achievement as being environmental, divisive and undesirable. They have been asked to try to establish equality. The only way that can be achieved is by lessening attention to very able children and concentrating on the less able in a corrective exercise. They stop pursuing excellence and go for equal mediocrity.

Originally, all education aimed at scholastic excellence. Now, from honourable motives, many sincere educationalists treat excellence as an unfair advantage. This educational trend appears first in a group of egalitarian bigots but many of these honest but misguided folk have penetrated to influential positions in the educational establishments in many western countries. There has been a good swing toward equality of educational opportunity and an unfortunate swing beyond the optimum.

The results have been modern schools where one of the vital roles of past schools has been set aside. Many schools now are no longer acting or reluctantly acting as a filter to find and foster great talent. School used to be a trawl net for the rare high flyer as well as an educator of the average and an aid to the retarded. Now they concentrate on the normative exercise and forget the selective one.

So it is only those very able children whose parents are aware and motivated that are given the educational opportunity they and society need to have. The talents of less privileged, brilliant children and those with imperceptive, uncomprehending or unmotivated parents are lost to society.

But our society is a homeostatic entity and overswings are in the end corrected. We begin to see the beginnings of a trend in this direction. It is the Gifted Children's movement.

I have said something about the simultaneous rise of the Gifted

Children's movements in various countries and my own original connection with them. The affinity between Mensa and these movements is obvious and our roles in various countries have been mutually supportive.

The various strands of the movement are in my opinion at the experimental stage so far. There seems to be no clearly defined body of accepted doctrine about how to solve the problems of gifted children. There is little agreement even about whether there are problems and if so what they are.

But the universal spread of the movement in many countries on both sides of the Iron Curtain cannot be ignored. There is a very serious problem. We have tried remedies. But there are not any 'correct' ones which apply widely. There is little research; we are feeling our way, not well comprehending. Human talent is as protean and diverse as humanity itself and the means of fostering it are likely to be equally diverse.

I am certain, despite doubts about detail, that there is a need for the movement. My reason for believing this lies in the large volume of literature on the subject that has accumulated over the years. It is the diversity of this literature that convinces me that so far we have all too clear a problem without a clear solution.

The most important report in this field is 'The Marland Report'. It is a report delivered in 1972 by S. P. Marland Jun., the United States Commissioner for Education, to the Congress of the United States.

The report shows that there is a great deal of uneasiness among the researchers who were set to look at the problem about the direction and emphasis of educational effort in America. There is a real fear that a great deal of excellent talent, especially from less privileged families, is being neglected and lost. In his covering letter to the President about his report on gifted and talented children Marland says, '. . . In this painstaking study, the Office of Education has called on the best minds within our agency and in the fields of special education. It has confirmed our impression of inadequate provision for these students and widespread mis-understanding of their needs.' The report later says, 'We know that gifted children can be identified as early as the pre-school grades and that these children in later life often make outstanding contributions to our society in the arts, politics, business, and the sciences. But, disturbingly, research has confirmed that many talented children perform far below their intellectual potential. We are increasingly being stripped of the comfortable notion that a bright mind will make its own way. Intellectual and creative talent cannot survive educational neglect . . . This loss is particularly evident in the minority groups who have in both social and educational environments every configuration calculated to stifle potential talent.'

This is the USA which is acknowledged to have an excellent and successful educational system. Marland's warning words apply with extra force in those countries in the Western World where the educational egalitarianism I describe above has advanced even further.

My impression of the Gifted Children's Movement in several countries is that it is driven by the alarm of middle class parents at the anti-excellence ethos that has invaded the educationalists in these countries. This affects their own children. The fact that those most hurt are the less privileged bright children whose parents are often indifferent is overlooked.

In view of the enormous scale of the problem we may safely be confident that the sort of parents who are in touch with a Gifted Children's Association are those that would probably solve the problems anyway. It is the brilliant slum child who will be ignored by anti-selection, anti-elitist teachers and find no friends.

When Marland sent for me he suggested that one thing Mensa could do was to provide what he styled as 'mentors' for bright under-privileged children. One of the clearest results of his research is that where bright children from unpromising backgrounds had, despite all, reached their potential, there was almost always to be found in the environment a guide or mentor of high intelligence and education who had acted as friend, supporter and motivator for the child. Only five percent of poor bright children achieve their potential but of that five percent no less than seventy-five percent had such a mentor in the background. Who can doubt that these mentors would be found to be members of what I call the World Culture in chapter 8. Where the bright make contact with the World Culture like Philip Powell, they join it and serve it. Mensa should set itself to meet these children's need.

Mensans should be trained to help, then actively seek and help, the bright under-privileged child. Under proper educationalist supervision they should then try to introduce such children to the World Culture, that is motivate them towards education. Our retired and independent members would find satisfaction in filling such a benevolent civilisation-supporting role for some child. There are few joys like that of serving the growth and development of the mind of one of these Golden Ones, as Plato called them.

The problem and the need is great, so I would urge attention in the first place only to those children of exceptionally high ability. If the little effort that can be generated is applied otherwise the children with the biggest problem, the really high flyers, will be crowded out. One of my criticisms of the Gifted Children's Movement is that its members and officials spend too much attention on the middle and lower ranks of the able. The problems there are less severe. It is the very exceptional child who most desperately needs the help we can provide.

I would like to see a general policy that, if the parents consent, any child old enough to be tested could become a member and benefit from the contacts that thus would be made. There is a sense in which the intelligentsia of each generation is found, fostered and formed by the previous one. That is the heredity of the World Culture of which I write. That is how it preserves its form through time. This is the vital role that modern Procrustean education neglects. It has to be fulfilled. Mensa can and ought to exert itself here.

Perhaps being the custodian and transmitter of the World Culture is the most important task of all for members and especially for Mensans because they are, as it were, generalist members of it rather than incidental members because of their education or training in some special field.

In America almost all the bigger Mensa chapters have a Gifted Children specialist and there is a nation-wide network of local co-ordinators who link with the local associations for the gifted and help Mensa parents with problems in this field. But more, much more needs to be done. Mensa is naturally well disposed towards the problem because, as I have said, we are no more than a society of grown up gifted children ourselves.

8

Mensa and the World Culture

I want to introduce a concept that may not seem to be much related to Mensa at first sight. I hope I may be able to show the relevance of this idea.

Having had the good luck to back the outsider Mensa and got a winner, I have had the delight of seeing its growth and of participation in a unique pattern of growing world-wide contacts.

After an unpromising start in a London slum I found myself in intellectual contact with good minds from a wide range of cultures in many parts of the world, a wider range than is normally available in international contacts, even in today's merging world. Most international contacts are between those in the same trade or business or those who have one interest, profession, belief or religion in common. Mensa is other than that. It is multidisciplinary.

In my professional career I had world-wide contacts but they were meetings and exchanges between experts and specialists, wood scientists and technologists. So in my two roles, as an innovating industrialist and as a Mensa pioneer, I have had international contacts. I am in a position to compare the usual type with the new Mensa type.

Mensa contacts, I observe, are of quite a different nature. They are protean, as is Mensa itself, their diversity is greater, they are warmer and more intimate. This seems to be marked by better comprehension and more rapport than in relationships arising from shared special interests. Norman Douglas said, 'There is a kinship, a kind of freemasonry, between all persons of intelligence, no matter how antagonistic their outlook.' I have tested this hypothesis and failed to falsify it.

The gradual realisation of the differences between Mensa and normal contacts led me a few years ago to put forward what I believe to be a useful conceptual framework in which to understand the development of our present world civilisation which has puzzled me.

There have been large civilisations before but there has been nothing which remotely compared for size, scale and complexity with the present world-wide trading and intercommunicating informational network.

Looking at this from the broadest perspective we see the earth's surface is divided into a patchwork of nations which claim to be autonomous competitive human social administrative areas. The authorities in each nation claim absolute sovereignty and self-determination. The United Nations agree international laws but nations do not accept them as commanding the same unquestioned authority that national laws do. They feel free to choose which of them they will observe and which they will ignore. The United Nations cannot be said to have established world law and order. There are international laws which are usually honoured but they are seen as mutual agreements, not ordinances.

However, arising much earlier, and spreading spontaneously, are another set of behaviour-regulating practices which govern the dealings between the peoples, institutions and governments of the nations. These are more widely accepted, rarely infringed and have a much more detailed and influential role in regulating the behaviour of people and institutions. It is their existence which made even the attempt to frame laws in UNO possible.

What are these behaviour-regulating systems which keep our vast world society stable and viable? They are of course the set of commercial, legal and industrial practices, norms and usages which have grown up through the millennia in many places. These ancient mores are so firmly and universally established that all but a handful of primitive societies observe them with great fidelity. What I have found mysterious is the way that, a few hundred years ago, these systems began to link up to form a world-wide system.

These commercial systems are not the only world-uniting ones. In the field of science there is in each separate discipline a world network which transcends national, racial, cultural and tribal structures. In art, world jurisprudence, philosophy, news-gathering, transport, sport, entertainment, holidays, invention, technology, and many other fields the same complex coalescence has happened.

By grouping all these similar developments together and relating them we can see that there has arisen, unbidden, unplanned and unpredicted, a supervening World Culture which overlies, underpins and transfuses the older local, national and tribal cultures. The World Culture is supported and transmitted to new generations by a world network of the informed and educated. To be informed, people have to be informable, intelligent. The potential Mensans and the Mensans around the world have become infected by a World Culture. They are contributing and participating in parallel membership of that as well as the culture to which they were born. Standing a little taller they have reached over the bounds of bigotry to take the hands of those beyond in an undeclared, because unconscious, fellowship.

A visitor from a distant world would look at the lack of authority of the United Nations, man's tribal competitive past and the national claims to complete sovereignty. Seeing these he might ask why the peoples are no longer in the same state of periodic conflict in which they have been for millions of years. What has changed that would not be expected to make conflict worse? More contact and more wealth could easily have meant more chance to fight and more to fight about. Such a visitor would see evidence of strife here and there but would be puzzled at the generally peaceful way the network of nations supported and worked within an immensely complex international trading, artistic, educational, and scientific, system. 'Why', the space visitor would ask, 'do not the powerful nations set out to conquer the others? They always did in the past.'

I have seen some local strife with small and medium wars in the thirty-four years since the last great one but I share the posited space stranger's surprise because, despite the miserable division in UNO there is this strange, tacit, peaceful trading world cultural contact and co-operation. We cannot explain it as a result of any element common to all the various cultures because they are so many, so various and so little compatible.

A great variety of entirely different cultures, religions, ideologies, philosophies, mores and customs influence and control the nations and other divisions of humanity. Although these do have common elements the dogmas are in serious conflict (witness the bloody disputes in the past and even, in diminished form, today). But .where we, the space stranger and I, might have expected continuous dreadful wars in a lawless anarchic world we have had a norm of peace and good relationships leading to a knowledge and technology explosion and a level of prosperity where the influence of the world culture is strong, which would have amazed the ancients.

The wars, and the blood-lettings, since 1946 have not been so much between nations as between those within nations who are of different cultural backgrounds, or of different religions and races. It is the ancient disputes which fester, Jew versus Arab, Hindu versus Muslim, Singhalese versus Tamil, Protestant versus Catholic (still) in Ireland, black versus white in many places, Luo versus Kikuyu in Kenya, Matabele versus the northern tribes in Zimbabwe, Shiite versus Sunni in the Muslim world, Malay versus Chinese; these are just a few of the problems. The list is endless.

The world-wide conflict between the different economic classes which Marx predicted in industrial societies seems a mild and quiet affair beside this kind of friction. Often it has seemed that Marxists have had to give their 'class struggle' a racist or culturalist flavour (entirely contrary to internationalist Marxist teaching) to get it going at all. Even the great rift between the rich 'North' and the poor 'South' so confidently dramatised by some politicians seems to be a noisy but purely verbal scuffle. The bloody affrays between more ancient rival cultural and racial factions are all we have left on earth of physical conflict between the members of that combative, territorial hunter-gatherer species, homo sapiens. After several million years of uninterrupted human strife I find this pleasing and surprising.

It is only the bigots of the traditional, long established cults,

religions and sects and racial groups who remain ready to maim
and kill to save souls. With fervour and sincerity they murder to
establish 'the right way'.

Since World War II there has been little conflict between the
nation states of the world where these ancient have not been, or
have not been exploited as the motivating drive.

What has made the difference? Certainly it has not been
planned. No one man, institution, ideology or religion has been
behind the birth and vast growth of this complex world wide
network of interweaving relationships. Like Topsy 'it just
growed'. Teilhard De Chardin pointed with surprise to this
unexpected convergence of hitherto diverging cultures as being
as mysterious as life itself. I think we have not thought enough
about it.

One great influence seems to have been the emergence and
mutual contact of a world wide cadre of intelligent, educated and
informed human beings. They have made the change possible.
Such people, as I have said, are able at least to peep over the
confining walls of cultural bigotry, nationalism, and every other
kind of cosy exclusive 'us against them' unity. Modern communications have made this contact possible but the communications could not have improved without the rapport that I describe.
It was a self-reinforcing, spontaneous world-wide phenomenon.
This world communications network was a self-organising system.

Those people all over the world, in many disciplines, who have
participated in this cultural coalescence have been acting to
promote their own interest or increase their understanding. They
have not seen the totality of that in which they are participating.
The merchants, the shippers, the authors and journalists, the
scholars, the scientists, the traders, the artists have co-operated,
as do those who work in the market, without a plan, for a thousand
small individual selfish reasons. The result has been, by the
operation of a Smithian hidden hand, the rise unnoticed of a new,
world-wide, supervening culture which is shared by at least some
of those of all the participating cultures. This phenomenon needs
a name and I call it the World Culture.

You will see my drift. I see Mensa as a tiny unconscious but exemplary part of it. All over the world I find myself in touch with Mensans of whom the overwhelming majority could be correctly classified as participating members of the posited World Culture. So far, the World Culture has been unselfconscious but Mensa and other groups like it may herald the birth of something that corresponds to consciousness in the World Culture. The wide interactions that Mensa brings about are not constrained by any particular discipline or interest. Mensa is more truly adogmatic, interdisciplinary and universal than its best competitor, the university. Mensa includes those of the able and informed that the university excludes. The autodidact and the 'opter-out' from the academic race are found in Mensa. The uneducated self-starter entrepreneur and the bright failure are found there too.

All those who have the kind of competence that is more in demand in an age of higher technology are fully represented in the broader ranks of Mensa than in the world of academe with its stereotyped and often biassed traditional selection prejudices. In one country university selection is biassed towards the so called 'upper' classes, in another towards the obsolescent manual working class and in others towards those of the 'right' race, language, religion or wealth. In Mensa any bright person can get into our world-wide agora. Even the one barrier – a small subscription – is not compulsory.

My concluding point is that if this World Culture is real and has been so productive of advantage for humanity as it seems to have been without plan or understanding, will it not be of even more benefit when it is recognised and positively served by the participants? It has done us very well without conscious human supporters or friends; what will it do when its advantages are seen and its spread and penetration fostered and encouraged by the world's intelligentsias?

The benevolent operation of the market, which better than any central regulation optimises the satisfaction of human desires, preceded the insights of Adam Smith. But its operation was helped by the understanding he brought. His visions inspired the political defence of the principles he advanced when they were under fire from uncomprehending centralists. May it not be that the active understanding and defence of the undogmatic, provisional principles of the World Culture are going to be needed in the future fight against the revival of fundamentalist dogmatism and centralism? Who better to champion so diffuse and tenuous a cause than the bright, open, comprehending minds of Mensans? There will be no simple formulas, slogans or policies for World Culture defenders. No reassuring simplistic theories. No comforting thought-economising creeds and dogmas to cling to. World Culture defenders have a strange undefined, undefinable and insubstantial territory to defend and they have, so far, no allies, nothing to attract the zeal and fanaticism which is so useful to the dogmatic causes. They have a tough fight. But where else can champions be found? I predict that and hope that Mensa can enter the fight to preserve our present World Culture because of what I have observed in thirty years' service to it.

Bigotry and extremism can survive on Mensa soil but the Mensa ground is arid and stony for such plants. It is my confident conclusion that the one thing that Mensans have in common, a good intelligence, is the best protection there is from excess of zeal, bigotry, fanaticism and every other kind of mental rigidity. The essence of intelligence is the ability to learn and the first essential of that is mental flexibility. A Mensan will give you an argument but his ears or her ears are open. His argument is the better because in the Mensan head is a listening brain. If you have a good argument the impossible happens; someone admits they might have been wrong. How often does it happen outside the ranks of really intelligent people?

Even the determined bigots in Mensa, and of course we have them, even those that prefer the security of dogmatic thought prisons, even they, in Mensa have to live in a barrage of sharp corrective intellectual challenge from their fellow members. They have to fight for a rigidity that is always under challenge.

Of course Mensa so far is only an infinitesmally small sample of the highly intelligent but it is the right kind of sample: very mixed, very representative, international, and ubiquitous. Mensa has the tenuous social, but intellectual, unity that is needed for the difficult role I suggest. It is small but growing.

My thesis is that the concept of the World Culture fills a gap for Mensa and other organisations like it that may follow. It provides

Mensa with a possible role without committing it to a position with fissile implications.

I propose that the set of 'intelligent people' contains sub-sets of 'the unbigoted' and 'the educated' whose intersection is the richest substrate for the development of that world-wide cadre which is, as yet, barely aware of its own existence, yet which is the essential underpinning feature of the world coalescence of cultures which I am trying to describe.

Rejecting the idea that intelligence tests make a random selection it is clear that the Mensa sample must contain many of the intersecting set, many of those of the cadre, or potentially of the cadre, which supports the emerging World Culture. Wide personal experience amply confirms that view. I propose that Mensa should see itself as a part of and a proselytizing supporter of that culture which seems as yet, to have no other conscious friends.

Now I must deal with another problem in this context: the Three Worlds.

The Third World is accepted as the name of that set of countries which are euphemistically and often untruthfully called the 'developing countries'. It is not clear which of the other two worlds claims to be the First World but I shall cheekily claim that title for the open societies called the 'West'. The centralist countries based on Marxist-Leninist ideology will have to make do as the Second World. My criterion is very simple and completely democratic. I work out the ranking by observing which way the feet vote and which way the walls face.

Allowing for my western chauvinism which must be obvious by now, I think it can be conceded that while there are manifestations of the World Culture in all three worlds, the First World has a greater and richer sample of what I have been trying to describe (rather than define). But, unquestionably the World Culture is very strong indeed in the Second World, the Soviet World. In many fields the Soviets are vastly important contributors to it. In art, literature, in all the sciences, space exploration, trading, industry, sport and many other fields the Soviet contributions are good and often excellent. Only the state-imposed, single ideological bigotry limits world cultural development in the Second World.

In the Third World progress is slower because of the widespread religious, cultural and ethnic chauvinisms which bind the minds of their intelligentsia. And they have not yet got the vital message of 'the best man for the job'. Mental testing could do more for the Third World than almost anything else as a quick fix for bribes and nepotism in personnel selection. It has also been set back by an over-zealous (but perhaps justified) repudiation of 'colonialism'.

Anticipating the inevitable criticisms of the conceptual framework I propose, Soviet-type Marxists will see my concept of World Culture as simply another name for 'the bourgeois capitalist ideology' which they condemn and attack. The rather different Third World Marxists will simply add the words 'Western Colonialist' before the word 'bourgeois' in the phrase above. They will do this despite the fact that they are co-operating participants in the World Culture and benefit from it and contribute to it considerably. They will write their condemnations on typewriters and word processors arising from that culture, within a set of idioms and ideas developed by it (probably at the London School of Economics), and publish it through media which would never have existed without it. They will be attacking it from within. Their attacks will merely strengthen it, make it more protean, more true to iself.

More dangerous, potentially destructive of the World Culture, will be the attacks from the fundamentalist religious bigots, most of whom are to be found only in the Third World. I cordially accept the description 'Satan' as the name for the World Culture which will be applied in those places. From bigots of this order the word is a compliment to that to which it is applied.

But we must not neglect the problem or fail to see the danger. The advantages that come from the spread of the World Culture are uneven. The changes are traumatic and disturbing as well as beneficial and essential to biosphere survival. Resistance is natural and healthy, especially when change is too fast. Supporters of the World Culture ought to pay much more attention to the side-effect problems that arise as it spreads its influence. Its spread is good, but only good on balance. There should not be too much hurry.

Immigrant minority groups of other cultures who come to the First World, and even to the Second World, having voted with their feet for the host country and culture, are likely, I fear, to be among those who reject the World Culture concept. They, or rather their intellectuals on their behalf, will identify my concept World Culture, with what they have called the 'dominant' culture of the host culture which they feel rejects them.

The idea of a multicultural society is usually the host culture's answer to the cultural clashes that arise with massive immigration. But looked at with clear eyes it is a non-starter. In intellectual, middle and upper class circles and in Mensa universally you will see what looks at first sight like the perfect working of a multi-racial multicultural society. It is nothing of the kind. It is simply a small local manifestation of the World Culture. There is no race or ethnic or cultural problem at all in such circles. There never has been.

But the idea that any society as a whole could work on such lines is illusory. What happens where there is a mixture of different ethnic/cultural populations is that they localise, form local enclaves. The most ancient and stable of these can be seen in Morocco and Tunisia where there are Arab, Berber, Riff and Jewish quarters in each large town. America is doing well at copying this stable, viable pattern. Americans do not like to admit it but look for yourself if you doubt it. Newer to the game Britain does not do so well but that is the way it is.

In the North African countries, apart from the race/culture enclaves, there is usually a World Culture quarter also where all the international hotels, businesses, banks and the World Culture community is to be found. It is called the European Quarter but that is not what it is at all. This quarter is simply the World Culture Quarter and it is of course truly multicultural and multiracial. Outside such quarters, much as we might like it, multiracialism and multiculturalism cannot be shown to be working anywhere. The name of the World Culture quarter in an American city is Downtown. The university is another World Culture centre.

All this bears out my point that, so far at any rate, humanity has not passed the stage at which the World Culture is sustained only by educated, good minds. I wish it were not so. My proposal is that Mensa should become the champion of the World Culture which I see as the last hope of the biosphere.

9

About Mensans

Here I try to give an impression of what it is like to belong to Mensa. 'Try' is the right word because the diversity of experience in Mensa is greater than that in any other such body in the world.

If Mensa has given reason to doubt the old adage that great minds (as far as they are represented in Mensa) think alike it is a solid proof that, at any rate, the owners of bright minds by no means think and behave alike.

Never averse to a challenge however, I try to convey at least the atmosphere and the flavour of Mensa occasions. Further, I can give some exemplary stories to show the range of variations that the Mensan must expect when he join his fellows in our world-wide 'think-link'.

'Expect the unexpected' seems perverse advice but it is right. Yet it is somehow misleading. To expect surprise is to be nervous and uneasy. In Mensa you can expect to be pleasantly surprised, gently shocked. But only when you are ready. The newcomer need not fear to be challenged, disturbed or least of all made to feel small. Rare exceptions apart, members tend to be urbane and civil, especially on first encounter. But they are rarely over-conventional or insipid and practically never boring. As soon as the first civilities are over there is likely to be a gentle mutual probing of minds and attitudes as the Mensans size each other up. Almost all intelligent people have learned to dissimulate to some extent, to test comprehension before they raise the level of discussion. Gradually newcomers will find themselves drawn out and politely explored. Your contact is almost always able to talk effectively on a whole range of topics, so a mutual interest is always quickly found. One of the risks for the expert in Mensa is that of finding a hearer who is unexpectedly equally expert or more so. Tread cautiously in taking an authoritative role.

There is of course a great deal of raillery, joking and the scoring of verbal Brownie points, and the extremes of verbal victimisation can be severe. But this is directed at familiars or affectionately recognised butts who accept that beloved social role. Perceptive and witty verbal aggression is common but it is used with sensitive discrimination where it will be well taken. The butts are those who can hand it out as well as they can take it. And the wit, though sharp, is almost never cruel. The sharper wit-wars are always between seasoned combatants who like each other and know each other well. It is in Mensa, as anywhere else, a sign of acceptance to be included in the mutual insult network. The difference is that the Mensa insults are never crude, and almost always teasing, challenging, provocative and very funny.

At best, where you get a chain of fast, apt responses, each superbly capping the last, it can be really uproarious. And one is never safe. In the middle of the most serious talk or lecture, when everyone is paying close attention, a chance slip will be made or an opening left and the jocular tennis rally will supervene with the wits vying to cap the last quip. But these sudden squalls are, if the subject is really interesting, quite brief and the speaker can soon recapture attention from everyone.

The new member's nightmare, the traumatic, feared aspect of Mensa, is the first contact. People generally get into new social groups by the ancient method of personal introduction. The tyro is taken by a senior to a meeting where there is a special introductory treatment to a group which has already established its mutual relations.

In Mensa this kind of introduction is rare. The initial recruitment process is largely postal. The first human contact is with a group of other candidates, all strangers to each other, at a supervised test session. Or it may be with a small group who are tested by a proctor.

These test sessions are, I fear, rather daunting occasions with something of the atmosphere of public academic examinations (with which Mensa people are likely to be familiar). Some are better and they feature a friendly talk about Mensa and even a social drink together afterwards. This should be more common.

For lack of the traditional introducer, many of the shyer members who loyally pay their subscriptions for years never take the next step and actually attend a meeting. New entrants will usually be approached by the leader of the nearest local group and sent a special invitation. Some Locsecs are keen, persistent and welcoming and even go to the trouble of delegating an introducer or pairing newcomers for mutual support. They get a good response and a lot of participation. Others are less energetic or easily discouraged by slow or shy responses.

Either way the expected trauma is the first meeting. The new member sets off with some trepidation and without knowing what to expect. It is natural to fear that somehow one will not be found to be up to standard. If one goes to a special 'new members' meeting (and this is a very usual introduction), one fears to be in the 'one of a crowd of strangers' position that is so unusual as an introduction. There is the fear of a silent circle of strangers waiting for someone to break the ice. If one goes to an established meeting there is the problem of being 'the stranger at the feast' without a friendly introducer. These are the natural expectations and the fears of the tyro member. They are unfounded.

Mensa, truly, is nothing like that. I have been at countless meetings of both types and never have I seen a meeting that justifies any of those fears. It is a bit startling to see, time and again, a group of new members, all strangers to each other, get into noisy and animated conversation immediately the small problem of mutual identification is over. The Locsec or leader often has a problem to get attention in the clamour.

The new member coming to a familiar group is normally given a judiciously warm welcome, not cool, not embarrassingly effusive. Conversation is likely to be in larger groups than usual and is often general so that joining a group is not a problem. No one needs to feel out of it for long. The accepted practice is that all groups are open. People join or leave them at will without comment or excuse.

That is a description of the most usual introduction to Mensa. It might be a lunch or dinner. It might be a coffee evening at a member's home or a pub meeting. Numbers vary from five to fifty with the smaller groups predominant.

To take a meal together is a very good introduction as it brings people into groups automatically. The members come from all social backgrounds and so dress is usually very informal and the restaurants chosen tend to be economical so that no-one is excluded. Except those who can afford and prefer something better, that is the majority.

Recently there has been a corrective trend in the dinners to provide something for that neglected majority as well. Some, not all, of the Mensa Dinners have reverted to the Berrill type and become more formal occasions with the men in dinner jackets and ladies dressed for the occasion. Here there is usually a formal chairman. The rule is general conversation. All talk to all, not chat to neighbours. Good surroundings and good food are arranged. This type, called 'Black Tie Dinners', are becoming popular despite the need for pre-booking and the greater cost. They are often oversubscribed. The comfortable limit in numbers is about twenty-five but they are better at sixteen or so. This Berrill-type dinner was run very successfully in France under the name, 'Diner-Debat', and was revived in England in 1980 with great success.

SPECIAL INTERESTS GROUPS

Special Interest Groups (or SIGs) in Mensa are simply Mensa circles which have an interest or enthusiasm in common. They meet, correspond, circulate journals and pursue their interest by and through their Mensa contacts. To tell about this very important aspect of Mensa activity is difficult because its range and variety is so very great. I have discovered that high intelligence does not create unanimity in opinion but the reverse, more and more diverse opinions, 'pluralanimity'. The interests of Mensa members show this same protean quality.

In the latest list of special interest groups in the USA there are 142 active groups. They range from less than half-serious ones like the Apathy SIG which died, 'The Degenerates' and the Vampire SIG, through the range of all the normal hobbies and interests to some more esoteric ones like Skydiving SIG, Brain

Research SIG, Fortean Mysteries SIG, Assassinations (Research), Biorhythmic Cycles SIG, Mentors, and SUFCA (Save Us From Computers Amen).

It is my serious expectation that many of the influential movements and societies of the future will originate in Mensa SIGs.

Another very early, popular type of event which always brings a crowd is a Lecture/Discussion. Mensa members prefer the kind of participative lecture where almost everyone gets a chance to speak and so the lecturers and speakers are invited to 'lead a discussion' rather than to give a lecture. My own version of these has been a continuous feature of British Mensa for thirty years. The event went, at one time, under the name 'Conversazione'. Now it is called a 'Think-In'. Never a bore, Think-Ins at their best can be very good indeed. A pleasant lecture room, with comfortable chairs, is chosen. It should be somewhere where members can meet socially for a bite or a drink before or afterwards. Often there is a chance to eat together beforehand. Any member can organise a Think-In and members pay on entry to cover the cost of room hire (unless a local member has the space at home).

The subjects of discussion are enormously varied but usually topical, in the sphere of public interest and such as to inspire debate. To 'think-in' is not to be educated or instructed. It is dynamic participation in the formation of informed public opinion on questions which are not yet fully resolved. The lecturer is there to set the scene for the Mensa interaction and to be ready to apply the needed factual corrections to the debate. Think-Ins are not unwaveringly serious, there is always a lot of laughter, but there is often a reported output and the underlying intention is to tackle serious intellectual questions without undue solemnity.

Mensa has more and more residential weekends such as those run for thirty years by Eric Hills in England. The American development of these is the Regional Gathering and that is like a slightly smaller version of the Annual Gathering of which an impression will be gained in the historical section of the present book. The Regional Gathering will usually have a local flavour and a general holiday atmosphere with a lot of hotel room parties, quite a bit of free drinking in the 'hospitality suite' (an extra hotel suite taken for the purpose), a games room, a computer room, and numerous rap sessions and small lectures and discussions (or workshops) in various meeting rooms. Larger lectures happen but are more rare. Breakfasts are taken individually but lunches and dinners are usually large group affairs with a certain amount of speechifying, presentations and amusing diversion.

The newer type of institution, the week-long discussion-type holiday, is a very extended version of the Think-In or residential weekend format. Mensa at Cambridge and one or two in Holland, Austria, and France are the only ones of which I have experience. The American version is the Annual Colloquium. I append exemplary accounts of particular Mensa At Cambridge, Black Tie Dinner, and Think-In meetings which I have reported before. These should give an impression.

This is the account published in the *International Journal* of Mensa At Cambridge this year:

Like the American MAC (Mensa Annual Colloquium), the British one, Mensa at Cambridge, started as an answer to the justly and constantly repeated challenge, 'With All Those Brains In Mensa, What Do You ACTUALLY DO?'

The fifth Mensa At Cambridge marked a new stage in the rise of what has become a British national institution, an Annual Week Long Feast Of The Intellect to which the nation's media pay increasing attention. There must be over a hundred clippings about this year's conference. They are still coming in September.

In Cambridge in July the sun is no brash and glaring youngster; he is a kindly and comfortable old English gentleman. He smiled benignly on the lovely old colleges and the calm river Cam covered with its tangle of ridiculous punts, punt poles and people. Old Sol's vague, welcoming smile impartially greeted a hundred and thirty witty, friendly, quick thinking Mensans from a dozen countries as they wandered over the laughing confusion on the river, over the Mathematical Bridge and settled into non-standard, idiosyncratic, comfortable rooms all over the muddled rambling courts and buildings, medieval and modern, of that most beautiful College on the Cam, Queen's.

The theme this year was TWENTY TWENTY VISION. John McNulty, and Margaret Clarke found a panel of sages prepared to risk crystal-ball-gazing as far into the misty future as Orwell did.

What could these gazers make out in the swirling vapours? Much. Much to astonish. Much to talk about.

The keynote this year, and the innovation was increased participation. Mensans listened and absorbed. Then they thought. Then they came back, reacted. One began to have vaunting thoughts. Mensa Founder Berrill was rightly derided when he suggested in the early days that Mensa might advise authorities and governments. He may not have been wrong but untimely. A really independent disinterested forum which is free from all bias except intelligence CAN make a useful contribution. Perhaps a fool-free agora, where independent, international public opinion can come struggling into life, perhaps it can serve. Especially when those who assemble can first listen to experts and savants.

'THE FUTURE, IF ANY,' then, was the theme, and the first speaker was that redoubtable, witty, young, balding-redhead, marathoning, micro-wizard, poet-tycoon, British Mensa Chairman, Sir Clive Sinclair, Founder and patron of Mensa At Cambridge.

Professor Sir Clive, spoke well, his message was hard hitting and shocking. The trend lines point plainly. By 2020 Mankind will have A Rival Intelligence on earth. No. Not bug-eyed monsters in space ships, his own artefact Artificial Intelligence. Responding, Clive said it's risky to believe in an immortal soul which informs the undoubted mechanism of brain. There is no evidence. Safer to work to the reasonable hypothesis that mind is mechanism. If so it can be functionally replicated. Cut false security based on faith. Better to plan for Very Clever Computers, Metacomputers. But do not be frightened Artificial Intelligence will, in the short term, lead to a Golden Age for man and for life on earth.

Christopher Lee is the BBC Defence Correspondent. He

walked us along the Projections of Destruction and uncovered to our horrified eyes the Very Nasty Things that were under the mossy stones of the Future. We averted our gaze a bit. Here is a field where intelligence is frustrated into silence. But the story was not all black. The assembled Majority View was optimistic.

In Britain, when our own Mensan, athletic, young, supple, thin, fluent, penetratingly bright, Dr Madsen Pirie, talks about the future you bloody well listen. Because, like friend Clive, he is out there making it happen.

Madsen runs the Adam Smith Institute which in the last five years has become Britain's most influential Think Tank. It is almost a regiment of Think Tanks. By influencing thinking not by the exercise of power. It was Madsen's speech which captured most of the headlines. It was superb. I was his chairman. During the prolonged applause when he finished I passed him a note with one word on it. 'Masterly'.

He sketched a future where the talents and enterprise of able people has been released in a less governed society. The two kinds of Big Boss, those of overbloated Big Firms and of the Mass Unions had faded from the scene as the Underground Economy has grown up to take over.

Food, goods, are provided by robots. Service leisure and arts industries flourish in a work-world made up of myriads of small highly specialist firms run on terminals in people's own homes. Machines work. People organise, deal in information.

The real boss of any English University is the Vice Chancellor. The mere Chancellor is a King or Union Boss or something minor.

The Vice Chancellor of Cambridge University, Professor John Butterfield is a chubby, honest, kindly, gentle, lovable man who happens to be of incisive, brilliant intelligence. He spoke of the difficult future of medicine as we climb up the slope of diminishing returns in the medical sciences. He was frank and honest. We shall have problems. We loved him.

The Boss of one of the National Opinion Polls, John Barter came with a mass of data which he put over skilfully. He had

compared Mensan with unselected opinions about Twenty
Twenty. Surprise. Our views were not outstandingly different
from unselected opinion.

Autodidact, brilliant, non-institutional, accepted, outsider
Brian Ford is first a scientist, then a science historian and
expert, and then, supremely, a communicator. Walking a fast
Marathon as he spoke, he bewitched us there in the absurdly
colourful and glorious Elizabethan Old Hall, with an entranc-
ing wizardry of words which made us love, adore, and at last
understand how wonderfully clever and complex are the Simple Creatures, the Procaryotes. A silly old Eucaryote like your
President has always been suspicious of, and disliked bacteria.
I shall not discriminate any more. I abjure Eucaryionism and
declare my biological brotherhood with all protozoans nucleate
or not. Brian predicts a great future in the new age of biotech-
nology for our new friends.

This is an account of a Black Tie Dinner at the National
Liberal Club this year:

But let me tell you about a Black Tie Dinner, or President's
Dinner, that was held at the National Liberal Club on the 20th
September. We limit numbers so that conversation can be
general. Nineteen of us sat at a square table. At a long table it
gets too difficult for the chairman to prevent a departure from
the 'one at a time, all talk to all' tradition. The girls looked
modestly resplendent, in colourful long dresses revealing lovely shoulders, cleavages and smiles. The men, mostly young,
were witty, looked good in stylish modern dinner jackets and
spoke well with confidence. The beautiful brunette opera
singer's incisive, original, thoughtful words on the modern
novel were given close attention, especially by the three writers.
A stunningly beautiful, perfectly dressed lady's opinions about
work satisfaction were expressed with such unstudied and
sincere eloquence that we found it hard to see her in her
normal surroundings as an engineer supervising the construc-
tion of an oil rig in mountainous seas off Scotland.

The successful young man whose discs are making a name in the pop music scene was clearheaded about the impact of mass communications on the traditional art forms, as were the headmaster, the inventor, the homemaker, and the head of an international social work agency, though they were not in agreement. They all tore into each other and the succulent, flavoury goose with equal gusto. There was, as always, a network (to coin a collective noun) of softies including your unhumble President, but the subject of programs never came up, except at the beginning when we all tell who we are and what we do. Although strangers to the keyboard and monitor seem to be thin on the Mensa ground, we are not just another Chip Shop.

There was a lot of laughter and many telling sallies. Mean leg length was markedly extended as the kidding developed. When the wine had flowed a bit it became uproarious as the competition in wit became less restrained.

Then, suddenly, we were all very serious when a topic touched us close. Job satisfaction was the topic and we all had our own tale to tell about the two great problems for the bright. Getting it and giving it. When we are young we are often underextended, bored and desperate to use all our talents. With time, most of us solve that, but we never forget. When we get to be bosses, with all the pressing demands on the top person, we find out how difficult it is to find the answers and still preserve the organisation and keep it to its norms and objectives. An important problem aired, minds changed.

Black tie elegance would not work around your way? We thought that, too. But we tried it, and it did.

And this is the report of a typical Think-In meeting in London in 1983.

Here is some really new thinking about world politics! Barry Buzan is a Lecturer in International Studies at Warwick University. This is a very condensed account of his recent fascinating talk to a London Think-In. His book, People, States and Fear *(Wheatsheaf Books), is just out.*

The relevance of the topic lies in the need for a sense of progress in international relations.

At present, international relations contains no criteria around which a sense of progress could be built.

Consequently, international relations are seen as a largely formless web of events. A situation approximating chaos is seen to reproduce itself endlessly.

Without a sense of what constitutes progress, there is no basis for policy except national self-interest.

That basis simply reproduces the conditions for chaos.

Therefore, we need idealist images of order to provide a macro-framework for international policy.

The problem with existing images is that they are too far removed from the realities of the international system to have any significant impact on behaviour.

Purpose here is:
1. to outline existing structures and images.
2. to criticize their adequacy as the basis for a sense of progress.
3. to suggest an alternative view.

The Three Major Images of International Order

1. THE REALIST IMAGE

Represents the traditional orthodoxy in International Relations.

Rests on analysis of the international system as an anarchy in that there is no superordinate political authority, the units are sovereign.

Anarchy is preserved by the struggle of constituent units to preserve themselves and is therefore very stable as a system structure.

Anarchy creates a free market in the distribution of power, and power is therefore the essence of international relations.

The realist image is based on the state as the principal unit in the international system. The focus of analysis is on how well particular states do, and the concern with power means that the system is characterised in terms of the most powerful states within it (e.g. bipolarity, multi-polarity, etc).

The realist image is widely seen as a statement of the problem. It accepts what is, and has no idealist pretensions.

Although it contains a strong and valuable sense of the prevailing structure, it is self-reinforcing because it directs attention to competitive state policy.

2. THE INTERNATIONALIST IMAGE

represents the mainstream idealist reaction against realism. Because it is formed against the realist position, it is conceptually enslaved to it. It reacts excessively to its proposed faults.

This image is based on a vision of world government of some sort. It is based on an analogy with the state as the solution to the Hobbesian anarchy of the state of nature: just as the state produced political order for individuals, so world government would solve the problem of international anarchy.

Anarchy is equated with chaos, and is seen to be the definition of the problem.

The internationalist image dominated idealism until quite recently, but is now widely held to be bankrupt among those who think seriously about the problem.

Attempts to implement it have been overwhelmed by the structural dynamics of international anarchy.

The balance of power prevents universal empire.

Nationalism, the defence of sovereignty and the lack of agreed organising ideology, prevent the emergence of world federalism.

International organisations in practice have become important facilitators to the state system, acting to support its weaker members and to provide some desired common goods.

Whatever the merits of the internationalist image, there is no prospect of its implementation within the foreseeable future, and it therefore it cannot serve as a useful guide to policy.

The internationalist image does not take sufficient account of the actual political dynamics of international relations to be credible.

3. SOCIO-ECONOMIC IMAGES

These are a variety of images all based on the assumption that social and/or economic structures will somehow supersede and obviate the political structure of the international system.

They were mainly liberal and Marxist in origin:

Liberal economics assumes the separability of politics and economics and the triumph of materialism over other values.

The image is of interdependence giving rise to a world society in which states fade into irrelevance.

The problem is (a) the apparent health of the state, and the growth of its numbers and (b) the unresolved question of political order that underlies the growth of a world economy (the underwriter problem).

This was an image of the 1960s which is crashing along with the global liberal economy on which its hopes rested.

Marxist images of international order are notoriously vague. Proletarian internationalism contains an image of a world society in which states have crumbled away. As with the liberal image, economics is seen to triumph over, and supersede, politics.

The immediate reality wherever Marxists have obtained political power is a drive to build strong states. In the real world. Marxists are among the most strident supporters of the realist image.

We conclude that none of the available images provides an adequate basis for political action.

The realist image capitulates to a structure of disorder.

The internationalist image is too detached from political realities to be credible.

The socio-economic images simply avoid the question of political structure and so are not complete.

AN ALTERNATIVE IMAGE: MATURE ANARCHY

Assumptions:

1. Any useful image must be based on the political reality of an enduring anarchic structure.
2. Anarchy does not necessarily mean chaos. It can be seen as a

preferred political order and can be a vehicle for many idealist objectives.

3. The differences between individuals and states as units makes it inappropriate to draw analogies between anarchies composed of individuals and anarchies composed of states. States are better suited to anarchic systems than are individuals.

4. A global free trade economic system is not politically sustainable.

The image:

A world system based on regional blocs, each centred on a locus of industrial capacity (available nodes are: US, USSR, Japan, EC, possibly India and China).

These blocs might have imperial, hegemonic or confederal structures. They would be economically self-centred and capable of mounting credible nuclear deterrence.

The blocs would pursue self-reliance even at some cost in economic efficiency. There would be a need to avoid excessive fragmentation in protectionism and excessive vulnerability of global free trade.

International organisations would continue to play a harmonising and joint functions role.

Rules of conduct and system norms would be encouraged as a complement to mutual deterrence and economic self-reliance. These would include:

Respect for cultural and political diversity and the right to non-interference on internal affairs.

Mutual recognition of territorial boundaries and sovereign equality.

Peaceful settlement of disputes.

Responsibility to collaborate on problems of joint or planetary interest.

All of this is possible with no violation of the principle of anarchy. Indeed, it takes the positive side of anarchy – the cultivation of diversity as a political preference – and builds on it, rather than over-stressing the need for unitary systems as a way of overcoming the problem of political fragmentation.

*Possible problems of implementation:

1. the scale of policy-making required (e.g. EEC)
2. the inner-directedness of states as actors their consequent low priority to external affairs, and insensitivity to/distortion of feedback/input.
3. the implication of a neo-colonial future for many third world states.
4. the sanctioning of nuclear proliferation and the maintenance and extension of armed deterrence.

THE PEOPLE IN MENSA

By deliberate policy people, except in the obvious way, are more various in Mensa than anywhere else. I believe that it is because they are more intelligent that they are more various. The function of high intelligence is as much to generate options as it is to choose among them. Originality and creativity are set up as valuable qualities which are thought of as independent variables different from intelligence. But the evidence shows that intelligence as usually measured tends to correlate well with measures, such as they are, of creativity.

Marland reports that creativity is a tenuous concept. The various tests of creativity that have been devised correlate very poorly with one another. But they all correlate much better with intelligence tests. So Mensans and their ideas and attitudes vary more than others.

How about classes of people? Ethnic classes? We have no means of knowing because we do not ask but all groups are visible. Nat Weyl, judging only by names, came to the conclusion that Jewish-sounding names were over-representated (compared with the population norm). His survey also showed that the most serious over-representation in religious matters was a gross proportional surplus of Unitarians in American Mensa.

WOMEN IN MENSA

In Mensa women are under-represented. They seem to prefer it that way. The suggestion that the bar should be lowered to increase the proportion was strongly opposed – by the women members. Everywhere, in every country, the proportion is the same. Only one member in three is a woman.

We have no explanation but Professor Alice Heim may have.

She points out (*Intelligence and Personality*, Nichol & Co.) that the sub-set of humanity, woman, is deficient in members of other smaller sub-sets. Among women, those who are very bright, those who are very dim, those who are colour-blind and those who are criminals, are under-represented. Alice Heim seems to be fairly confident that the lack of very high and very low scorers on intelligence tests among women is a natural and expected consequence of what she calls 'the mediocrity of women'. She does not think this is explained by the social environment allotted to women in our society. She finds the phenomenon too universal for that. She goes on to say that with regard to verbal skills there is a clear sign that women are superior, and says that attempts to prove that this may be due to the environment are unconvincing.

Her third point is that girls tend to develop earlier intellectually than boys and this follows with physical and emotional development. In the days of the 11+ examination; on face value more girls ought to have obtained grammar school places. However, a year or two after the age of 11 the boys put on an intellectual spurt and come into their own academically. And this was allowed for, so that the results fitted what was expected to be the case later on. Heim says that creativity is greater in people who are nearer to the middle of the spectrum of sexual tendencies. Creative men tend to have more femininity in their psychological make-up than less creative men, and creative women tend to possess more masculine traits than less creative women. This is difficult to prove or refute because there is semantic circularity in the idea.

Finally I quote from Alice Heim: 'First, the top rungs of the achievement ladder are certainly occupied by men, and this is very likely a basic psychological fact – as opposed to a sociological one – since the bottom rungs of this and other ladders tend also to be occupied by men.'

Which way is Mensa going?

Mensa is like the hologram. It is an exciting idea in search of a use. A central role has brought me thousands of letters from members. They were of an extraordinary diversity. There is no dominant theme, but a persistently recurring one has been the 'Now we have it, what do we do with it?' approach. We have built up a world-wide association; should it have a policy? Should it become a pressure group, or a lobby with declared aims? The facile answer is that Mensa is not an organisation but an association. People are used to the idea of an organisation formed to further some policy. There are few institutions without at least an ostensible one. It is natural to expect that Mensa should conform to this model. But the association of Mensa members is not based on any purpose or policy, other than association itself. It is based on an objective criterion of selection, an assessment of the applicant's ability to think effectively. Mensa aims to be a forum of the intelligent of every persuasion, so it is simply and permanently not possible for Mensa to have any controversial collective views or policies.

Because the accusation of 'elitism' against Mensa is frequent and appears to be reasonable, let me talk about organisations in general.

The very existence of a committed organisation, one with objectives, is an indication that the policies are not uncontested. There are usually non-members, opponents or people with other priorities.

Organisations are formed to deal with areas of policy where there is disagreement with those not joining. Parties, factions, companies, groups, almost all institutions are formed with limited aims which are in competition with the aims or priorities of other parties, factions, groups, companies or institutions. Suppose Mensa were the same. If Mensa adopted, for instance, the policy of abolishing all experiments on animals, we should have a divided Mensa: the no-experiments faction and the rest. That would be a contradiction of what we have done so far. If we were to follow that road Mensa would divide into a proliferation of antagonistic groups loosely based on the original idea. This is a possible, even a likely course for Mensa, but not one that recommends itself to me at least.

My very strong recommendation to my Mensa colleagues is to hold on to our tenuous but strangely strong, tacit accord. Even at the cost of outward contention we should cling to our hidden protean unity.

Mensa has its own ways. It has its own kind of one-headedness. Some condemn us because we are uncommitted on the great political questions of the day. But Mensa is collectively a-political, because it is poly-political not because it is apathetic. Mensa has no collective aims because its members have all sectional aims.

As a self-appointed Mensa apologist I am in the odd position of having to put up a defence of the process of classification. Mensa is based on the classification of people, discrimination in fact. People are encouraged to be discriminating, but told that it is always wrong to discriminate. Mensa discriminates, so I shall try to answer this serious charge. In a mixed society where the mere recognition of occupational cultural and ethnic classifications is seen as divisive we forget the reason why mind must classify.

Neither human intelligence (nor any conceivable intelligence) can deal with the bewildering array of events and entities in the universe without simplification by classification. Looked at closely enough, everything, every event, every person is unique.

Our brains, whether we like it or not, have to simplify their data processing by sweeping similar things into heaps and labelling the heaps or classes with words. Mind has to classify if it is to comprehend and predict. The comprehension and predictions are limited by the validity, tolerance and usefulness of the classes chosen as the basis for thinking. All classification falsifies reality because, at the limit, each event and entity observed remains unique.

Further, it is not given to us to know *ab initio* which systems of classification help understanding and prediction and which do not. With taxonomies (systems of classification), Man proposes; experience disposes.

So, I maintain, all associations are the result of some classification process, and all serve the interests of some class in this wider sense. It may be the class of those interested in angling. It may be that of those interested in social reform, chess, politics or the rights of animals or bacteria. Institutions serve classes. All of them.

Now there is a modern trend, inspired by Marx or by fear of his ideas, which repudiates any classification of people whatsoever. Mensa had to answer or shut up shop.

Marxism itself, of course, though its final aim is a classless society, encourages and sharpens 'class consciousness' and indeed advocates class war.

So, perhaps as a defence, perhaps in reaction, it is popular, in recent years, to reject outright any attempt to understand the differences between people which would involve classifying them in any way whatever.

At first sight this is an attractive idea. Do away with any nasty, divisive classifications, treat people as ants or as clone-mates and all conflict will be resolved; we shall love each other and live in sweet harmony, prosperity and peace. Like ants.

The wicked, divisive, elitist, selection system which we, in Mensa, employ comes under attack by those who fear for our safety in the inevitable street fights between those above and below our arbitrary cutoff.

This blatant defence of classification, especially in the sensitive field of mental excellence, will, I know by experience, be condemned as a manifestation of racism, fascism and elitism, so I must say here, again, that I speak only for myself. High intelligence is no defence against stupidity, and self-humiliation is the special fault of the able. I know that among the diverse opinions in which Mensa rejoices, there will be some who condemn my lack of humility on Mensa's behalf.

It ought not to be, but it is necessary to say this. There are classifications systems which are manifestly unjust because they are used to make decisions which are inappropriate. To decide the appointment of doctors or dustmen on the basis of the colour of the hair or skin is unjust because pigmentation is a bad guide to the usefulness of people in these occupations. However, to decide such appointments without the guidance that comes from appropriate classification would be equally unjust. There is nothing wrong with discrimination in favour of the class of those strong enough to lift dustbins in one case, or the class of those with medical qualifications in the other.

It would be as unjust to everyone to insist on giving opportunities to mixed-ability surgeons or bridge designers drawn in fair proportion from all classes of intelligence, knowledge and skill as it would be to them to choose them on the basis of the wealth and social class of their parents.

I should not need to emphasise the point but I am afraid it might be wise to do so. Once feudalism collapsed in the developed world there was no way we could do without the classification of human beings. It is essential to the correct functioning of the extended complex, interwoven society which is the source of livelihood and prosperity wherever they exist. Our system is based on the amplification of intelligence and ability in a system for the division of labour where the underlying principle is that of finding the best person for the job. Classification of both jobs and people is involved.

Wrong and therefore harmful systems of classification are those based on parental status, social class, ethnic origin, sex and age where these factors are inappropriate. (There are choices where such factors *can* be relevant. Being a practising Protestant might count against an aspiring pope without unfairness. It would not be 'discrimination' to choose a black-skinned actor to play Othello.)

The habit of unduly extending the case against the evils of inappropriate discrimination merely weakens it. The serious problems of discrimination in society would be easier to deal with if we all stopped paying insincere lip-service to the doctrine that *all* discrimination is evil.

We live in a vast, complex, interrelated society in which very large numbers of people, each unique, have to be fitted into roles where the rest can best be served. There are, like it or not, great differences in the ability of different people to train for and fill these highly specific, often demanding roles. The notion, so popular today, that society can accomplish this vital social sorting-out without classification (i.e. discrimination) is warm-hearted but empty-headed, emotional nonsense of a very damaging kind.

The great adventure and discovery of the open society is that it swept away systems of human classification which were no longer appropriate. Innovators and entrepreneurs were set free to experiment. The modern pluralist state is successful because any system of classification may be tried out.

There is freedom of association. Any group of people may come together to try out any lawful scheme. The fundamental life-enhancing principle of trial and error is evoked. All gain. Even the losers in the prosperous countries are rich compared with those countries where tribal and tradition classification systems still rule.

Out of the vast number of experiments some good and useful systems and institutions are offered for selection by the rest of us via the market mechanism (or the slower but necessary democratic one).

The open society will have failures; some bad and harmful institutions will be offered for modification or rejection by the body politic. The myriad resulting organisations and institutions come into healthy competition within a long-evolved benevolent framework of law, custom, practice and world culture traditions.

Institutions survive and evolve like any other living entity, because they are there. No one asks a dog, a flea or an elephant what its purpose is. They have one obvious purpose, to exist and replicate. There are human institutions like that. The Oddfellows, the Kiwanis and the Buffaloes are examples. So may Mensa be without need for apology.

The members of Mensa are a classified selection. They are not selected for what they think but *because* they think, and think for themselves. What does Mensa do now and what can it do in the future?

Today Mensa serves its members in obvious ways. It provides a place where good talk can be heard. It establishes a frankly intellectual forum where members may provoke, stimulate, encourage, and correct each other's thinking, ideas, creativity, invention and projects. It also creates a multi-disciplinary, trans-world agora for the exchange and development of ideas, plans, schemes and dreams.

It is also, very simply, a club where congenial and usually, interesting people can meet, marry, make friends, partners, and hay.

Further, Mensa's network spans the earth. Travelling members can meet a ready-made circle of colleagues in other countries with whom there is a natural initial link. Further still, like many international clubs, it forms an interdisciplinary medium of commercial and business contacts.

That is a lot, but apart from that Mensa is much more: it is a ubiquitous university, in the older sense of that word. It creates groups which initiate many projects which are of use to the participants and often generally.

I know from the sample that I have observed that Mensa is the unacknowledged source of an unknown but large number of inventions, articles, books, scientific papers, new companies, associations and projects which would have been impossible without it.

Equally, Mensa has a very large number of marriages, sports teams, drinking groups, parties, jaunts, jamborees and celebrations to its unacknowledged credit. There is much good (and little bad) here.

All these justifications for existence are normal and simple enough, but are they, in the general view enough to justify our continuance?

MENSA RESEARCH

Berrill's original objective, research, has never played the part we early members expected. Berrill did quite a number of opinion surveys but they could not be taken seriously as research projects.

I myself tried to do a number of surveys and learned about and used statistical sampling methods for the purpose but these too were amateur affairs.

The only sustained effort in this direction has been reported in the *Mensa Research Journal* published at first by American Mensa Ltd., under the editorship of Vern Schuman. This started sometime before 1970. It was later taken over by the Mensa Educational and Research Foundation when this was set up. The journal has now been edited for many years by Dr Max Fogel. The *Mensa Research Journal* is a professionally produced journal with accounts of many serious researches in fields relative to the Mensa theme.

The one serious large scale research which was internationally funded was that mentioned in the text by Professor Philip Powell entitled *Elementary Education, Personal Adjustment and Social Achievement of a National Sample of Gifted Adults.* This was published by the World Congress on Gifted and Talented Children.

I think that it ought to be a future aim of Mensa to do a great deal more in this field. We have a unique sample of people who were at one time gifted children. A great deal could be done to answer the questions about the way to deal with and get the best from such children and could be learned from good research based on our large sample with its great range of educational treatments.

INTELLIGENCE AND OCCUPATION

There is a very visible trend in societies in the developed world. It is the mechanisation and thus the disappearance of many jobs which demand little conceptual ability. Unskilled jobs for people are disappearing; jobs that require high intelligence and training are proliferating. It may be important that Mensa is a collection of the type who are now in more demand. There are already many who have found it useful to search in Mensa for the abilities they need. Mensa could form a Talent Bank upon which society could draw. Possibly we could extend the idea and have a computerised store of data about those of the members who opted for it so that it could be made available to talent seekers.

There is another thing which tentatively we might be able to claim as a plus for Mensa itself and for the world in general. I have heard this idea from several people and it fits in with my secret dreams for Mensa.

Remembering what the Queen and Dr Abbele thought: if there is any group of people who can reach across the cultural divisions, the religious, ideological, political and national bounds which separate humanity, it *might* be the more intelligent members of each group, cult and sect. They perhaps, may be able to grasp and understand the differences and, more important, see beneath the surface, to sense the hidden human unity beneath. I have a very strong impression that this is so. Bringing together the intelligent members of every culture and country around the world may form human links that help towards the hope for world peace.

Despite Mensa's natural, human and basically harmless internal troubles and squabbles that I have described, Mensa experience confirms this view. We may well say, 'If the more intelligent cannot comprehend each other and reach accord, who can?' So far, not without purely verbal quarrels, we have comprehended, reached accord.

But let me go beyond this thought. Let me invite myself to see visions, to dream dreams. My first steps on to this shifting ground take me this way. Is not what may seem to be Mensa's principal weakness really a hidden strength? Our protean quality, our uncommitted, provisional stance, our lack of bigotry, our refusal to be bound by a common dogma; these things may hold us back from concerted action, but that itself may be a protection and an advantage. Having got used to living with our disagreements and divisions we may survive the fissile stresses that have afflicted almost all similar organisations in the past.

And if we can do that may we not, as I have suggested, prove to be the best champion and defender of the new World Culture which I have described? The World Culture is a difficult idea to defend and, with the recent renewed outbreak of a virulent, dogmatic fundamentalist reaction to it in many places, it is in need of defence. I believe that it is very hard for really bright people who are exposed to our very mixed group of other bright people to fall victim to these extreme forms of dogmatism.

I dare to think that one-culture dogmatists in Mensa ranks will remain such a small minority that Mensa can take on the role of defending and advocating the Whole of which I believe it is itself a small part. The World Culture has exactly the same qualities of tolerance, diversity, provisionality, lack of dogma and of wide mutual intercommunication that we see, in part, in Mensa.

To foster intelligence for the benefit of humanity is already an accepted aim of Mensa. The best way to do that, and the fundamental future role of Mensa, might be to be a conscious force to further and support the earthly manifestation of Mind in the larger form, the present ubiquitous World Culture.

This will involve a greater role in the support of talent, excellence and ability than we have played so far. It means a posture defence of science and enquiry and of opposition to rigidity and dogma. It will involve the defence of the open against the closed society, the open against the closed frontier, the open against the closed mind. It will involve a feeling of identification with what was behind Wells' thinking when he spoke of World Brain, behind Shaw's when he spoke of the Life Force, behind Chardin's when he spoke of the Noosphere, behind Popper's when he spoke of World III and behind mine when I speak of the World Culture.

A test for your intelligence

The verbal and number tests. You have one hour. Then stop.

DIRECTIONS
Answer the questions as carefully and as quickly as you can. Begin at the beginning and go straight through. Some of the first questions are easy. Answer them carefully – there are no catches. The later questions get harder. You have *one hour. Do not spend too long on questions you cannot do.*

Look at these words:

>   apple, orange, <u>potato</u>, plum, cherry.

They are all names of fruits except 'potato', so 'potato' is underlined, as it does not belong with the others.

In each line below **underline the ONE WORD that does not belong there.**

1. house, school, dog, cinema, church.

2. carrot, cabbage, turnip, orange, potato.

3. mountain, valley, hill, peak, ridge.

4. hour, yard, foot, mile, inch.

5. walk, run, trot, gallop, rest.

6. dress, overcoat, necklace, trousers, vest.

Now look at these numbers:

$$3, 5, 7, .., 11, 13, 15.$$

There is a gap where the number is left out. It is 9, so the numbers should be:

$$3, 5, 7, 9, 11, 13, 15.$$

Now these:

$$64, 32, 16, .., 4, 2, 1.$$

The number left out is 8, so the numbers should be:

$$64, 32, 16, 8, 4, 2, 1.$$

Now do these the same way, putting in each gap the right number:

7. 4, 6, 8, .., 12, 14, 16.

8. 23, 20, 17, .., 11, 8, 5.

9. 4, 10, 16, .., 28, 34, 40.

10. 20, 18, 16, 14, .., 14, 16, 18, 20.

11. 2, 3, 5, 6, .., 9, 11, 12, 14.

12. 5, 7, 10, 14, .., 25, 32, 40.

Now look at this list of words. Each word has a number.

1.	wide	6.	empty	11.	lazy
2.	end	7.	swell	12.	big
3.	fast	8.	over	13.	long
4.	find	9.	like	14.	good
5.	right	10.	grand	15.	deep

'Quick' means the SAME as 'fast,' which is word No. 3. So we put:

'quick' means the SAME as word No. 3.

'Small' means the OPPOSITE of 'big,' which is word No. 12. So we put:

'small' means the OPPOSITE of word No. 12.

Now do these, putting in each time the number of the right word from the list. Some are SAME, and some are OPPOSITE.

13. 'lose' means the **OPPOSITE** of word No. . . .

14. 'broad' means the **SAME** as word No. . . .

15. 'above' means the **SAME** as word No. . . .

16. 'slow' means the **OPPOSITE** of word No. . . .

17. 'idle' means the **SAME** as word No. . . .

18. 'short' means the **OPPOSITE** of word No. . . .

19. 'shallow' means the **OPPOSITE** of word No. . . .

20. 'expand' means the **SAME** as word No. . . .

21. 'discover' means the **SAME** as word No. . . .

22. 'bad' means the **OPPOSITE** of word No. . . .

23. 'begin' means the **OPPOSITE** of word No. . . .

24. 'correct' means the **SAME** as word No. . . .

25. 'vacant' means the **SAME** as word No. . . .

26. 'different' means the **OPPOSITE** of word No. . . .

27. 'contract' means the **OPPOSITE** of word No. . . .

28. 'finish' means the **SAME** as word No. . . .

Now look at this:

hat, head (face, hand, <u>foot</u>, dress, mouth, <u>shoe</u>).

A hat is worn on the head, and a shoe is worn on the foot, so 'shoe' and 'foot' are underlined.

Do these others in the same way, underlining just TWO words in the brackets connected in the same sort of way as the two words outside the brackets.

29. apple, fruit (oak, grass, field, orange, tree, wool).

30. sit, chair (table, cloth, bed, blanket, wake, sleep).

31. girl, sister (father, brother, mother, boy, man, son).

32. tongue, taste (walk, ear, leg, arm, see, hand).

33. cruel, kind (angry, generous, sorry, timid, selfish, shy).

34. stay, go (come, depart, depend, remain, stand, run).

35. same, opposite (black, round, white, blue, square, green).

36. water, liquid (thought, steam, taste, emotion, ice, fear).

Here is a letter square:

R J N Y K
G E P U B
M Q F T S
O A H C V
X L D W Z

See how the letters are arranged. Thus P comes just after E. C is just below T. S is between B and V. **Now answer these questions:**

37. What letter comes just above the letter just after H? ......

38. What letter comes just before the letter just above A? ......

39. What letter is midway between G and B? ......

40. What letter comes between the letter just below A and the letter just above C? ......

41. What letter comes just above the letter that comes just before the letter just below S? ......

42. What letter comes between the letter between R and M and the letter between F and D? ......

43. What letter comes just before the letter just above the letter between Q and T? ......

44. What letter comes just after the letter that comes just above the letter just before the letter just above F? ......

45. What letter comes just above the letter which comes just after the letter which comes between the letter just above F and the letter just below M? ......

46. What letter comes just below the letter which comes between the letter just after the letter just above G and the letter just before the letter just below B? . . . . . .

Now in each line below there are **TWO** words this time which do not belong with the other four words. **Underline these TWO words in each line.**

47. water, beer, bread, lemonade, cake, milk.

48. sit, run, rest, stop, stand, look.

49. malice, jealousy, greed, kindness, envy, stupidity.

50. tall, arrogant, timid, proud, fierce, boastful.

51. now, here, then, where, when, while.

In each line below fill in the right number in the gap:

52. 4, 9, 16, . . , 36, 49, 64.

53. 2, 6, 12, . . , 30, 42, 56.

54. 41, 38, 36, 33, . . , 28, 26, 23.

55. 2, 3, 5, . . , 17, 33, 65.

56. 3, 5, 4, 6, . . , 7, 6, 8, 7.

57. 99, 80, 63, . . , 35, 24, 15.

Look at this list of words:

1. brave	6. scatter	11. argue
2. evade	7. join	12. content
3. hinder	8. tremendous	13. leave
4. lessen	9. crooked	14. hurry
5. agree	10. proud	15. wander

In each case below put in the number of the right word from the list:

58. 'obstruct' means the SAME as No. . . .

59. 'wry' means the SAME as No. . . .

60. 'differ' means the **OPPOSITE** of No. . . .

61. 'courageous' means the **SAME** as No. . . .

62. 'concentrate means the **OPPOSITE** of No. . . .

63. 'lag' means the **OPPOSITE** of No. . . .

64. 'enormous' means the **SAME** as No. . . .

65. 'seek' means the **OPPOSITE** of No. . . .

66. 'connect' means the **SAME** as No. . . .

67. 'help' means the **OPPOSITE** of No. . . .

68. 'dissatisfied' means the **OPPOSITE** of No. . . .

69. 'depart' means the **SAME** as No. . . .

70. 'diminish' means the **SAME** as No. . . .

71. 'tiny' means the **OPPOSITE** of No. . . .

72. 'divide' means the **OPPOSITE** of No. . . .

73. 'disperse' means the **SAME** as No. . . .

Now underline the TWO words in the brackets connected in the same sort of way as the TWO words outside the brackets.

74. envy, jealousy (love, hate, greed, cruelty, selfishness, terror)

75. island, water (sea, land, ocean, lake, hill, valley).

76. ear, music (colour, picture, eye, sound, song, red).

77. then, now (future, when, present, where, gift, past).

78. dispute, concur (agree, connive, disdain, differ, deter, depart).

79. perhaps, however (likely, possibly, certainly, nevertheless, because).

80. sun, earth (moon, star, night, light, earth, sky).

81. hour, second (foot, yard, length, inch, time, minute).

A certain tank holds 20 gallons of water. When a tap over it is turned on water flows from it into the tank at the rate of 4 gallons a minute. When a plug in the bottom of the tank is pulled out water drains away from the tank at the rate of 6 gallons a minute.

Now answer these questions:

82. With the tank empty and the plug in, the tap is turned on. How many minutes will it take to fill the tank?

...... minutes

83. With the tank full, the tap is turned on and the plug pulled out. How many minutes will it take to empty the tank?

...... minutes

84. With the tank empty and the plug in, the tap is turned on for 3 minutes. It is then turned off and the plug pulled out. How many minutes will it then take to empty the tank?

...... minutes

85. With the tank full, the plug is pulled out and the tap turned on. After 4 minutes the tap is turned off with the plug left out. How many more minutes will it then take to empty the tank?

...... minutes

86. The tank is full. The plug is pulled out for 2 minutes. The tap is then turned on for 3 minutes with the plug still out. How many gallons will be in the tank at the end of this time?

...... gallons

87. The tank is empty with the plug in. The tap is turned on for 4 minutes. The plug is then pulled out with the tap left on for another 6 minutes. How many gallons will be in the tank at the end of this time?

...... gallons

INTERPRETING YOUR TEST RESULT

You should have finished the test within the period of one hour allowed otherwise the results are doubtful.

Determine your raw score by adding the points as instructed on the answer sheet. There is no penalty for errors; only correct answers are counted.

Enter the SCORE/AGE/IQ TABLE at your present age if you are below 14 and at the age 14+ if you are older. Read your percentile rating and your IQ opposite your raw score.

If your percentile rating is 98 or better you would probably qualify for Mensa if you were to take the supervised test. If you are on the 95th percentile it is usually worth a try as there is a margin of uncertainty which is unavoidable in this inexact art. A score of about 132 would qualify for Mensa membership.

If you live in the British Isles and want to apply to Mensa or get a brochure and test please write to: MENSA FREEPOST WOLVERHAMPTON. The full address is Mensa, Bond House, St John's Square, Wolverhampton WV2 4AH.

Overseas enquirers will find the nearest appropriate address on page 307.

Enquiries from countries where there is no national Mensa branch should go to the International Mensa Office at 50/52 Great Eastern Street London EC2A 3EP UK.

THE ANSWERS
The key and the scoring scheme

To be counted correct an answer must be exactly as given in the key below – no more and no less – except that in items 37–46 answers may be in block capitals as in the key, or in small letters

KEY

1. dog	31. brother, boy	61. 1
2. orange	32. walk, leg	62. 6
3. valley	33. generous, selfish	63. 14
4. hour	34. depart, remain	64. 8
5. rest	35. black, white	65. 2
6. necklace	36. emotion, fear	66. 7
7. 10	37. T	67. 3
8. 14	38. M	68. 12
9. 22	39. P	69. 13
10. 12	40. H	70. 4
11. 8	41. T	71. 8
12. 19	42. Q	72. 7
13. 4	43. E	73. 6
14. 1	44. N	74. greed, selfishness
15. 8	45. P	75. land, lake
16. 3	46. F	76. picture, eye
17. 11	47. bread, cake	77. present, past
18. 13	48. run, look	78. agree, differ
19. 15	49. kindness, stupidity	79. possibly, never-theless
20. 7	50. tall, timid	80. moon, earth
21. 4	51. here, where	81. yard, inch
22. 14	52. 25	82. 5
23. 2	53. 20	83. 10
24. 5	54. 31	84. 2
25. 6	55. 9	85. 2
26. 9	56. 5	86. 2
27. 7	57. 48	87. 4
28. 2	58. 3	
29. oak, tree	59. 9	
30. bed, sleep	60. 5	

TOTAL:
This is your 'raw score' (number of answers completely correct)

SCORE AGE IQ TABLE

	AGE	10		10½		11		11½	
score	IQ	Percentile	IQ	Percentile	IQ	Percentile	IQ	Perc
10	85	16th	83	13th	80	9th	77	6th
12	87	19th	85	16th	82	11th	79	8th
14	89	23rd	87	19th	84	14th	81	10th
16	92	30th	89	23rd	86	17th	82	11th
18	94	34th	90	25th	88	21st	84	14th
20	96	40th	92	30th	89	23rd	86	17th
22	98	45th	94	34th	91	27th	88	21st
24	100	50th	96	40th	93	32nd	90	25th
26	102	55th	98	45th	95	37th	92	30th
28	104	60th	100	50th	97	42nd	94	34th
30	106	65th	103	58th	99	47th	96	39th
32	108	70th	106	65th	102	55th	98	45th
34	111	77th	108	70th	104	60th	100	50th
36	114	84th	111	77th	107	67th	102	55th
38	117	87th	113	80th	109	72nd	105	63rd
40	119	89th	115	84th	111	76th	107	67th
42	122	93rd	117	87th	114	82nd	109	72n
44	125	95th	120	91st	116	85th	111	76th
46	127	96th	123	94th	118	88th	113	80th
48	129	97th	125	95th	120	91st	115	84th
50	131	98th	127	96th	122	93rd	117	87th
52	133	98th	129	97th	124	94th	120	91st
54	135	99th	132	98th	126	96th	122	93r
56	137	99th	135	99th	129	97th	124	94t
58	140	99th	137	99th	132	98th	126	96t
60	143	99th	139	99th	134	98th	129	97t
62	—	—	142	99th	137	99th	131	98t
64	—	—	145	99th	140	99th	133	98t
66	—	—	—	—	144	99th	136	99t
68	—	—	—	—	147	99th	138	99t
70	—	—	—	—	150	99th	140	99t
72	—	—	—	—	—	—	143	99t
74	—	—	—	—	—	—	145	99t
76	—	—	—	—	—	—	147	99t
78	—	—	—	—	—	—	149	99t
80	—	—	—	—	—	—	150	99t

BELOW THIS LINE IT WOULD BE WORTH A TRY FOR MENSA

	12 Percentile	IQ	12½ Percentile	IQ	13 Percentile	IQ	13½ Percentile	IQ	14+ Percentile
5	5th	74	4th	73	3rd	73	3rd	71	3rd
7	6th	75	5th	74	4th	74	4th	72	3rd
9	8th	77	6th	76	5th	75	5th	73	3rd
0	9th	79	8th	77	6th	76	5th	74	4th
1	10th	80	9th	79	8th	77	6th	75	5th
3	13th	81	10th	80	9th	78	7th	76	5th
5	16th	83	13th	82	11th	79	8th	77	6th
6	17th	85	16th	83	13th	80	9th	78	7th
8	21st	86	17th	85	16th	82	11th	79	8th
0	25th	88	21st	87	19th	83	13th	80	9th
2	30th	90	25th	88	21st	84	14th	81	10th
4	34th	92	30th	90	25th	86	17th	83	13th
6	40th	94	34th	92	30th	88	21st	84	14th
9	47th	96	40th	94	34th	90	25th	86	17th
1	52nd	98	45th	96	40th	91	27th	87	19th
3	58th	100	50th	98	45th	93	32nd	89	23rd
5	63rd	102	55th	100	50th	95	37th	91	27th
8	70th	105	63rd	103	58th	97	42nd	94	34th
0	74th	107	67th	105	63rd	100	50th	97	42nd
2	79th	109	72nd	107	67th	103	58th	100	50th
4	82nd	111	76th	109	72nd	105	63rd	102	55th
6	85th	113	80th	111	76th	108	70th	104	60th
8	88th	115	84th	114	82nd	111	76th	106	65th
0	91st	118	88th	116	85th	114	82nd	108	70th
2	93rd	120	91st	118	88th	116	85th	110	74th
4	94th	122	93rd	120	91st	117	87th	112	79th
7	96th	125	95th	123	94th	120	91st	114	82nd
9	97th	127	96th	125	95th	123	94th	116	85th
1	98th	129	97th	127	96th	125	95th	118	88th
3	98th	131	98th	129	97th	127	96th	120	91st
6	99th	134	98th	132	98th	130	97th	124	94th
9	99th	137	99th	134	98th	132	98th	126	96th
2	99th	139	99th	137	99th	134	98th	128	97th
4	99th	142	99th	140	99th	136	99th	131	98th
6	99th	144	99th	142	99th	138	99th	133	98th
9	99th	146	99th	145	99th	141	99th	138	99th

Appendix

1 April	Mensa Magazine Volume 1, No. 1
May	Mensa Magazine Volume 1, No. 2
June	Mensa Magazine Volume 1, No. 3
1 July	Mensa Magazine Volume 1, No. 4. First list of 22 members.
August	Mensa Magazine Volume 1, No. 5. Mensa Quarterly starts. Volume 1, No. 1; good Berrill photograph.
November	First Annual Gathering of Mensa. Second Membership List, 33 members.
6 December	14 members at dinner at 'Jill-on-the-Green' restaurant.

1948

April	Dinner at Trocadero. 35 present. Good meeting.
Summer	Various odd dinners. Some very odd.

1949

	Badge, 'Ornamental Tile', several interrogatories sent to members.
	Dinners at Café Royal and Cumberland Hotel.
	Mensa Quarterly.
	V. Serebriakoff applies some time in autumn.
November	Annual Gathering. Council appointed by referendum.

1950

	Berrill becomes disillusioned. 'Council' meets.
January	V.S. accepted by Berrill.
April	Mensa Quarterly. Mensa numerals. 169 members.
May	Mensa Quarterly. V.S. suggests postal debates.
August	Mensa Quarterly. 199/258 reply to Berrill.

November	Annual Gathering at Charing Cross Hotel. Attendance about 60. A 'Commission' decides on 'Mensa Council'.
1951	
	New council chosen.
	Activity and recruitment wane.
	Monthly Dinners at 'A La Brioche'.
February	Mensa Quarterly, Volume 3, No. 1.
July	Mensa Quarterly, Volume 3, No. 4, page 1. Berrill's 'Personal Message' very negative.
4 November	Annual Gathering at Charing Cross Hotel. Attempt to depose Berrill fails. Council resigns and circulates, proposing rival organisation.
1952	
January	Mensa Quarterly, Volume 4, No. 1. Berrill resigns as Secretary. 76 replies to circular re: new council.
20 January	Quarterly gathering. 27 attend.
April	Mensa Quarterly, Volume 4, No. 2 – V.S.'s piece 'What should be our policy'.
April	Quarterly gathering. Monthly Dinners continue.
July	Mensa Quarterly – piece by V.S.
October	Mensa Quarterly, Volume 4, No. 4 (one page)
1 November	Annual Gathering at Charing Cross Hotel, small attendance. During the year, membership falls. No recruitment. Ware lapses.
1953	
April	Mensa Quarterly. 'Cri du Coeur' for successor by Joe Wilson.
July	Mensa Quarterly, Volume 5, No. 2. First Marlow picnic.

5 October	V.S. marries Win Rouse, the *Corps d'Esprit*.
	V.S. becomes third Secretary of Mensa.
November	Mensa Quarterly, Volume 5, No. 3.
20 November	Annual Gathering at Charing Cross Hotel.

1954

	V.S. is working at recruitment. No publication.
7 November	Annual Gathering at Charing Cross Hotel. Informal committee accepted; V.S. confirmed as Secretary.

1955

November	Mensa Proceedings, Volume 6, No. 1, edited by V.S. and Glyn Emery.
20 November	Annual Gathering at Charing Cross Hotel. Dr Carter gives first Annual Lecture on 'Eugenics'.

1956

June	Marlow picnic. Charney Basset weekend.
November	Mensa Proceedings; Editor V.S. says 'Miracle continues'.
20 November	Annual Gathering at Charing Cross Hotel. S. Andreski gave Annual Lecture. Numerous new members. Dinners at 'Beguinots' continue.

1957

	Vigorous recruitment. Midlands Mensa begins. Office run by Joyce Mumford. Little publication.
November	Annual Gathering at Charing Cross Hotel.

1958

	Dinners at Schmidt's Restaurant, very crowded.

	Many discussion meetings in people's homes.
September	Mensa Proceedings, piece about being 'swamped'. 14 meetings that month; Birmingham meetings.
16 November	Annual Gathering and AGM at Charing Cross Hotel.
	Annual Lecture by Professor Philip Vernon. 60 members present.

1959

January	Mensa Correspondence, monthly journal started by Brian Mager.
March	Mensa Proceedings, V.S. talks of 'Breakthrough'.
	Long description of organisation.
April	Publicity article in *The People*.
May	Discussion as to what members call themselves – this led to 'M' and 'Fem' and 'Mensan'.
June	Mensa hits Berrill's 600 members target. Recruitment taken over by professional Mrs Hayes. 6 meetings.
19 July	Berrill at Sheffield Park outing. 9 meetings in month.
2–5 October	First residential conference at Braziers Park.
1 November	English Speaking Union. Annual Gathering and AGM.
	Wilson in Chair. Treasurer Spicer. Membership Mumford.
	Groups Salzedo. 750 members.
	Burt gave Annual Lecture. Berrill gave lecture.
	V.S. reports attempts in USA.

1960

| January | Professor Sir Cyril Burt announced as President. |

	A. A. Hyatt trying to form American Branch with NAGC.
March	Big TV break: 'Tonight' in England.
April	Massive publicity continues TV and Press.
May	Eustace, 2nd Editor of Mensa Correspondence, resigns.
June	17 meetings called. Eric Hills takes over Local Groups.
August	Win Serebriakoff edits Mensa Correspondence. Call by Stickland for a Constitution for Mensa. Constitution sub-committee announced.
	V.S. edits Mensa Correspondence; it goes into print.
	American founder, Peter Sturgeon, begins to call meetings in New York.
18 October	15 members at Sturgeon's New York meeting.
October	Mensa Correspondence; 20 meetings called.
	Second residential conference announced. Mensa Register started.
28 October	Sturgeon entertains second meeting of Mensa in New York.
November	Mensa Correspondence; V.S. starts new supervised test procedure.
3 November	Annual Gathering and AGM at Russell Hotel.
	180 present. Big press break.
18 November	Sturgeon calls third American Mensa meeting chez Abe Kipnis.
December	Wayne Green hosts meeting of American members in New York.
18 December	*New York Times* story on Mensa followed by letter from P. Sturgeon. NY WCBS Radio story. Flood of enquiries to Mensa from America.

10 British Regional Groups function at year end.

17 November	Annual Gathering at Conway Hall. Annual Lecture given by Professor Medawar.
November	Annual Gathering and AGM Committee appointed Chairman J. Wilson, Secretary V.S., Treasurer S. Russel, J. Simpkins Sparrow, Stableford, D. Cass, Phil Simpson, Peter Sturgeon who reported as American Secretary. 641 members. Activities Bulletin started. V.S. reports visit to Holland and meeting with Koops and Naber also Count Soltikow. Many foreign offers. American talk of secession. 200 attended AGM.

1963

January	Mensa Correspondence; article by Margot Seitelman.
March	Burt launches premises fund. V.S. on holiday meets G. Fischhof in Italy; plans Austrian Mensa.
15–16 June	First American Annual Gathering. Huge success. 160 members attend.
July	American *Charisma* published.
August	David Mason, Editor Mensa Correspondence, reports of American Committee at Annual Gathering – Brian Heald, Peter Sturgeon, Alf Rubinstein, Emerson Coyle, Herb Arhend, John Codella. First Meeting of Dutch Mensa.
October	Mensa Correspondence; International Structure announced. World membership 2,632; US about 1,000. Development Officer Stableford reports work in Holland, Germany, Brazil and France.
November	Annual Gathering at Conway Hall. Karl Popper.

Coverage by Panorama TV. Peter Sturgeon
present.
Art exhibition.

1964

American membership 1,400.

April   Journal called *Interim* starts. First article
                 'Echo 3'.

20 June   American Annual Gathering at Biltmore
                 Hotel, New York. V.S. present. Enormous
                 publicity including *Time* magazine. Chopper
                 trip for *LIFE* Magazine.

July   *Interim*; election of International Committee
                 announced.

August   *Interim*; V.S. reports completion of Mensa
                 Book and announces foundation of Austrian
                 Mensa by Dr G. Fischhof.

September   *Interim*; V.S.'s report 'On having your head
                 turned' in USA. Peter Sturgeon's report.

October   V.S. gives International Secretary's report
                 on new structure; gives up as General
                 Secretary of British Mensa after 9 years.
                 New British Committee – Chairman E.
                 Hills, Secretary Carol Irvin, Treasurer N.
                 Schulman.

20–22 November   Annual Gathering at French Institute. See
                 AGM report interim files. Turnover
                 £18,000. Talk of constitutional problems,
                 Review Committee etc.

December   International Election Ballot result, Sereb-
                 riakoff Panel 820, Kaufman Panel 160.
                 Mensa addresses in UK, USA, Austria,
                 France, Rosemary Bertrand, Germany, Dr
                 Steiner, Netherlands, Naber, Belgium,
                 Sweden, Albrecht, Australia, Marjorie
                 Meakins, Rhodesia, A. P. Bowl.
                 First International Constitution accepted by
                 referendum.

1965

	American membership 4,400.
May	*Interim*; Hamilton article.
June	Mensa Founders to meet in Germany. Mensa structure under fire from provincial and American critics.
	Premises fund £2,000.
	American Annual Gathering at Biltmore Hotel, New York, 275 present from 22 states. Codella Chairman of American Mensa, with Singer, Hamilton, Heald, Yee, Truelove, Glor Rubinstein, Martinson, Willoughby.
August	Reg Candy takes over British Mensa office.
	European Founders' Meeting: Serebriakoff, Naber, Albrecht, Fischhof, Bertrand, Steiner, Eberstark.
September	Postal ballot re: Victor and Win Serebriakoff's tour.
	Treasurer Steven Russel dies.
October	Victor and Win in big publicity tour of USA; Johnny Carson and many other shows. 35,000 applications, over 5000 new members in USA.
	Interim, A4 size. Max Wyman, Editor, reports Founders' Conference.
November	British AGM at Institut Francais. Marghanita Laski and J. Cohen lecturers.
	V.S.'s 'A Mensa Analysis and History' published.

1966

	World membership about 11,000.
	American membership peaks at 8,000.
	Period of harassment of American Committee chaired by Codella.
June	Troubled Annual Gathering in New York.
August	Codella resigns.

November	V.S. publishes 'How Mensa is Organised'. London Annual Gathering. Motion of 'no confidence' in International Committee.

1967

	American membership peaks at 11,000.
June	American AGM. Chairman Ahrend, with Coyle, Frisch, Turchin, Rubin, Lowenstein, McGowan and Jack.
	Canada split away with 514 members.
	British journal *Intelligence*.
	Report of International General Council.
July	Report on Lugano meeting. 3rd aim.
August	Report that American Annual Gathering rejects 'no confidence' motion.
September	American Bulletin – talks of Friedman, Rubin to International General Council in England.
October	General Secretary three year report.
November	British activities bulletin separate from the International Journal, which remains so until *Mensa* in 1982.
	British AGM Lecture by Simon Hoggart. Committee.
	International Election V.S.'s panel lose. Mayne/Frisch panel takes over.

1968

January	American bulletin takes front page. American membership constant at 11,000 after split-off of 504 Canadian members.
February	British Mensa to Wolverhampton.
March	Defeat of Serebriakoff slate: Mayne, Frisch panel 2,210. Wilson, Serebriakoff 1,660. Reconstruction panel 876.
	Magnificent Manchester weekend.
April	*Intelligence* article 'On being kicked out', V.S.
May	Mensa Journal, article by I. Robinson 'Welcome Stranger'.

June	American Annual Gathering at Tarrytown; 225 present. Article by Mayne 'On being swept in'.
June	'British Mensa' full list of new International General Council.
July	No Mensa Journal.
1, 2, 3 November	British AGM at Victory ex-Service Men's Club. Criticism of International Journal. Sydney Irving elected Chairman.

1969

	American membership 11,000.
January	British Mensa attacks on International Editor. His apologia. Regional British committee meetings.
February	American Bulletin, 'Censorship of International General Council?'
April	Nigel Searle appointed Secretary British Mensa.
May	American Bulletin; Karl Ross takes over as Assistant Editor. Young Mensa Conference, Birmingham.
June	American AG at San Francisco; 250 present. Chairman Rubin, with Friedman, Sprague, Hume, Truelove, Kuch, McCorquodale, and Miller. International Journal 'Honours Founder' dinner row. Peter Devenish wins and creates Mensa symbol.
July	Mensa looks conservative in survey. Eric Hills appointed International Ombudsman.
September	Athertons take over Mensa Journal.
October	London Dinner; Ware installed as Vice-President.

12 December	British Annual Gathering at Victory ex-Service Men's Club. Committee: Simpson, Northcote Parkinson, Lishman, Odell, Gallant, Atherton, Barbara Courtney-Wildman, Eddie Meadows.
December	Revival of 'Think-Ins'.

1970

January	Picture of new British Committee in Bulletin.
March	International General Council realignment. Weil takes Chair, Van den Bosch Secretary. American membership 11,000.
April	Mensa Journal; nominations called for International Election.
May	American Bulletin, Marvin Grosswirth's 'news and views' starts.
June	Ombudsman's report on Portos. International General Council disputes article by Margot Seitelman.
	American Annual Gathering in Philadelphia. Chairman Rubin. British Mensa financial reports.
August	Report of Philadelphia Annual Gathering.
October	Mensa Journal. *Daily Mirror* quiz; 47,000 replies.
	Mensa Journal, V.S.'s Unity Slate returned unopposed. Serebriakoff, Van den Bosch, H. Blumenthal, Visser, Fogel Allen, Alan Henderson.
November	American Bulletin, amendments to by-laws. Mensa Journal mention of Mensa Japan.
27 November	British Annual Gathering at Victory ex-Service Men's Club. Committee: Lishman Chairman, Atherton, Meadows, Allen, Odell, Murphy, B. Courtney-Wildman, Radford, Southworth, Gallant and Tubbs.
December	Sir Cyril Burt in Mensa Journal on heredity.

1971

	American membership 11,000.
February	Mensa Journal lists new International Committee.
April	Mensa Journal lists new Committee. Sprague challenges Rubin for American Chair.
May	R. Lehr takes over as Chairman in France; Paris International General Council meeting.
June	American Annual Gathering in Houston; 200 members.
	Rubin Chairman, with Kuch, Friedman, Robinson, Truelove, Jacobs, Fowley, Miller.
July	Large American Bulletin. Mensa Journal reports fast growth under R. Lehr in France.
1–4 October	Silver Jubilee Celebration, London and Oxford.
	Plaque 12, St John Street.
10 October	Sir Cyril Burt dies at 88. Mensa Journal; Burt on Jubilee.
November	British Annual Gathering.
	V.S. elected to British Committee. Take up of quiz idea mentioned.
	Enoch Powell at AG.
	Committee: Lishman Chairman, Atherton, B. Courtney-Wildman, Southworth, Gallant, Allen, Haynes, Rees, Serebriakoff, Radford.
December	Atherton gives up as Mensa Journal Editor. Tony Buzan takes over.

1972

	American membership peak 13,000.
February	American Bulletin discusses new President.
March	Odell reports 5,000 entries on Superbrain and 4,000 on Gold Block.
April	International meeting at Aachen.

May	American TV guide quiz.
	Mensa Journal edited by A. Buzan; articles by Professor Skinner, Brian Ford, Heinz Norden.
June	Annual Gathering at Denver; 200 members.
	V.S. tour of Denver, Portland, Chicago, Kansas City and Louisville.
	Odell takes over 'British Mensa Magazine', French Member Terrassier starts Gifted Children's Movement in France.
	British Mensa affiliates to Arts Theatre Club.
	Think-Ins at Arts Theatre Club.
November	British Annual Gathering at Victory ex-Servicemen's Club.
	Committee: Atherton Chairman, Haynes, Southworth, Boyce, Collins, Gallant, Lally, Middleton, Radford, Rees, Roberts and Serebriakoff.
	Peripatetic British Mensa meetings start: Sheffield, Birmingham, London, Manchester.

1973	
	American peak membership 16,368.
April	European Mensa Conference, Vienna.
June	American Annual Gathering at Louisville; 400 members.
	Grossworth Chairman, Kuch, Lowenstein, Robinson, Truelove, Jones, Weyl, Cook and Uhl.
	Political troubles and lawsuits in American Mensa.
	V.S.'s international slate re-elected against opposing panel.
1 November	British Mensa Annual Gathering at Victory ex-Servicemen's Club. Committee: Kirby Chairman, Lambert, Collier-Bradley,

Capelin, Clayton, Gallent, Lally, Maxwell, Rees, Wolfe and Yare.

British magazine ceases due to finance.

1974

American peak membership 17,000

Readers Digest quiz.

April   British magazine reappears.

Professor Buckminster Fuller accepts as President.

May   Channel Islands Mensa breaks away from Britain after a referendum.

V.S. tours USA.

June   American Annual Gathering at Chicago; 350 members. President Buckminster Fuller speaks.

November   British Mensa Annual Gathering at Victory ex-Servicemen's Club. Committee: Atherton Chairman, Boyce, Collier-Bradley, Brewis, Lovegrove, Odell, Yare, Molyneux-Roberts, B. Courtney-Wildman, Winter.

1975

American peak membership 20,000.

British membership 2,750.

Peripatetic American Mensa, Chicago, Atlanta.

Paris Congress.

June   American Annual Gathering at San Antonio; 500 members.

Fallon Chairman, Werba, Fowley, Robinson, Gardner, Sprague, Cornish, Cook, Jacobson.

British Mensa Newsletter enlarged and printed.

Attack on Odell who resigns in August.

November   British Mensa Annual Gathering at Victory ex-Servicemen's Club. Committee: Middleton Chairman, Atherton, Collins, Boyce,

Gallant, Roberts, Southworth, Brewis, Lovegrove, Winter.

1976

American peak membership 22,000.
British membership 1,351.

February   Dutch Mensa Wijk at Duurstede Anniversary.

March   British Super Brain in newspapers.

June   Third Congress International, Toronto.

American Annual Gathering at Valley Forge; 600 members. Celebrate 200th USA Anniversary.

V.S.'s tours including Toronto; American Mensa meetings in Louisville, Washington, Houston, Los Angeles.

Problems continue in British Mensa.

Serebriakoff Panel elected for IGC: G. Hopkins, A. Gardner, D. Warren, A. Hill, G. Werba, Phil Powell, G. Atherton.

Opposing Panel: led by Kleinjan and Officier.

November   British Mensa Annual Gathering.

Committee: Winter, Chairman, Francis, Simpkins, Brewis, Ashford, Boyce, Collier-Bradley, Coates, Courtney-Wildman, Wall, Clift, Lewis.

1977

American peak membership 24,000.
British membership 2,090.

March   Mensa Journal; article 'Burt-bashers'

April   International General Council meet in Paris. Think-In on Brain.

June   American Annual Gathering at San Diego; 750 members.

Fallon Chairman, Werba, Fowley, Frommer, Gardner, Sprague, Mosley, Humes,

	Saper, Wright, Kollar, Vickers, Rickard, P. Victor.
23 July	4th International Congress at Bristol.
November	British Mensa Annual Gathering.
	Committee: Collier-Bradley, Hodkinson, Simpkins, Yare, Brewis, Courtney, Blanchard, Spanchak, Boyce, Collins.
December	Newsletter reports British Chairman and Secretary resign at AGM after big row.

1978

	American peak membership 30,000.
	British membership 2,210.
	American Mensa meetings: Chicago, New Orleans, Minneapolis, Portland.
	British Mensa gets use of National Liberal Club.
March	Mensa Journal reports meetings: Geneva, Santa Barbara, Catskill, Channel Islands, Dundalk, Paris, London.
28, 30 April	French Gifted Children's Congress, Nice. Big Mensa participation.
June	American Annual Gathering at Cleveland; 850 members.
3, 5 November	British Mensa Annual Gathering at Birmingham.
	Committee: Collier-Bradley Chairman, Courtney, Simpkins, Boyce, Yare, Rayner.

1979

	American peak membership 33,000.
	British membership 2,545.
March	M. Clift, Editor of British Mensa newsletter.
	Second *Readers Digest* article.
June	American Mensa Annual Gathering at Kansas City; 900 members.
	Werba Chairman, Saper, Frommer, Sample, Noble, Blair, Atman, Humes, Gentry,

Mann, Wantland, Vasiliauskas, Rickard, Felt.

American Mensa meetings: Louisville, New York, San Francisco, Phoenix.

November British Mensa Annual Gathering at Liverpool.

Committee: Collier-Bradley, Yare, Meredith, Boyce, Rayner, Serebriakoff, Sinclair, Lewis.

This was the revival committee in the UK.

Troubled meeting; Clift sacked but sense restored.

1980

American peak membership 43,380.

British membership 3,418.

Redpath takes over British Mensa newsletter.

April American Mensa meetings: Charlotte, Huntsville, Los Angeles, Phoenix.

V.S. retires from work at 66.

June American Mensa Annual Gathering at San Francisco; 1,050 members.

August First 'Mensa At Cambridge'.

November International General Council meeting in Athens agree new draft Constitution.

International level big constitutional wrangles.

British Mensa Annual Gathering at Aston University, Birmingham.

Committee: C. Sinclair Chairman, Yare, Meredith, Serebriakoff, Lewis, Boyce, Napier, Rayner.

1981

American peak membership 47,000.

British membership 5,010.

17 January Werba etc. at Blackheath.

February	V.S.'s US trip including Baltimore. Disaccord.
3 May	Irish Annual Gathering at Dublin.
June	American Mensa Annual Gathering at Louisville, 1,100 members.
	Werba Chairman, Saper, Frommer, Oakes, Noble, Coons, Atman, Shaughnessy, Kupper, Mann, Hawkins, Vasiliauskas, Rickard, Felt.
	American Mensa meetings: San Diego, Milwaukee, Fort Myers.
July	British Mensa newsletter, August editorial attack on V.S. by Gabe Werba.
July	Mensa At Cambridge.
19 August	International Gathering at Graz.
31 October	Miami Pact.
November	British Mensa Annual Gathering.
	Committee: C. Sinclair Chairman, Yare, Meredith, Schulman, Lewis, Boyce, Napier, Rayner. V.S. elected Editor.
December	Mensa Journal reports Miami Pact, signed by Werba, Noble, Fallon, Sinclair, Gardner, Serebriakoff. V.S. plans for new-style British newsletter.

1982

	American peak membership 49,000.
	British membership 7,809.
	G. Atherton gives up and resigns as Editor of Mensa Journal. Constitution passed and International Committee dismissed. New Board installed by referendum, chosen by National Representatives.
	Brock Chairman, L. Rickard Treasurer, Kleinjan Administration and Chestapalov Development.
April	Mensa Journal; V.S. writes 'I go consenting'.
June	American Mensa Annual Gathering at

	Trenton, NJ; 750 present. C. Sinclair, V.S., J. McNulty, M. Pirie.
July	First meeting of the International Board of Directors, Toronto. V.S. appointed Third President, Ware appointed 'Fons et Origo'. Aukland meeting planned.
November	British Mensa Annual Gathering at Brighton. Very good atmosphere. Committee: C. Sinclair Chairman, Yare, Meredith, Boyce, Rayner, Schulman, Logan, Pirie.
December	British newsletter becomes *Mensa*; 36 page glossy magazine.

1983

	American peak membership 49,000. British peak membership 9,130.
February	London International General Council meeting; Chairman Sir Clive Sinclair reports.
June	American Mensa Annual Gathering at Phoenix; 850 present. Noble, Chairman, Shaughnessy, Man, Felt, Rider, Coons, Atman, Crutcher, Kupper, Brasgalla, Hawkins, Frommer, Mathison, Mattson.
1 July	Buckminster Fuller dies. Mensa At Cambridge gets big publicity.
October	Nice meeting of International Board of Directors and Aukland meeting of International Board of Directors.
November	British Mensa Annual Gathering. Committee: C. Sinclair Chairman, Yare, Meredith, Rayner, Schulman, Logan, Pirie, McNulty.

1984

	American peak membership 50,000. British peak membership 12,987.

	American Mensa meetings: St Louis, Syracuse, Orange County.
April	Mensa Journal has long list of international events; so does May issue.
	Marvin Grosswirth's death reported.
June	American Mensa Annual Gathering at Washington.
	Mensa professional Editor takes over, S. Clarke.
	David Tebbutt takes over International Journal.
October	*Mensa* glossy coloured.
	International meeting in Kerkrade, Holland.
2, 3, 4 November	British Mensa Annual Gathering at Bristol is highly successful.
31 December	V.S. completes his second Mensa history: *Mensa*.

Addresses

INTERNATIONAL
Mensa International, 50–52 Great Eastern Street, London EC2A
3EP, UK. Tel: ((44)) (1) 792 6576.

AUSTRALIA
Anne Huckle, 16 Elliott Avenue, Carnegie, Victoria 3163, Australia. Tel: ((61)) (03) 568 7500.

AUSTRIA
Mensa Oesterreich, Postfach 502, A-1011 Wien, Austria. Tel:
((43)) (222) 224 6603.

BELGIUM
Didier Racheneur, BP 1824, B-1000 Brussels, Belgium.

BRITAIN
British Mensa, Bond House, St John's Square, Wolverhampton,
UK. Tel: ((44)) (902) 26055.

CANADA
Mensa Canada, PO Box 505, Station Street, Toronto, Ontario
M5M 4L8, Canada. Tel: ((1)) (416) 497 7070.

CHANNEL ISLANDS
Philip Poole, 'Heathlea', Pont Marquet, St Brelade, Jersey,
Channel Islands. Tel: ((44)) (534) 43907.

FINLAND
Soumen Mensa r y, PL 21, SF-00531, Helsinki 53, Finland. Tel:
((358)) (90) 494487.

FRANCE
Henri Delekta, 34 Rue St Emilion, Mont St Père, 02400 Château
Thierry, France.

GERMANY
Deutsche Mensa, Hofholzallee 102, D-2300 Kiel 1, West Germany.

GREECE
Hellenic Mensa, 9 Alyos Street, 115 20 Athens, Greece.

INDIA
Mensa India, Jnana Prabodhini, 510 (New) Sadashiv Peth, Pune 411 030, India.

ISRAEL
Mr J. Eliezer, 84 Hagana Street, Raanana, Israel.

ITALY
Mensa Italia, Via Cassia 1328, 00123 Rome, Italy. Tel: ((39)) (6) 376 5965.

IVORY COAST
M. Jerome Aka Ahui, BP 1761, Abidjan 01, Ivory Coast.

JAPAN
Reiko Muta, 301 Sunny Heights, 34–21 Tomigaya 2-chome, Shibuya-ku, Tokyo 151, Japan. Tel: ((81)) (3) 469 7043.

MALAYSIA
Malaysian Mensa, PO Box 10015, Kuala Lumpur 01-02, Malaysia.

NETHERLANDS
Mensa Nederland, Postbus 100, 3500 AC Utrecht, Netherlands. Tel: ((31)) (30) 522096.

NEW ZEALAND
Mensa New Zealand, Box 35080, Browns Bay, Auckland 10, New Zealand.

NORWAY/SWEDEN
(Acting) Bengt A. Baldesten, Emaljvägen 12, 175 73 Järfälla, Sweden.

SOUTH AFRICA
Mr P. Ross, Box 6074, Roggenaai 8012, South Africa.

SPAIN
Mensa Espana, Sevilla 28 3° E, Zaragoza 6, Spain.

SWITZERLAND
Mensa CH, Case Postale 539, 1211 Geneva 1, Switzerland.

USA
American Mensa, 2626 E 14th Street, Brooklyn, NY 11235 USA.

Index